FRAMED

The Corruption and Cover-Up behind the Wrongful Conviction of William Michael Dillon and His Twenty Seven-Year Fight for Freedom

As Told by William Michael Dillon
Written and Narrated by Ellen Moscovitz

Copyright © 2014 William Michael Dillon and Ellen Sue Moscovitz
Revised 2015, 2022

All rights reserved. No part of this book may be used or reproduced in any manner whatsoever without written permission, except in the case of brief quotations in critical articles and reviews.

Published: Flying Free Productions LLC 2022.

Printed in the United States.

ISBN: 978-1-915930-28-6 PAPERBACK
ISBN: 978-1-915930-29-3 EBOOK

Cover Art by David Ter-Avanesyan

www.frameddillon.com

Order direct: store.bookbaby.com

*To Charles Rogers
and Roseanna Rogers.
May they always be remembered
as guardians of truth.*

> *JUSTICE IS A WORD.*
> *IF YOU WANT THE SOUL OF JUSTICE TO BE THERE,*
> *YOU HAVE TO PUT IT THERE.*
>
> **~ William Michael Dillon**

NOTE:

This book is a work of narrative nonfiction. All quoted trial testimony and police interviews are derived from actual trial transcripts and written police reports. Other quoted material is derived from police interviews, videotapes, newspaper reports, sworn depositions, official hearings, interviews, public records, and other printed sources. Some names may be spelled in multiple ways in order to remain consistent with the transcripts.

No claim is made that all quoted, off-the-record, conversations are verbatim. The quoted, non-recorded, conversations are accurate in substance and as the author(s) remember them. They are not written to represent word-for-word transcripts. The author(s) has retold them in a way that evokes the feeling and meaning of what was said, and in all instances, the essence of the dialogue is accurate.

Any errors or omissions are inadvertent.

ACKNOWLEDGMENTS:

For their encouragement and wise counsel, we thank all who have helped to make this book a reality.

Former homicide detective and novelist Marshall Frank for his encouragement, advice, and never-ending belief that we could get this project done.

Author and TV producer Gary Yordon for being our first adviser with ideas on how to get the book started.

Attorney Don Rubright for his legal oversight, editorial assistance, and belief in our mission.

Attorney Thomas Julin for his legal oversight and generosity.

Attorney Joan Weiss for her legal oversight, editorial critique, and advice.

Bill Greenleaf for his editorial expertise and invaluable mentoring.

Catherine Turner for her professionalism and expert proofreading skills.

David Ter-Avanesyan for his captivating cover design

HMDpublishing for the brilliant typesetting

Al Filger for his enduring friendship, inspiration and support of this project.

Melissa Mizelle for her friendship, caring spirit and heartfelt feedback on the first draft.

Susan Karpe for her friendship, encouragement and honest feedback on the first draft.

And never to be forgotten...

All the wrongfully convicted prisoners still behind bars, for their never-ending inspiration.

CONTENTS

Prologue 9

Part I

01. Prisoner #082629 13
02. Anything Goes 19
03. The Making of a Suspect 25
04. On the Brink 31
05. Tracked 37
06. Arrest 41
07. Wild Card 49
08. The Affair 55
09. An Aging Jury 61
10. Tall Tale 67
11. No Evidence 71
12. The Half-Blind Eyewitness 75
13. Ace in the Hole 83
14. Brilliant Theater 91
15. Inconceivable 111
16. Witness for the Defense 117
17. A Carefully Orchestrated Trap 135
18. A Small but Welcome Victory 157
19. Asked and Answered 169
20. Closing Arguments 181
21. A Unanimous Decision 187
22. Denied 189

Part II

23. What Nightmares Are Made Of 197
24. The Lords of Justice 203
25. The Last Stop 211
26. Lifeline 215
27. Epiphany 223
28. Chokehold 229
29. An Angel 233
30. Evidence Lost . . . and Found 239
31. Freedom 253

Part III

32. Stuck 261
33. Another Recantation 271
34. No Time to Waste 277
35. Peeling the Onion 283
36. Tools 291
37. Fishing Expedition 303
38. Stalemate 313
39. Moot Point 319
40. Death on the House Floor 325
41. Burned 331
42. Second Chance 339
43. Better than Johnny Cash 345
44. Smoke and Mirrors 353
45. The Power of Innocence 363
Epilogue 367

PROLOGUE

The first time I met William Michael Dillon, he was leaning on the bar across the room and chatting with a colleague of mine. The date was March 20, 2009. The event: the annual Innocence Project Conference. About 150 guests, many of them ex-cons and their attorneys, were assembled at Cabo, a bright and lively two-story "Mix-Mex" grill in the heart of downtown Houston, Texas. Though a buffet had been set up in the lounge between floors, most of the guests had gathered on the top floor, which consisted of a large bar that spanned the width of the restaurant, a dining area with oversized red booths, and a huge outdoor patio that overlooked the sparkling downtown lights.

I was networking through the crowd in my capacity as president and CEO of DNA Diagnostics Center, an Ohio-based DNA testing company that was sponsoring the event. By the time I spotted Bill, I had already listened to countless gut-wrenching stories of how innocent men—and a few women—had been wrongfully convicted of heinous crimes, only to have society and the legal system abandon them. Their stories weren't new to me. I'd been running DNA testing businesses for more than two decades and had seen my share of injustices. Thus, I'd always had a soft spot for the Innocence Project's mission and had recently authorized free DNA testing in fifteen post-conviction criminal cases that were being investigated by the Ohio Innocence Project, along with reporters at the *Columbus Dispatch*. I viewed my involvement, and by extension my company's involvement, as a way to give back to the community in which we operated, while standing up for justice, regardless of the outcome of the testing.

Now I was in a restaurant full of a hundred or so free souls who'd previously been in bondage. Many of these former prisoners had been convicted decades earlier before DNA testing had been developed and used in the courtroom. For most, there had been no way to prove their innocence. Meeting the people whose specimens we had tested offered a vivid reminder of the vital role our industry plays in America's fragile justice system.

As I approached Bill, he extended his hand and greeted me in a friendly baritone voice.

"Hi."

Between his sun-bronzed skin and his rugged good looks, I assumed he was an attorney from the local Texas chapter of the Innocence Project. He wore horn-rimmed glasses, which framed a set of smiling blue eyes.

"So," I said casually, "what's your story?"

"I spent twenty-seven-and-a-half years in prison for a murder I didn't commit," the towering stranger answered matter-of-factly.

Given the setting, I suppose I shouldn't have been surprised by his response. But his answer caught me off guard.

Perhaps sensing my shock, Cassie Johnson, the woman he was chatting with, stepped in. Cassie, a leading forensic scientist from Texas, was an attractive and engaging woman who had a zest for her work. I was trying—unsuccessfully, as it would turn out—to recruit her into my company.

"Ellen, this is Bill," she said. "He was one of the dog handler cases."

The dog handler Cassie was referring to was none other than John Preston, a notorious charlatan who, before being discredited, was a self-professed, man-trailing expert who claimed his dog had never been wrong and could track scents up to eight years after the fact. Preston and his "wonder dog" had helped put numerous people behind bars—some of them on death row.

"Was he one of yours?" I asked.

"Yes," Cassie answered. "We had to use MiniFiler to test the DNA."

Cassie was using lab lingo to explain that it had been a tough case—one that had required her team to use the latest, most sophisticated technology to perform the DNA testing.

Bill then began to explain how Preston and his German shepherd had helped make him the prime suspect in a grisly first-degree murder case in Brevard County, Florida. After listening to his story, which read like a Hollywood script with all of its sex, lies, and danger, together with an unlikely hero who triumphs over the corrupt forces determined to destroy him, I felt like I had been punched in the gut. Here was an obviously intelligent, well-spoken man who, despite being convicted for something he had never done, despite being the victim of untold cruelty and spending the better part of three decades in prison, showed no trace of bitterness. He simply wanted to move on with his life and live it the best he could. I knew instinctively then, as I do now, the world needed to hear his story.

~*Ellen Moscovitz*

PART I

CHAPTER 1
PRISONER #082629

Even the sign had bars on it.

As the secured van entered the maximum security prison in unincorporated Bradford County on March 12, 1982, William Michael Dillon, one of the eight prisoners aboard, looked up at the arched sign overhead just in time to note the vertical bars running the length of the sign, which read ominously *Florida State Prison*. It wasn't so much a welcome as it was a warning. Bill, a directionless kid in the body of a strapping twenty-two-year-old man, had hardly begun to glimpse his future when it disappeared and was replaced by the cold, hard lines of the state penitentiary.

The enormous sign was suspended high above the entryway, which in turn was flanked by armed guards. Ahead of Bill lay a flat, sprawling campus covered in barbed wire and cordoned everywhere by impossibly tall fences. Even the buildings' windows were covered in wire mesh.

The van backed up to a ramp, and Bill, shackled and chained, was unloaded with the others and led through the doors of Florida's most notorious prison. From there, the prisoners were marched to a second-floor holding cell. Only vaguely aware of the horrors that awaited him, Bill flinched as the steel doors slammed shut behind him. He was trapped. Shrieks of condemned men living in a concrete fortress sliced through the dense sweltering air. As the stench of sweat and urine burned the back of his throat, he fought the urge to vomit. Images of his life flashed before his eyes, reminding him in an instant of everything he would never have: a family, children, the simple joys that came with freedom. Just months earlier, he'd been entertaining dreams of playing Major League Baseball. Now, he hoped only to survive.

He glanced nervously around the 10 ft. x 6 ft. cell, which was reinforced with steel bars. Concrete walls. Hard concrete floors. No seats. The only amenity was a small commode mounted to the floor in the corner.

"We got eight new cocks!" someone yelled from somewhere down the grim hallway. An older prisoner translated for the group. A heavyset man with a graying beard, he had been in prison before. "That means we're fresh meat," he whispered, his voice laced with fear.

Another prisoner approached their cell. He was in charge of issuing the prison blues: three sets of pants, shirts, socks, and underwear. "Mind your own business if you want to survive," he said. "There's a lot of fuckin' crazy people in here."

He took their measurements and faded into the gray darkness.

Next, a woman dressed in a nurse's uniform appeared.

Her escort was a male officer who put everyone on notice. "Don't disrespect our women!"

Tall, with long dark hair, she called each prisoner individually by name and asked him to step up to the bars, where she fired off questions about diseases, current medications, and whether or not the prisoner was considering suicide. In front of the officer and the group of prisoners, she was direct and to the point, the owner of a frigid stare. But when Bill's turn came to speak with her individually and away from the group, she seemed genuinely concerned about his safety.

"How did you get yourself into FSP at such a young age?" she asked as she crinkled her brow.

"I was convicted of murder," Bill said swallowing hard.

"But why did they send you *here*?" she probed.

"Gotta . . . a life sentence," Bill stammered, not understanding the depth of her questions and deeply unnerved by his own words.

After the nurse left, a short, uniform-clad lieutenant by the name of Roberts stepped up to the cell. "How many of you want to go to protective custody?"

Before anyone could answer, he sternly explained to Bill and the others that they had just entered a maximum security facility. "They're extremely violent in here," he warned.

Everyone but Bill—or Prisoner #082629, as he was now known—took the lieutenant's advice and asked to be entered into protective custody.

Bill had other concerns. To begin with, retreating to a tiny cell with only a small window, cloistered from the rest of the prison, wasn't an appealing option for a man with claustrophobia. At least a standard cell had bars instead of walls. Secondly, he knew he would eventually have to join the rest of the prisoners. Better to face whatever torment awaited him now, he thought, than to prolong the inevitable. The alternative was to be labeled a coward, which he had a hunch would only make things more difficult for him.

"You should go," Lieutenant Roberts said. "They're just not right in here. You're too young. You won't do well."

But Bill, facing a life sentence, refused the offer. So long as he just minded his own business, he told himself, he could stay out of trouble. He would go out of his way not to create any animosity toward anyone.

Bill was left in the cell while the others were herded to "PC," giving him one last chance to change his mind before being released into the general population. But he stood firm.

As Bill was led through the three-story stronghold on his way to Cell L1 North 3, he felt his body begin to shake. This was where he would spend the rest of his life. Though above ground, the building was dark and dank, a muggy hellhole, like some stone dungeon in a Third World labor camp. Three tiers of cells surrounded an open square. Rows of steel bars lined the balcony, known as the quarterdeck, that ran in front of the cells.

Bill carried a small, standard-issue cardboard shoebox containing what were now his only worldly possessions. The prisoners wailed and whistled catcalls at him as he passed their cells, causing icy chills to run down his spine. His hair, now soaked with sweat, tumbled down over his forehead, and he glanced furtively as he walked, fearfully absorbing what he could.

When he reached Cell L1 North 3, he found it hidden out of sight of the officer's station. The guard escorting him lifted the lever of the one-man cell and slid the heavy door open. A steel bunk sat against the wall to his right, its mattress consisting of a two-inch pad thrown on top. Nearby, a porcelain sink hung from the wall. A bare toilet was bolted to the floor below it.

Bill caught a glimpse of light, no more than a wisp, shining through a small, barred window, which was partially covered with a flap of metal attached to the frame. He couldn't see any glass behind the bars, which meant there would be nothing to block the cool March air, or come hurricane season, there'd be nothing to stop the wind from whistling into his cell. Out the window he could see row upon row of neatly spaced rectangular buildings in the middle of a huge flat field—no tree in sight. A tall, circular guard tower dominated the yard and enjoyed a 360-degree vantage point high above the rows of barbed wire and concrete cells.

Bill stood motionless and continued to stare out the window, knees wobbling, his whole body captivated by the assault to his senses.

Another prisoner, an older man who, as Bill would learn later, had come off death row, stopped at his cell and broke his reverie.

"Do you want a knife?" he whispered.

Dumbfounded, Bill replied, "Do I need a knife?"

"You do," the older man insisted.

"Then get me a knife," Bill said, choking on the words.

The prisoner nodded and disappeared, and Bill resumed his vigil by the window. But before he could register the gravity of his situation, he heard the sound of shoes scuffing the floor behind him. A second later, someone hit him over the back of the head with something hard and heavy—a bar pipe—and he was wrestled to his bunk by a group of prisoners. These were big men: strong, violent, ruthless.

Dizzy and confused, Bill didn't know what was going on, but he fought back desperately, flailing his arms and kicking wildly. His attackers, not bothering to be quiet, pinned him to his bunk. One of them put a cold blade to his chin and sliced it while another pressed a blade to his throat. Warm blood trickled down his neck. He continued to struggle, continued to try to break free, but his efforts were futile. They had him pinned with his face smashed against the cinder block wall. He felt the sheer force of their sweaty flesh against his as he was pressed into the metal framework of his bunk.

Bill, still struggling to understand what was happening, felt a surge of adrenaline—and a corresponding rush of super strength. Like a diver being attacked by a shark in the water, he was doing whatever he could to survive, swinging and hitting in every direction, and for a moment he thought he was going to overcome the assault. But finally the pain was too much, and he blacked out as the sounds of the savage gang-rape echoed through the tiers.

He had been in prison less than one hour. And in that time, he had gone from a person to a number, from a free man to the victim of inhuman, remorseless violence. No doubt there were some on the outside who thought he deserved such a cruel fate, but he knew something they didn't. He was innocent.

CHAPTER 2
ANYTHING GOES

In the summer of 1981, had anyone told Bill Dillon that his days of freedom were nearly over, he would have snorted in disbelief. Although technically an adult—at least according to the legal definition—Bill, at twenty-one years old, had more in common with a seventeen-year-old kid. His family had recently moved to Florida's Brevard County, and Bill, after a frustrating stint in the army, had returned home to lounge on the beach, play baseball, and party. When he wasn't watching the waves, he was couch surfing with friends, most of whom were more supportive of his hedonistic lifestyle than his parents, who were eager for him to get on with his life and start acting like a responsible adult.

He would have been hard-pressed to find a more agreeable locale than his current stomping grounds. Each evening, after the hot Florida sun retired from the sky, the Brevard County nightlife sprang to life, offering endless opportunities for entertainment and gratification. There was something for everyone along the strip that stretched from Cocoa Beach to Canova Beach and ran parallel along Highway A1A and the Atlantic Ocean. The corridor included the small towns of Indian Harbour Beach, Satellite Beach, and a handful of other seaside communities, each of which seemed to melt into the next along the coastline.

Dotting that coastline was an assortment of colorful watering holes. The Dragon Lady Den proudly displayed a large, vibrantly painted dragon curling its body up a post. The A Frame Tavern, about three miles up the highway to the north, attracted the beer and wine set, mostly locals, who came to socialize and drink away the stress of their daily lives. And then there was the Pelican Bar and Lounge, which was usually bursting at the seams with partying, smoking, pool-playing beach bums, tourists, and locals, each of whom came to be part of Brevard County's nightlife and listen to little-known rock bands willing to play for tips. Like the other bars along the coast, the Pelican hosted a patchwork of people—mingling and meeting, seeing and being seen—from all walks of life.

If Canova Beach attracted all kinds, those enjoying the nightlife typically had three things in common: sex, drugs, and rock and roll. Indeed, the eighties, still in its infancy, had ushered in a new "anything goes" era, and in Brevard County, it was a well-known fact that gay men used Canova's densely wooded beachfronts as a protected refuge, a place where they could meet secretly and have a rendezvous. A favorite hotspot, dubbed "Queer Pier" by the locals, was a clearing in the beachside woods where the old Canova House had once stood before a fire destroyed it. A thicket of tropical flora shielded the clearing from public view. Only a small dirt path, well worn from frequent use, could be seen from the parking lot overlooking the beach. Every night, a parade of men disappeared into the woods—only to reemerge minutes later after consummating their sexual trysts.

Gay or straight, most in Brevard County knew how to party. Bill, always looking for a good time, fit right in. He was a carefree spirit—holding an assortment of odd jobs and working only sporadically, fleshing out his resume with stints as a carpenter's apprentice as well as a mechanic at a bowling alley. Though lacking direction, he had plenty of creative ambition, imagining he might be an inventor or a musician someday. In fact, he often dreamed about singing and learning to play an instrument.

At six feet, four inches tall, and weighing in at nearly two hundred pounds, Bill was also a gifted athlete. He had tried out for the Detroit Tigers' farm team earlier in the year and had earned a callback to the second round of tryouts, now fast approaching.

It was August, and Bill, temporarily unemployed, was spending the waning days of summer at the beach. Without a job, he was having difficulty making rent at his little apartment in Satellite Beach—and was currently locked out by the landlord. He dutifully contacted his probation officer, Randy Amos, to inform him that he likely would be staying at the Bocci brothers' apartment until he had enough money to continue paying the rent. He often slept on a friend's couch despite the fact that his family lived in the neighborhood. As a somewhat hyperactive young man enjoying a prolonged adolescence, he liked to be where the action was. Most of his waking hours were spent on recreational pursuits like chasing girls, smoking the occasional joint, or hanging out at the music bars on the beach. Bill loved rock and roll, with country music running a close second. A typical night of barhopping meant catching a different band at each venue he visited and soaking up as much music as he could absorb.

On one such night, a sweltering evening during the first week of August, Bill dropped in on the Pelican Bar. Rick Springfield's number one hit "Jessie's Girl" was blanketing the airwaves, and Bill was eager to hear some live rock and roll.

He entered and greeted a group of regulars at the bar. Then, across the room, he noticed an intoxicated man making unwanted advances toward a woman Bill had never seen before. She was a slim brunette with cropped hair and, at that moment, wide, fearful eyes.

Bill's protective instincts kicked in, and before he knew it, he was coming to her aid.

The drunk left without a fuss, but the frail-looking woman appeared shaken from the encounter. She told Bill her name was Donna Parrish, and Bill offered to drive her home.

After dropping her off at her place, Bill met Donna several times over the next few days. She told him she was twenty-four, although he felt certain she was older. She had a young son, no longer in her custody, and lived with her mother. Donna told Bill that she needed to get her life on track, which at the time, like Bill's, was heavy on fun and light on responsibility. Donna, by her own admission, seemed to have no trouble earning men's attention and prided herself on being able to use her female charms to get what she wanted.

Bill soon realized he wasn't all that compatible with Donna, but despite his misgivings, he felt compassion for her situation and thought perhaps he could help her somehow. Maybe, he thought, he could help her find the proverbial light at the end of the tunnel.

On August 16, just two weeks into what was turning out to be a strange and stormy relationship, Donna decided to take Bill to visit her friends George and Linda Plumlee at the Ocean Star Motel in Cocoa Beach. Bill was at his parents' house when Donna pulled up in a red Ford Mustang she had borrowed from the Plumlees, with whom she had stayed the night before. It was noon.

Bill turned to his sister, Debbie, who had promised to make him a home-cooked meal and was frying pork chops on the stove. "I'm sorry," he said. "I gotta go."

He kissed Debbie on the forehead, apologized once more for canceling their plans for a meal, and grabbed a cold, leftover hotdog on his way out the door.

The Ocean Star Motel was a two-story building with rooms on either side. Since the motel was laid out on a north–south axis, neither side enjoyed a view of the ocean, but a deck on the second floor offered glimpses of it. The sandy beach was just steps from the first floor.

As Bill and Donna pulled into the parking lot, he noted the sign out front, which was aqua green like the Atlantic and boasted white lettering.

The two arrived just in time to find the Plumlees, an older retired couple, in the middle of a fight. It was obvious by their slurred speech and combustible behavior that they'd been drinking.

After less than an hour, Bill took Donna aside. "I don't want to be here," he said. "I'm leaving."

With that, he walked down to the beach and sat on the sand. However, with no money and no wheels of his own, he was stranded.

Donna showed up a few minutes later with a borrowed blanket in hand, and Bill, forgetting for a moment the nasty scene back at the motel, stretched out on the blanket beside her. It didn't take long before the two, partially hidden between two sailboats, gave in to their desires in broad daylight.

Afterward, Donna disappeared to return the blanket to the Plumlees. Bill, after pondering his options, decided he'd hitchhike back to Satellite Beach.

Just then a man who looked to be in his mid-forties appeared. He had dark hair and was holding a Löwenbräu beer in his right hand.

"Hey," he said, "don't you know everybody can see you down here? Here's something to cool you off."

He handed Bill a beer and introduced himself. His name was Charles Rogers. Roseanna Rogers, his wife, managed the motel. Moments earlier, he explained, he had been standing on a wooden platform overlooking the beach and talking with another motel guest when he had spotted Bill and Donna getting amorous. He had decided to come down to the beach to intervene about the time he'd overheard other guests talking about the situation. Bill and Charles made small talk for a few minutes, and then the older man left.

When Donna returned, she suggested she and Bill walk to the phone booth in the parking lot and call someone with a car since the Mustang would be staying with the Plumlees. Bill agreed, but their plan fell apart when no one would agree to pick them up.

Wondering what they were going to do, Bill turned to see Charles Rogers approaching.

Charles quizzed Bill and Donna about their predicament. They were stranded, they told him, and had no place to stay. After walking back to his apartment to consult with his wife, Charles returned a minute later.

"Are you two hungry?" he asked.

Bill opened his mouth to say no, but he hadn't eaten anything since the hotdog. "Yes," he answered.

Charles smiled. "I've got a pot roast in the crock-pot. Why don't you come and join me and my wife."

Bill and Donna agreed and followed the man to the very first room on the far side of the motel, away from the ocean. Once inside the meagerly furnished motel apartment, they met Roseanna, a lovely woman with long, curly blond hair. She was clearly much younger than Charles but radiated the same warmth and kindness.

Bill and Donna, famished, eagerly sat down to dinner, and over the course of the evening, they learned that Charles and Roseanna would be celebrating their wedding anniversary the next day. Charles was an avid racing fan and had spent the day relaxing beside the radio, listening to NASCAR.

After dinner, when it became apparent Bill and Donna had no transportation and no money to get home, their new friends suggested they spend the night. So the two couples stayed up late into the night talking and drinking while Charles and Roseanna's ten-year-old son slept in the next room. Bill, Donna, and the Rogerses were so tired by the end of the night that they fell asleep in their clothes.

The next morning, August 17, was a Monday, and Roseanna woke Bill and Donna and explained that she had to get to work early cleaning the motel's rooms because she and Charles were expecting a visit from Charles's boss later. Crunched for time, she politely asked the young couple to leave.

After saying goodbye to Charles and Roseanna, Bill and Donna parted ways, with Donna opting to stay behind and Bill electing to hitchhike to his parents' house. Despite their steamy moment on the beach, they were already arguing again.

As Bill started for the highway, he couldn't help thinking that his two-week relationship had already gone on too long. Donna's constant complaints, her contention that the world was against her—all had conspired to make her less attractive. The only thing holding him to her now was their mutual attraction. She was always ready and willing, always eager to go party and have fun. But clearly that wasn't enough to sustain their fling.

Bill arrived at his parents' home just as Hurricane Dennis began ravaging the Atlantic coast. Desiring to be on his own, he spent the next few rainy days holed up in an apartment rented by two acquaintances, Joseph and Matt Bocci, who also happened to be the neighborhood marijuana dealers. Although he'd had enough of Donna, she was persistent. Every time he turned around, she was there, frustrated that he was attempting to put space between them.

Deep down, Bill knew he couldn't keep up this lifestyle forever. He'd ridden the summer of 1981 like a world-class wave. But even the biggest wave had to break, and eventually he would have to get serious. With no money and little training, he felt uncertain about his future. Maybe he would get certified as a mechanic, thus coming full circle and accomplishing what had inspired him to enlist in the army in the first place. Maybe at his upcoming tryout with the Tigers' organization he would win a position and carve out a career in baseball. Or maybe he would answer the siren call of music and learn to play the guitar.

All he knew for sure was that the future was his for the taking.

CHAPTER 3

THE MAKING OF A SUSPECT

Before Hurricane Dennis made landfall, the summer of 1981 had been an unusually dry one in Brevard County. In fact, Florida had been enduring drought conditions since early spring. Thus Hurricane Dennis, although the most damaging storm that hurricane season, offered one bit of relief: rain.

By six o'clock in the evening on Saturday, August 22, the storm had already moved up the East Coast and then turned back out to sea. The worst was over.

With a joint in one hand and his eyes fixed on Canova Beach below, Bill Dillon was seated beside Joe, his younger brother, in Joe's open-top Monte Carlo. The view from the parking lot was always stunning, but never more so than in the wake of a big storm.

Bill and Joe were planning a carefree night on the town, and Bill had just exhaled a long string of smoke when he spotted an older couple approaching Joe's car. The woman veered straight toward Bill, who was lounging in the passenger's seat, while the man walked around to Joe's side of the car.

Tall and statuesque, the woman had light blond hair, which she wore past her shoulders.

"Afternoon," she said in a friendly voice. "I'm Detective Christine Barringer." She nodded to the man. "This is Steven Kindrick. We're with the sheriff's department. Do you mind identifying yourself?"

"My name is William Dillon, ma'am," Bill said, hurriedly snuffing out the lit joint in the palm of his hand and then cuffing it out of sight. "And that's my brother Joe."

"Mind if we ask you a few questions?"

Bill broke out in a cold sweat. Two years earlier, at the ripe old age of nineteen, he had been convicted of marijuana possession. Now, just two weeks from successfully completing probation, he was in danger of being busted a second time, this time by two plainclothes police officers.

"No," he said.

To Bill's great relief, neither officer appeared to notice the joint.

"We're investigating a murder that took place near here," Barringer said. Her tone remained friendly—almost chummy. "Do either of you know anything about what happened? Maybe you've heard something or know someone who's said something about it."

Bill had read about the murder earlier in the week and knew it had been a grisly one and that the police were searching for leads. According to the newspaper, a forty-year-old construction worker by the name of James Edward Dvorak had been beaten to death in the woods just a few feet away from where they were parked. But that was the extent of his knowledge.

"I don't know anything about it," Bill said. "All I know is that it happened over there." He pointed to the wooded area, which, only a few days earlier, had been cordoned off with yellow tape.

Barringer raised an eyebrow. "How do you know that?"

Bill nervously squeezed the joint tighter into his singed palm. "I read about it in the newspaper," he said, neglecting to mention that he'd actually seen the yellow crime scene tape while driving by earlier in the week.

Barringer's friendly demeanor vanished. "Step out of the car," she ordered.

Bill felt his heart in his throat. Had she smelled the joint? He did as he was instructed and got out of the Monte Carlo.

Barringer, meanwhile, produced a Polaroid camera, and before Bill could wonder what was really going on, she asked, "Can I take your picture?"

"Sure, I guess," Bill responded in a confused tone.

The detective snapped a photo.

If Bill had been nervous before, now he was sweating bullets.

"How 'bout you come down to the station with us and answer some questions," Barringer suggested.

Bill stared at the officer anxiously. "I don't have time right now. I'm going across the street to the Pelican. Anyway, I don't know anything about a murder. I can't help you."

The officer persuaded Bill to come down to the station the next morning, still pushing the issue and suggesting he might be able to help with the investigation since he was familiar with the area.

"Sure," Bill said. By now he just wanted to leave. All he could think about was the joint in his hand. Could they smell it? Were they about to bust him?

Barringer and Kindrick, appearing satisfied with his answer, nodded and continued on their way.

Bill exchanged a wide-eyed glance with his brother and then hopped back into the Monte Carlo. He'd come *this* close to being caught with marijuana in his possession. The only logical course of action seemed to be a celebration at the Pelican. He still had time to shoot a few rounds of pool with his brother before the drinking crowd arrived for the night.

The mercury had already climbed to a sweltering ninety degrees by the time Bill woke up the next morning at eleven o'clock. He shook off a mild hangover and headed for the beach. Without a job, without a class schedule or any kind of daily itinerary, he typically drifted from hangout to hangout and party to party, particularly on the weekends, when nearly everyone was looking for a good time. The fact that he had promised to drop in at the police station completely escaped his mind.

As they often did, the next few days went by in a blur, and it was Tuesday, August 25, before Bill remembered his promise to Detective Barringer. He was hanging out at Buccaneer Beach, enjoying the noon sun, when friends told him that the police had been there earlier and were looking for him.

"They were showing people your picture," one of his friends said to hammer the point home.

"For what?" Bill asked. He had completely forgotten about the murder.

No one seemed to know, so Bill walked across the street to Sambo's, a casual diner with a counter and booths that faced the highway. Four open-air pay phones stood side by side in the parking lot outside, where they were covered by a small roof.

"This is William Dillon," Bill said after dialing the county sheriff's station. "Are you looking for me?"

"Where are you?" asked the officer on the other end of the line.

"I'm at Sambo's, across from Buccaneer Beach. They said you were looking for me."

"Stay there," the officer instructed in a stern voice. "We'll be right over."

Bill didn't have much time to wonder what all the fuss was about because within minutes two police cars were hurtling toward Sambo's with their sirens screaming and their cherry lights flashing. They skidded to a stop in the parking lot, and the first officer out of his car marched directly over to Bill.

"Are you William Dillon?"

"Yes," Bill said, bewildered.

"We'd like to bring you in for questioning regarding the murder of James Dvorak. Who do you want to ride with?"

Bill, still shocked, spotted Detective Barringer among the officers surrounding him. "I'll go with the lady," he said.

Bill's mind raced as Barringer drove him to Satellite Beach's nondescript sheriff's station on A1A.

"You're not a suspect," Barringer assured him. "But you might be able to help us with our investigation."

Bill nodded quietly. The thought hadn't crossed his mind that he might be a suspect.

Once inside the station, Bill was taken to a desk near the back, where Barringer offered him a piece of paper to sign. Too inexperienced to ask for an attorney—and too nervous to read the fine print—Bill hurriedly complied without knowing what he'd just signed. He looked up from the paper to see Barringer and the others watching him carefully.

The blond-haired detective then began to question him. "Where were you nine and a half days ago?"

Bill searched his mind but came up empty. "I don't know," he finally said.

Bill offered an apologetic shrug, suddenly wishing he kept a calendar or, for that matter, wore a watch. "I honestly can't remember."

A phone on Barringer's desk rang, and she'd hardly put the phone down when it rang again.

The interrogation went on for several minutes, with the detective asking questions and Bill answering them the best he could—all while Barringer fielded one call after another.

Finally Bill, under pressure from the detective, dug deeply into his memory and offered a handful of possibilities of where he *might* have been on the night of August 16. He listed the names of several friends he'd been hanging out with lately, but he couldn't say precisely who he'd been with or when they'd been together. He certainly couldn't remember what he'd been doing on August 16, now nine days past.

He was adamant about one thing, however.

"I had nothing to do with the murder," he said.

At four o'clock in the afternoon, after a full hour of questioning, Detective Barringer finally called it quits. "You can go," she said.

Bill stood up to leave.

The detective motioned to the piece of paper Bill had signed, which was still sitting on the desk, and said, "You can wad that up and throw it in the trash. We won't be needing it after all."

Bill felt a surge of relief. With the detective placated, he could finally be on his way. He crumpled up the piece of paper and tossed it into the trash. As Bill turned to leave, he was curiously stopped in his tracks and commanded to repeat the procedure, but this time the detective insisted he crumple it up even more before he tossed it away so nobody could read it.

It was a strange request—the perfect capper to a strange day. Bill reached into the trash can, retrieved the piece of paper, and crumpled it a second time for good measure before depositing it once more into the garbage.

Whatever, Bill thought. *I just want to go home.*

After finishing with the interview, Bill called his mother to come pick him up. It wasn't an easy phone call to make. Bill's relationship with his parents had been strained for some time. But when the chips were down, there was really only one person to call: Mom.

Amy Dillon arrived at the station flustered and furious. A born and bred Englishwoman from Liverpool, she had been raised in a no-nonsense, working-class environment. Bill knew he drove her crazy with his antics. He was the rebel. She was the strict and proper matriarch. She clearly couldn't understand why he hadn't gotten on with his life yet. This kind of embarrassing episode—being hauled into the police station for questioning—could only cause confusion in his mother's otherwise neat and tidy life.

"This is what happens when all you do is chase girls and go to parties!" she chastised him on the way home. "You need to stop smoking pot! You need to change your life before it's too late!"

Although he resented the lecture, Bill couldn't deny his mother had a point. As mad as she was at him for disrupting their family's life, not to mention humiliating her and his stepfather, she was also obviously concerned about his life's trajectory.

Bill ate dinner at his parents' home, where he was offered a bed for the night. Still reeling from the day's events, he was thankful for the comfort and security his parents provided. He had just begun to unwind when, at nine thirty that night, there was a loud knock on the door.

Joe Dillon, his stepfather, got up to answer it.

A second later, Bill was staring past his stepfather at two police officers on the front porch. Behind them, two additional officers stood at the ready. A pair of squad cars waited at the curb.

"Mr. Dillon," one of the officers said. "We're here to speak with your son. We'd like to take him to the police station in Melbourne for some more questions and some tests. If he passes those tests, we won't bother him anymore."

Bill's stepfather, visibly unnerved, turned to Bill. "What do you want to do?"

By now, Bill had had enough. "Dad," he said confidently, "I had nothing to do with the crime. I can pass any test they got. I want to go and clear this thing up."

He then followed the officers to one of the patrol cars parked in front of his parents' home. In a few hours, he thought, all of this would be behind him.

CHAPTER 4
ON THE BRINK

Born August 31, 1959, in Lancaster, California, Bill Dillon never met his father, an airman stationed at Edwards Air Force Base. Bill was a baby when his parents divorced, and the man who took his father's place—Joe Dillon Jr.—married his mother when Bill was still a very young child. So for the first decade or so of his life, Bill assumed that Joe was his biological father and that his family was like any other. Debbie, his only sister, was two years older than him. And his two brothers, Joe III and David, were five and six years younger, respectively.

The four children, like most military brats, knew several homes, thanks to Joe's career in the air force. Bill's earliest years were spent in the Mojave Desert, which provided him with a vast playground right outside his back door. The family went camping at Big Bear Lake in the San Bernardino Mountains and waterskiing at scenic Lake Arrowhead.

One day, Bill brought home a stray Dalmatian puppy he'd found on his way home from school. The bedraggled puppy was sick and had a bad eye, but young Bill was determined to nurse him back to health.

"Mom! Dad! Look, I found a puppy. He needs help!" Bill pleaded.

Animal lovers, Joe and Amy, nevertheless, informed him that the dog couldn't come inside—it was too ill. All the more reason to take care of him, Bill thought. He built the puppy a doghouse out of a plastic garbage can and kept him outside. Every day, he applied drops to the puppy's bad eye and fed him bologna and water. Sadly, the Dalmatian didn't survive for long, but from that moment on Bill was a passionate animal lover. He would go out of his way to ensure that even the lowliest of creatures was protected, often carrying a wasp across the house on a postcard in order to set it free and prevent his mom from swatting it with a newspaper.

Shortly after Bill turned thirteen, the whole family packed up and moved to England. Joe Jr. had been transferred to the Royal Air Force Mildenhall station, near Suffolk, England. Though nominally a British base, it supported a large US air operation. The weather in southern England was miserable—damp and gray most days—but Bill and his siblings soon found themselves enjoying it. Different food, customs, and traditions all made an impression on the Dillon children. A girl who lived down the street owned horses and taught Bill how to ride. Bill was in his element, surrounded by animals and living out his cowboy fantasy in the middle of the English countryside.

Not long after the move, Bill found some old school report cards hidden in a cabinet in the den. The first names atop the report cards were familiar: Debra and William. But the last name was foreign to him: Collins. He confronted his sister with the cards and was devastated to learn that Joe Dillon Jr. was his stepfather. His biological father—William Lee Collins—had divorced his mother and left the family shortly after Bill's birth. A trembling Bill demanded to know more. What was his real father like? Why had he never been allowed to meet him? Didn't his father want to see him?

Although keeping such information from children was common practice at the time, Bill felt betrayed. He didn't immediately bring the issue to his mother. But in the weeks and months that followed, he grew distant from his stepfather. Joe Dillon Jr. was an extremely kind man who had adopted both of his new wife's children as his own. Bill, however, was finding it increasingly hard to accept his love and discipline. In Bill's mind, Joe was the interloper, an impostor of sorts, the man who had taken the place of his real father. As a result, they clashed often. Bill would later learn that his mother had been deeply hurt by his biological father and had grown to hate him over the years. And any hope of meeting the man had been lost years earlier when William Collins had died in a car crash—on Bill's seventh birthday. For the moment, Bill knew only that he resented Joe for taking his father's place.

After finishing middle school, Bill completed his first three years of high school at Lakenheath High, about three or four miles from Mildenhall. Bill was receiving a first-rate British education, which would in the years to come serve him well. He had a thirst for knowledge and never missed a day of school.

Bill's favorite class was chorus. He was learning to sing and develop his musical talents. Desperate to play an instrument, he repeatedly asked his parents for one, but they refused, feeling that he wouldn't take care of it. Bill nevertheless kept plowing ahead with his musical interests and joined a school band as its lead singer. He was chosen to sing a duet of Bob Dylan's "Blowin' in the Wind" with a classmate at a big performance for the whole school. At home, meanwhile, country music was playing, thanks to his stepfather's love of old country classics. At the time, most of his peers were listening to rock and roll. Bill knew all the top one hundreds, but country spoke to his soul.

Just before the start of Bill's senior year, Joe was transferred once again, and the family was uprooted and moved, this time back to the States, to Minot, North Dakota. A frustrated Bill wanted to stay in England and graduate with his class. He knew no one in North Dakota and would have to start all over making friends. In fact, no one in the Dillon family wanted to move to North Dakota. It was cold, boring, and isolated. The military brass promised a girl behind every tree, but after arriving in Minot, Bill saw that they had been lying. There were no trees, much less girls, in Minot.

With few distractions around him, Bill managed to narrow his focus to two simple objectives: graduate and get out of North Dakota ASAP. He accomplished both by the end of the school year and, at the age of seventeen, joined the US Army, with the goal of becoming a certified mechanic while proudly defending his country. After finishing basic training and Advanced Individual Training (AIT) at Fort Leonard Wood, Missouri, all of his friends were sent to Korea. Bill was assigned to Fort Greely, roughly one hundred miles south of Fairbanks and one of the coldest places in Alaska.

Bill's military career was only a few weeks old when he was driving on an icy ridge line with no guardrail near Black Rapids Ski Lodge. One second he was lumbering along in the truck and the next he'd hit a patch of black ice and was careening toward the cliff edge to his right. He hit the brakes to no avail. The ice, the weight of the truck, and the sheer velocity of such a huge rig all conspired to bring him skidding toward the edge of the cliff, and as he slid forward, he saw his life flash before his eyes. He braced the wheel, knowing the truck was about to plummet down the steep ledge.

By some miracle, the truck hit the one and only boulder that rested on the icy edge of the overhang and bounced back onto the road, flipping in the process. Now Bill's truck was careening upside down toward an oncoming tanker truck. The tanker screeched to a halt just in time, and moments later, the driver of a tractor trailer, which had been following Bill, was prying him free of the wreckage. The rest of the incident remained a blur until Bill woke up in the hospital not knowing whether he would live or die.

As Bill recuperated in the hospital, he began to see his brush with death as a message. God had never played a big role in his life, but in that instant, Bill realized he was not alone on that icy road. He was kept alive for a reason. It would now be his quest to understand the plan for his life. Unfortunately, the army didn't seem to share the same urgency. Instead of earning his certification as a mechanic, Bill was sweeping floors and changing the oil of armored vehicles. On enlistment, Bill had been promised an education. This was a dead end. Meanwhile, unionized civilian workers were earning premium pay doing the work Bill had signed up to perform. In fact, in direct conflict with what he had been promised, the rules expressly prohibited Bill from working on any engines due to the army's civilian contract.

Bill lived off base with four other soldiers. Like him, they were unhappy with the daily routine. As Bill reflected on his situation, he couldn't help noticing the irony: he had escaped the bleak North Dakota landscape only to end up somewhere colder and more isolated. With nothing else to do, he started partying with his roommates. They were joined by a local girl who often came over to cook for the young men. Bill and his roommates loved eating regular home-cooked meals, but the girl's mother wasn't so keen on the arrangement and demanded the girl stop hanging out at the house. Unfortunately, the girl, a naturally free-spirited young woman, ignored her mother's wishes.

The mother, not willing to give up on the girl, reported a number of things missing from her home, and sure enough, after an official investigation was conducted, the same items were found at Bill's house. None of the items were valuable. There were some bed linens and other household items intended to make her stay more comfortable. Bill and the others never thought about whether or not they had been taken with permission. But the mother's ploy was successful. Each soldier earned an official reprimand for being caught with stolen property.

Bill, already sour on his military career, grew more frustrated still. It was bad enough that he wasn't learning his trade. Now this incident had become part of his permanent record and would follow him throughout his career. As a patriotic young man who had always admired soldiers—so much so that he wanted to be one—Bill agonized over what to do. A few more months of menial labor convinced him it was time to get on with his life. After negotiating a settlement with the army, which agreed it had breached its contractual obligations, a disappointed Bill was allowed to leave the service with a general discharge, the status of which would be automatically upgraded to honorable within six months—or so he was told. Glad to be out of Alaska, he never did follow up on his discharge status—unaware that the oversight would come back to haunt him someday. At nineteen he was too immature to know that he would always regret his decision, but he made himself a quiet promise that someday, he would find a way to honor the soldiers and their sacrifice to the nation. What he didn't know was that it would happen in the most unexpected way.

So it was that in 1979 Bill headed south—way south—to the sunny climes of Florida, where his family was now residing. He moved in with his sister, Debbie, who was living on her own, right across the street from the University of Central Florida, in Orlando. Bill, after finding a job at a sub shop, worked during the day and went to college parties at night.

On September 9, while driving home from a bottle club at four o'clock in the morning, nine college kids packed into his car, Bill was pulled over by police and cited for drug possession. In his pocket: a joint and a Quaalude, which the students had given him in exchange for the ride. Ironically, Bill didn't use Quaaludes and had only intended to smoke the joint. In any case, the indiscretion earned him probation and a $135 fine. Since he was considered a youthful offender, he was offered a deal. If he pled-out to the joint, the Quaalude would never show up on his record. The alternative was to admit possession of the Quaalude—a third-degree felony that *would* end up on his record. Bill gladly accepted the deal and did his best to forget the incident.

Not surprisingly, Bill's parents were disappointed by the recent turn of events. First his untimely departure from the army and then the drug bust. Bill, however, had at least one thing still going for him: his right arm.

Bill could throw a baseball ninety miles per hour and had perfected his curve ball as well as a new pitch called a split-fingered fastball, which was his secret weapon. Due to his years in England, Bill didn't have much formal baseball training, but his raw talent was undeniable. Joe Dillon had a contact who alerted him about a scout, from the Detroit Tigers organization, who was coming to town. After hearing about his son, the scout granted Bill a "walk-on" opportunity to try out. After throwing numerous pitches at Cocoa Stadium in Cocoa Beach, Bill earned a callback. When he left the stadium, his feet could barely touch the ground.

He was one more tryout away from, hopefully, being signed into the Tigers' farm system. Encouraged by his success and the prospects of landing a minor league contract, he started going to the ball field every chance he got to practice his hitting and pitching.

Spared a certain death at the bottom of a steep ravine in Alaska, spared the ignominy of earning a third-degree felony on his record—Bill suddenly felt optimistic about his future. He had survived his share of adversity and was now on the brink of doing something special. A career in baseball was a distinct possibility. Indeed, it was more than that. It was meant for him.

CHAPTER 5
TRACKED

Bill Dillon's gaze shifted nervously from the door closest to him to the one on the other side of the patrol car, and as his eyes searched the back seat for a way out, he felt a sudden sinking sensation in his gut. Neither door had a handle on the inside. A metal screen stood between him and the front seat.

He wasn't sure how long he'd been sitting in the back of the patrol car. Bill had seen several police cars parked out front in the well-lit parking lot. But back here, in the courthouse parking lot where Bill was trapped inside the squad car, it was pitch-black. After parking the squad car, the officers escorting Bill had left him alone in the car and disappeared inside.

Since then he'd had nothing to do but wait, and for the first time since being questioned by the police back at Satellite Beach, he was beginning to feel afraid. As each second ticked by, slowly, inexorably, a sense of foreboding overtook him. The murder case—and the police's inexplicable interest in him—was suddenly all too real.

If he hadn't been arrested, why were the police treating him like this? His T-shirt, sticky with sweat, clung to his back as he stared longingly at the closed window beside him. If only he could crack it or one of the others. He needed air.

Suddenly an imposing silhouette of a man, not much more than a shadow, appeared from behind the courthouse. He slowly approached the squad car, and soon Bill was able to make out the form and figure of a large man he'd never seen before.

The man opened the door beside Bill. "Follow me," he said tersely.

Bill, bewildered, had no choice but to comply. He trailed the stranger into the darkness of the poorly lit courthouse, their footsteps throwing echoes down the long hall. Up ahead, a dim light shone.

The man steered Bill into the last room on the left, which was the foyer to the judge's chambers. Inside the foyer, there was another door, this one with a smoked-glass window in it. It was a tiny room, hardly big enough for Bill and his escort. On one side sat a wooden desk with a chair pushed under it, and on the other, a larger upholstered chair rounded out the crowded little room's limited furnishings.

In the warmly lit room, Bill got a better look at the hulking figure of his interrogator. With his light brown hair slicked back and a pair of thick black glasses perched atop his wide nose, he looked like a classic tough guy cop, complete with slightly disheveled suit and tie. He was a big man, with broad shoulders and a personality that oozed nothing but pugnacity.

"I'm Detective Charles Slaughter," he said. "I'm the lead investigator in the murder case of James Dvorak."

Bill nodded nervously.

Detective Slaughter arranged the larger of the two chairs at an angle facing the door.

Bill, assuming he was being directed to take a seat, started for the chair.

"Wait a minute," the detective said firmly. "Stand very still."

Bill did as he was told, all the while conscious of the smoked-glass window in the door that separated the judge's chambers from the foyer. He was standing directly in front of it.

Slaughter motioned to Bill's thick brown hair, which fell below his shoulders. He instructed Bill to take his right hand behind his head, grab his hair and pull it all the way over to the right. Bill, like most stylish young men in the early eighties, wore his hair long. With bright, piercing blue eyes, he looked a bit like one of the teen idols of the David Cassidy generation, and the long hair was integral to his appearance. He hadn't cut it since leaving the military, much to the displeasure of his mother, who was still trying to turn him into the clean-cut vision she saw in her mind.

Trembling slightly, Bill obeyed the order and swept his hair to the side.

Slaughter then positioned Bill sideways, with his left profile parallel to the smokey window so his hair was out of sight.

As frightened as he was, Bill was savvy enough to suspect the window was being used as a one-way mirror. In all likelihood, someone was on the other side of that window. But who? Bill felt his skin crawl as he imagined some stranger sizing him up from the other side of the window.

After a minute or two, Slaughter pointed to the large upholstered chair he had positioned in front of the door. "Take a seat."

"I need to go to the bathroom," Bill said.

"Okay," Slaughter said and then picked up the phone on the desk and repeated, "We're going to the bathroom."

The detective escorted Bill to the bathroom, and after Bill relieved himself, the two men returned the same way they'd come.

"We're here," Slaughter said into the receiver and then, after resting the phone firmly in its cradle, got comfortable behind the desk and proceeded to make small talk with Bill.

Two or three minutes later, an enormous German shepherd with an oversized head pushed through the door followed by its handler.

Bill instinctively pushed back in his chair, putting as much distance between himself and the dog as possible. But as a lifelong animal lover and someone particularly fond of dogs, he quickly recovered himself and snapped his fingers to call the dog over to him. The dog excitedly sniffed around the room and continued around the desk toward where Slaughter was sitting, at which point its handler abruptly pulled it back.

The handler, a medium-built man in his early to mid-forties, sported a tie over his short-sleeved white dress shirt and a smug look on his face. He looked Bill directly in the eye. "How does it feel to be tracked by Harass II?"[1]

"Tracked for *what?*" Bill asked.

"You'll see," the handler said.

---

1   Harass II, John Preston's tracking dog, was also known as Harrass II and Harrass 2.

CHAPTER 6

ARREST

Bill was still trying to figure out what the dog handler and his intimidating German shepherd had accomplished when Detective Slaughter escorted him back across the dark parking lot and into the police station. What did the dog handler mean by tracking him? From where? And with what evidence? Although unnerved by the experience, Bill felt reassured by the fact that he was innocent. He'd had nothing to do with the murder being investigated, which meant there couldn't be any evidence against him. He was led into a large room. Numerous desks had been lined alongside opposite walls, creating an aisle through the center of the room.

Slaughter sat Bill down in a chair in the center of the aisle, and Bill was soon surrounded by several officers and investigators. It seemed half the station's employees had stayed late in order to interrogate him. Before he could catch his breath, uniformed and non uniformed personnel began firing one question after another at him.

"How did you do it?" a plain-clothed officer asked.

"Were you just hoping to steal his wallet before things got out of control?" another officer, uniformed this time, asked.

"Did you meet him down on the beach or in the parking lot?" someone else asked.

Bill's head was spinning. Was this really happening?

"I didn't murder anybody," he said adamantly. "You've got the wrong guy."

His statement merely fueled their fire. The more he maintained his innocence, the harder his inquisitors pressed. They wanted a confession, not a denial.

"Just tell us you killed him," Detective Slaughter said. "Just tell us he made you mad."

"Maybe the fag came on to you," another detective suggested, "and you got upset. Just admit it!"

The questions and accusations kept coming, and as the hours dragged on, Bill found himself running out of patience. "I told you I can't remember where I was nine and a half days ago," he said, his voice cracking from tension, "but I know I wasn't killing anyone!"

Detective Slaughter, unrelenting until now, softened visibly. "Look," he said, pausing to wipe his glasses clean, "if you just confess, we can get you off on manslaughter. You'll only get five years—and be out on good behavior in eighteen months. It's a great deal. Take it if you know what's good for you."

Bill glanced up at the clock. It was nearing midnight. Were they going to keep him here until he confessed? Could they do whatever they wanted to do to force a false confession from him? He didn't know enough about the legal system to answer either question. All he knew was that he couldn't take much more of this. His eyelids were growing heavier by the minute. His stomach, meanwhile, was growling angrily, and his right leg, bouncing up and down in time to the pounding in his chest, was no longer taking orders from his brain. He'd long ago given up on stopping the tremor or the anxiety that was triggering it.

The interrogation continued. Several more hours passed before a clearly frustrated Slaughter finally asked Bill whether he would take a lie detector test.

"Absolutely," Bill said. Desperate to prove his innocence, he was certain that a lie detector test would do just that. Once he was cleared of any suspicion, he could be on his way.

"The fella who administers the test won't be in until the morning," one of the officers on hand said. "We can't let you go, so we're gonna put you in a jail cell. But we won't lock the door."

Bill, unaware that he couldn't be held without being charged with a crime, readily agreed. By now, along with being dog-tired, he was thoroughly intimidated. He didn't want to further annoy the police, and he didn't know he had any other options than to fully comply. After all, the detectives had told him they *couldn't* let him go.

As he stood up, he felt his legs nearly buckle from fatigue. He couldn't say for sure how long he'd been answering questions. All he knew was that he was exhausted.

After following the officer to the one-man cell, Bill willingly stepped inside. The officer who had escorted him to the cell left the door cracked just enough to show that it wasn't locked. With nothing left to do, Bill dropped his aching frame down onto the thin plastic mattress that topped the bunk and tried to get some rest. Confused and frightened, he drifted off to a restless sleep.

When Bill opened his eyes on August 26, it was five o'clock in the morning. He'd slept just two hours. He was disoriented at first, but he didn't need much prompting to remember the nightmare he'd just endured.

Bill glanced from the door to a small table that sat beside a hard metal bunk. Someone had left on the table a silver foil-wrapped hamburger from a fast-food joint and a soft drink with a straw already in it. Bill unwrapped the burger and took a big bite, only to discover that it was cold. Who knew how long it had been sitting there? The soda, in contrast, was warm and flat. Bill, parched from his ordeal, choked down one sip and grimaced. He thought maybe it was a diet soda, which had always tasted like chemicals to Bill. This one was curiously worse than usual.

Bill reluctantly pushed the meal away. As hungry and thirsty as he was, there was no way he'd be able to stomach either the burger or the soft drink.

An officer arrived to escort him to the polygraph room. Although hungry and in desperate need of a shower, Bill dutifully followed the officer to the testing room, where the test's administrator connected a few wires to Bill's stomach, chest, and head, plus another to a finger on his left hand.

The technician asked a series of questions to make sure the machine was working correctly. After a few more questions, the man asked Bill to deliberately lie to him with his next answer. It didn't take long before he appeared satisfied everything was working correctly. From there, he moved on to the real test asking Bill various questions about the murder and his whereabouts that night.

The whole test took all of ten minutes.

Afterward, another officer approached Bill with news of the results. "Well, Mr. Dillon," he said in a tone that teetered on downright cheerfulness, "we gotcha. You're lying."

No one bothered to show Bill the actual results. Instead, he was escorted to the interrogation room once more, and this time the detectives, even more determined to wring a confession from him, let him have it.

"We know you're lying!" one of the investigators barked at him. "The test results prove it! You tried to rob him, and you ended up killing him!"

Once again, the police were hurling a barrage of questions and accusations at Bill, and all he could do was maintain his innocence. The questioning, as relentless as it was fierce, stretched through the morning and into the afternoon.

But Bill refused to back down. "I didn't do it," he said repeatedly. Still struggling to remember where he'd been on the night of August 16 or the following morning, he gave the police a handful of names of people he might have stayed with during the time in question.

Unfortunately, his refusal to cop to the killing only seemed to make his interrogators angrier.

Finally, Detective Slaughter cut loose. "Well then screw it, you prick!" he bellowed furiously. "If you don't want to go about this the easy way, we'll just have to arrest you for murder! You could have been out in eighteen months! Now you're going to the chair!"

Perhaps sensing they'd pushed him too far, the police softened their approach. Sergeant Kindrick, the detective who, with Christine Barringer's help, had first interviewed Bill and his brother while canvassing the parking lot above Canova Beach, took over the questioning. Bill observed the group staring at him and for the first time he noted that an officer turned on a tape recorder. In stark contrast to Slaughter, Kindrick was gentle in his demeanor. Like everyone else, he wanted to know where Bill had been on Sunday, August 16.

By now, though, Bill was too flustered and too tired to remember anything accurately. He began by saying he'd been at the Bocci brothers' apartment.

"Matt Bocci can verify that I was there on Sunday," Bill said, "but see, what I'm trying to do is actually remember just exactly where I was. And it's not the easiest thing in the world to do, I'm telling you. If I knew just exactly where I was, I'd tell you."

"But you, uh, to the best of your knowledge or your recollection, you stayed at Matt's house, correct?" Kindrick asked.

"Yes," Bill said cautiously, "with Donna."

"Okay. Who else was there?"

"Uh, his brother Glenn."

In fact, Matt's brother's name was Joe. Glenn Zeller was Matt and Joe's roommate. But Bill, who hadn't known the Bocci brothers for very long, was drawing a blank under unrelenting pressure from the detectives.

"I thought his brother had a different name," Kindrick said.

"His brother does," Bill said, groping for the right one. "Mark."

"Mark?"

"Mark Bocci."

Once again, Bill got the name wrong.

Still struggling to remember, Bill added, "See what I'm trying to catch ahold of is because I told my Probation Officer that I'd been staying there and if I could just get to my...or talk to my Probation Officer and tell him what day I ...that I talked to him I can tell you just how many...what time it was exactly, but see I haven't been able to talk to anybody to find out just..."

"Do you know your Probation Officer's name?"

"Yeah, Randy Amos, but I don't know his home phone. He wouldn't give me his home phone.

"Well, I talked to Randy and I talked to you and I think it was uh, yesterday..." Barringer chimed in. " and you...and you told me that, uh, that it was Wednesday the nineteenth..."

"But..." Bill, confused, started to object.

"...that you and Donna hitchhiked over to Melbourne to see Randy." Barringer continued.

"We hitchhiked, we got a ride with Andy..." Bill said.

"And at that time you told me it was Wednesday."

"That was Wednesday?" Bill asked, trying to count days in his head. "So then it was... then it was Sunday night then... It was Sunday night because Donna came and picked me up," he said. "I know for a fact my sister was cooking...cooking a dinner one Sunday, because Donna and I'd had a fight the night before and I went home, and I slept in my brother's car because I wasn't allowed to sleep in the house… And Donna came by in a red Mustang that was a car of the people that she was staying with, was George and Linda. I don't know their last name, they were staying in the Ocean Star Motel in Cocoa Beach. And I went up there with her. She said, 'Come up here with me.' I went up there with her, and she made me sit around in the laundry room and outside on the beach all day long. And she was gettin' mad at them because they were getting' drunk. And they were giving her a hard time about me and stuff, and, you know, everybody seems to give her a hard time about me, I can't understand. But I waited around until about…about six o'clock, and then I got pretty teed off, and I told her, hey, you better come on, and whatever. So she just left. She just got dressed, and we were gonna go . . ."

Under severe duress, Bill didn't mention spending the night with Charles and Roseanna Rogers. Instead, he told his interrogators that Donna wanted to go to an AA meeting and that they hitched their way back to town, and eventually ended up at the Bocci brothers' apartment. From there, his account grew more disjointed, with Kindrick and Barringer taking turns guiding him back to the events of what *they* determined was Sunday night. As intent as Bill was to remember things correctly, the detectives seemed equally determined to trap him. The result was sprawling, incoherent narrative that at times was spot-on and at other times was simply muddled. He just could not recall which night was which.

"I'm trying to remember, I just can't… You know somethin' I don't think it was Wednesday that I called Randy… I caught up and this is where…where I'm lost., I'm caught up in when I called…" Bill said racking his brain.

Alarmed by where the interview was heading, Bill declared, "My memory is just…I don't know, it never usually fails me, usually doesn't." But at the moment, he was totally bewildered.

Officer Eugene arrived toward the end of the taped interview. Byrd was running for county sheriff, and Bill had been serving as a volunteer for his campaign that summer, posting signs all over town for the candidate. Bill, confident Byrd was just the person to clear up this whole mess, had asked Detective Slaughter several hours earlier to call Byrd. "Gene can vouch for me," Bill had said adamantly. "He knows me."

Now with Officer Byrd on hand, Kindrick suggested he turn off the tape recorder and give Bill and the officer some time alone.

"You mentioned earlier about you feeling uncomfortable around us, so, you know, Gene's here, do you wanna…"

"It's not really the fact that … feel uncomfortable, it's just the fact that, uh, that I'm not guilty of…"

"Of what's… what is, uh…"

"….investigated here."

"Would it make you more comfortable if you talked with him alone or?"

"Well, I could talk with him for a few minutes…"

…"Okay, the time now is seven fifty p.m. and we're gonna stop the interview for a little while. We'll shut it off."

After Kindrick shut off the device and left the room, Byrd pointed his index finger straight at Bill. "They got you, Bill. You might as well make it easy on yourself and confess. They got you!"

Horrified, Bill's heart sank. He'd failed to convince anyone of his innocence. Worse, his last, best hope had turned on him. He didn't understand the bizarre happenings and why Byrd seemed certain of his guilt right off the bat. Absorbing that disappointment, however, was nothing compared to what he had to do next: call his mom.

A pair of officers escorted Bill to the front desk. It was a little before six o'clock in the evening. No doubt his mother had just made dinner and the family was about to sit down to a meal together.

Bill picked up the rotary phone on the front desk.

"Hello?" his mom answered after the second ring.

"Mom," Bill said, his voice choking up, "they're arresting me for the murder. Mom, I didn't do it. They're threatening me, Mom."

He heard his mother gasp on the other end of the line.

"If you didn't do it," she said worriedly, "don't say that you did."

Bill opened his mouth to reply but was instructed to hang up.

Seconds later he was being locked in a cell. He walked stiffly to the bunk, sat down, and rested his head in his hands thinking he'd just broken his mother's heart.

CHAPTER 7

WILD CARD

Bill was handcuffed and driven in a squad car to the county jail, and as he stared out the window at the evening landscape, he watched his youth disappear one block, one stoplight at a time. Suddenly everything he had taken for granted—the freedom to move and make his own decisions as he pleased—was streaking past in an untouchable blur. Anger welled up inside him. How could the police interfere with his life like this?

The county jail, in contrast to the outside world, struck him as impossibly small, a static rendering of hopelessness. As he walked through the main door, he saw immediately that everything inside was painted a drab olive green. To his right were two phones on the wall, plus several large glass windows that separated visitors from the prisoners inside. Little round vents beneath each window allowed for communication, but physical contact appeared impossible.

Bill was herded into the dungeon-like bullpen, a sixteen-man cell currently overflowing with close to thirty prisoners. A few tables occupied the front part of the cell, beyond which several mattresses were strewn across the floor. The air, putrid and still, was suffocating. Bill was thankful when he was assigned an actual bunk in a four-man cell that opened into the bullpen.

Chow arrived a short while later, and the rest of the inmates gathered at the tables. But Bill passed on the meager meal. Sick to his stomach and still in shock, he wanted nothing to do with any of the other prisoners.

The bullpen's walls were bare, except for a television that hung from the ceiling in the corner. At ten o'clock that night, Bill watched in disbelief as his photo flashed across the TV screen, accompanied by the sensational headline, MURDER AT THE BEACH. William Dillon, the news reporter breathlessly announced, was the chief suspect in the brutal killing of James Dvorak.

Bill wiped self-consciously at his damp forehead. It seemed doubtful that his life could get any more surreal, but as he fought to catch a few hard-earned winks later that night in his bunk, his mind raced with what still lay ahead. He needed help—this much he knew. It was time to call an attorney.

The overcrowded Brevard County Jail served as a temporary domicile for two-bit thugs, petty criminals, and those awaiting trial for a variety of offenses ranging from shoplifting to rape or even murder. The small-town lockup grew in population every time a local detective, police officer, or sheriff's investigator apprehended a suspect. The Brevard County State Attorney's Office was then charged with prosecuting each of the accused. Thus, Bill Dillon was just one among many in the lockup awaiting trial. His was set for November 30, still three months away.

The next morning, on August 27, Bill was ordered by two jail officers to exit the bullpen.

"You're being moved," one of them said.

Bill's mind raced. *Where and why?*

Outside in the hallway, a young public defender approached Bill and his escort. He was short, with close-cropped hair. "I'm your attorney," he told Bill confidently. "Just be calm. Everything will be all right. They don't have shit. They got nothin'. We're gonna get ya outta here."

The officers then escorted Bill to a single cell away from the rest of the population. No one told him why he was being segregated from the others; he only knew that his new home had no phone or television and was secured behind two steel doors. As for Bill's new attorney, he never saw him again.

Bill was in his cell the next day, August 28, when the guard outside ordered him out of his cell.

"Come on," the guard said. "You've got a lawyer visitation."

Bill followed the guard to the glass, and there on the other side sat a complete stranger, not the public defender he'd met the day before.

"I'm Frank Clark," the man said through the vent beneath the glass. "The court has appointed me as your attorney."

"What happened to the other guy?" Bill asked.

"There was a conflict of interest. Judge Morton gave me your case."

Bill, confused at first, quickly warmed to his new attorney. Frank was older and more seasoned, a street lawyer who appeared to have earned his wisdom the hard way. For the first time in days, Bill felt a surge of optimism. It appeared he'd been appointed a highly competent attorney.

Frank seemed to share the previous attorney's confidence. "They don't have anything," he told Bill. He started working the case immediately, quizzing Bill about where he'd been during the time of the murder, what he'd told the police, and so on.

There was one bit of troubling news, however. A man by the name of Roger Dale Chapman, purportedly one of Bill's fellow inmates in the bullpen during Bill's first night in the county jail, had reported to the police that Bill had confessed to the murder. He had since been released.

Bill, dumbfounded, searched his memory but came up blank. He wasn't there to make small talk with strangers, and he certainly hadn't confessed to anyone. But Frank said it didn't matter. Chapman was being represented by the public defender's office and was going to testify as a witness for the state against Bill. Bill's previous attorney, who was from the public defender's office, had therefore been forced to give up the case due to the conflict of interest.

Bill was both astonished and angry. Why had this Chapman fellow lied to the police? What could have possibly motivated the man to spin such a tale?

He shook off the news and tried to focus on making a case with his new lawyer. Bill knew very little about the law, but he believed wholeheartedly in Frank Clark, who appeared convinced that Bill was innocent and was clearly there to help him.

On August 31, Bill celebrated his twenty-second birthday in jail. He wasn't sure whether he'd ever get used to it, from the slimy green mold in the showers to the dusty brown grime that coated everything else, including the concrete floors. There was a dingy string mop available, but Bill had yet to see anyone use it. He had been transferred to a single cell, past the bullpen, past the four-man cells, at the end of a long hall. No windows. A door made of steel. Isolated.

He and Frank Clark had a scant three months to prepare for the capital murder trial, and the two went to work gathering all the available facts. Frank warned Bill to be careful about what he said if he received a visit from Donna or spoke to her on the phone. At this point, the attorney said, there was no telling whose side Donna was going to testify for. Frank told Bill that Donna had been speaking to detectives. Other friends of Bill's—Matt and Joe Bocci, for instance—were answering questions from the police, as well. But Donna had already changed her story repeatedly while speaking to Frank, which wasn't a good sign.

In fact, Donna had only known Bill for two weeks before the murder, but it was possible the prosecuting side might try to portray her as his steady girlfriend and thus a credible witness. If she could nail down his physical location at the time of the murder, her testimony might weigh heavily with the jury, at least in theory. In reality, Frank told Bill, it was hard to predict how the jury would react to her testimony. If she couldn't keep her story straight, it was likely her testimony wouldn't be worth a hill of beans and thus neither side would benefit from it.

Soon after Frank had warned him about her, Bill received a visit from Donna, who left him with several phone numbers where he could reach her. No one could call Bill at the county jail, but he was allowed to call out, and in the days that followed, he called Donna several times.

In early September, Frank arrived at the county jail with shattering news for Bill: a grand jury had indicted him on first-degree murder. This meant that the jury, after meeting in secret to receive testimony and weigh the available evidence, had decided the state had enough to move forward with its case. What that evidence was, remained for the moment anyway, a mystery.

But, as awful as that sounded, Frank also had some good news: a couple by the name of Charles and Roseanna Rogers had come forward to tell Frank that Bill and Donna had been with them on the night of the murder. Frank explained that Charles and Roseanna had been shocked to read in the newspaper that Bill had been arrested, for they had already told the police that Bill and Donna had slept in their apartment on the night of August 16 and hadn't left until the following morning. After Bill's arrest, they had tried to contact the police and ask them why their statements were being ignored, but eventually they had been forced to seek out Frank directly; it seemed the police were uninterested in what they had to say.

"Thank goodness they came forward because Donna and I had finally figured that out," Bill recollected. "We were there all night, Frank."

Bill had spoken on the phone with Donna about his whereabouts on the night of the murder, among other things, and the two had slowly worked through all of the possibilities before settling on the Ocean Star Motel in Cocoa Beach. Donna had likely relayed the information to the police, which would explain why the police had initially questioned Charles and Roseanna. Bill, for his part, had failed to mention his overnight stay at the couple's motel apartment during his interrogation, but that was only because he'd been so overwhelmed during the questioning that he'd drawn a complete blank. Now, though, he had a better grasp of the timeline surrounding the night of the murder. Better still, he had an ironclad alibi. If Charles and Roseanna *and* Donna all located him at the Ocean Star Motel on the night of the murder, the prosecution's case—whatever it might be—would fall apart. He would be fully cleared of suspicion that he'd had anything to do with James Dvorak's death.

One of the phone numbers Donna had given Bill belonged to Joanne Stinchcomb, a friend of Donna's and someone Donna often stayed with when she wasn't sleeping at her mom's house. Bill, on one occasion, ended up speaking with Joanne when Donna wasn't around, and during one of their conversations, Joanne echoed the concerns Frank had voiced earlier. She told Bill that Donna was trying to get information for the detectives.

As if on cue, the next time Bill spoke with Donna, she seemed to be trying to trick him into making incriminating statements, and as time wore on, their conversations grew more worrisome. She would ask him whether he remembered doing something she knew very well he hadn't done, and he would reply strongly in the negative. At times, it almost sounded as if she was guiding the conversation and someone else was listening in. Was she reading from a script? Bill couldn't be sure.

With each passing day, Donna's motives seemed more and more suspect. Would she tell the truth? Would she get her facts straight in time to convince the jury?

After several weeks, Bill got his first clue. During a visit from his family in mid-October, Bill learned that Donna had engaged in an illicit affair with none other than Detective Charles Slaughter! The story was front-page news because Donna had, allegedly, called a reporter, Gina Thomas at *Florida Today,* and dished about having sex with the chief detective who was targeting her supposed boyfriend. Apparently, one night after questioning her, Slaughter had driven her home and had sex with her.

The revelation was nothing short of a bombshell. But as salacious as the news was, Bill was certain it would be good for his case. Donna, if

Framed | 53 |

she decided to lie on the witness stand and somehow implicate Bill in the murder, would have a hard time convincing the jury that she was in any way credible. The police, too, would look bad in all of this. How could they use as their key witness a woman who'd had sex with their lead detective? No jury would buy it. The judge would probably throw the case out.

According to the article, the affair was indeed a blow to the prosecution, which considered Donna a key witness. Yet the state was pressing on with its case. Worse, both Bill's attorney, Frank Clark, and Sheriff Miller were quoted in the article as saying they thought that Donna's accusations were "immaterial" to Bill's defense.

The paper reported: "Sheriff Jake Miller said he couldn't comment further on the matter, nor could he predict its effect on Dillon's trial. Slaughter, who Miller described as an excellent homicide investigator with more than a decade of police experience, also declined to discuss Parrish's allegations."

"His personal life is not our concern unless it reflects badly on the department," Miller said in the article. The article continued to report that, "Dillon's court appointed attorney, Frank Clark, said Monday that Parrish's accusations are 'immaterial' to his defense."

The article further reported that Brevard state attorney Douglas Cheshire said, "Parrish's allegations have no effect on Dillon's trial . . ."

Bill privately fumed. He could understand the outlandish spin that the sheriff and state attorney were putting on the matter. But what about the comment attributed to his own attorney? Whose side was Frank on?

When Bill met with Frank later, Frank explained his motives behind the quote: he didn't want to anger the prosecution. In any case, he told Bill more bad news: the police now thought that Bill had convinced Donna to call the reporter with news of the affair. Bill shook his head. As frustrated as he was with his attorney, he was even angrier with Donna. While he had been fighting for his freedom, she had been having an affair with the detective trying to put him in the electric chair. She was talking to the press, providing misleading information, and appeared to be relishing every minute in the spotlight. Bill believed she had been one of the key witnesses, if not *the* key witness, during the grand jury proceedings. She had been playing the police. But she'd also been playing Bill.

CHAPTER 8

THE AFFAIR

After the story of the affair broke, Bill and his attorney felt confident that Donna would not be a credible witness, regardless of how she testified at the trial. In fact, Frank told Bill that whichever side tried to use Donna as a witness would ultimately get burned. She had proven to be fickle, unpredictable, and loyal to no one. It would thus be best to keep a safe distance.

Unbeknownst to Bill at the time, however, was the state's own internal investigation of the affair. On October 23, the Bureau of Staff Services interviewed Donna at a secret hearing. Frank Billings, an inspector for the bureau, wanted to get to the bottom of exactly what had happened between Donna and Detective Slaughter.

After being sworn in, Donna was questioned about her interaction with the police. Although Detective Slaughter's conduct was at the core of the investigation, it turned out Thom Fair was the agent who had met with Donna the most.

"I've seen Thom Fair the most out of all of them," Donna told Billings in the police report, "because he's the only one I'll really talk to as far as uh, getting along with, because he knows me more or less as far as, he knows when I'm lyin' or tellin' the truth, cause he knows me as a person."

Donna described herself as "confused" during her first few interviews with the police but admitted that she'd been playing "head games" and "trying to pull the wool over their eyes." It wasn't until September 2, the night before the grand jury, that she started telling what she *claimed* was the truth. Fair was tough during the questioning, she said, but Slaughter was "the hardest, meanest detective on the force." During their long interrogations, Donna stated, he called her "a burnout, a drug addict, and a space cadet," among other things.

As the hearing went on, Donna told Billings that she'd had sex with Detective Slaughter on the night of August 31, coincidentally Bill's twenty-second birthday, and more importantly, three days *before* the grand jury was convened. After a particularly tough interrogation, during which Slaughter relentlessly grilled Donna, the detective offered to drive her home. Slaughter had a six-pack of beer in his car, along with a yellow notepad. While he drove and sipped beer, she scribbled down answers to his ongoing questions. They stopped at a 7-Eleven past Melbourne Beach for food and cigarettes, and Detective Slaughter, after giving Donna some money to go inside and buy whatever she wanted, told her to keep the change when she returned to the car. Suddenly in a generous mood, the detective offered to help Donna find a job. Then the conversation turned personal:

> **Donna:** He kept driving, and after a while I guess Charlie got tired of askin' questions, and we started talkin' about personal things. We talked about his divorce, why he got divorced. I talked about my divorce, and more. Before I knew it, we started talkin' about me and how he's talked about me as a person, and he told me the first time he saw me in the sheriff's office with this one shirt—I can't even remember. He said I had this shirt on, that, my uh—I guess I'll say breasts—were protruding, and he noticed it and it turned him on. He liked my butt. That's when he started gettin' personal.
>
> **Billings:** Previously you told me you had a sweater on.
>
> **Donna:** I guess it was a sweater, then. That's what he said: sweater. I just can't pick out the specific sweater he was talkin' about. I still to this day don't know what sweater he was talkin' about. So I said to myself, "That's why he gave me twenty dollars. That's why he's drivin' me down to the beach, and that's why he's bein' so nice to me, 'cause he's a horny old man that wants a piece, and the only way he thinks he can get it is to bribe me with all his comments, his compliments, his money, and his position in the squad." I put two and two together, and I got four.
>
> **Billings:** What happened then?
>
> **Donna:** I started thinkin' of a way to get out of it, 'cause I really didn't want to go to bed with the guy. I had no interest in him. I had a boyfriend. Uh, since Billy and I—since Billy's been in jail, I been datin' guys. I didn't need to be with Charlie, you know. If I wanted

to get laid—excuse my pun; I'm just bein' honest—I, I didn't have to go with Charlie. I could just go to the Pelican and blink at somebody. Sounds conceited, but it's the truth. But I went and I did it, you know. I'm sorry I did.

Billings: I need to know the specifics. What happened?

Donna: Well, we got to the beach, and he says, "Uh, excuse me. I gotta go to the bathroom." He got out of the car, and he walked up to the shack that has the men's rooms in it.

Billings: What beach are we talking about?

Donna: A beach that goes across this big bridge, and it's a huge beach out in the back off a dirt road—well, not a dirt road, but a dark road. He went to the bathroom. He came back into the car, got back into the car, and asked me to give him head, or you know, oral sex. That's when I hesitated and said, "Well, you know, I don't know if I really want to." And then I said to myself, "Hey, Donna, do it. Get it over with, and go home." So I did. Not all the way.

Billings: Was this beach south of the Sebastian Bridge? Did you go over the big bridge?

Donna: To my knowledge, yes. And there wasn't a car in sight.

Billings: You stopped, both got out of the car, and walked towards this bridge that went to the beach?

Donna: Yeah, and we—he went to the bathroom. He stood there for a couple of minutes, and said, "Let's get back in the car cause I'm cold," cause it was windy that night. It had rained that day.

Billings: What did he say to you?

Donna: He said, "Let's go back in the car, and let me see how good you are at uh, oral sex."

Billings: What did you say then?

Donna: At first I hesitated, and I said, "Well, Donna, you wanna get outta here. Just do it and get it over with." Not really wanting to, I did it anyway.

Billings: Did he approach you on the bridge?

Donna: Yeah, he kissed me. He kissed me on the bridge, stuck his hand up my shirt, and then I said, "Let's get back in the car. It's windy and I'm cold."

Billings: You got back in the car, and then you went north on A1A. What happened then?

Donna: He unzipped his pants and told me to put my head down, and he said, "Don't worry. No one can see you. It's dark."

Billings: What, in fact, did you do?

Donna: I started to, and then a couple of minutes later I stopped. 'cause I didn't like it. In other words, I wasn't into it. I was, had, had other things on my mind, which was goin' to the Pelican and havin' a few drinks and forgettin' about the day, 'cause it was a long day.

Billings: Did you actually engage in oral sex with—

Donna: We engaged, but as far as him havin' any type of reaction that a man has, no, he didn't.

Billings: At this point, was all the beer—

Donna: No. The beer was—there's still a couple of cans left in the bag. There was a bag, probably two or three cans in it. I'd only had two beers, but I was so tired that it, it made me kinda not drunk. It just made me feel good and tipsy. But I knew in my mind what I was doing. I wasn't, you know, out of it or anything.

Billings: After you decided not to have oral sex with him, what did he say to that?

Donna: He said, "Well, if you don't want to do it, why don't we just go back to my house? If my daughter's asleep, we'll go in my bedroom, and we'll have a lot more fun because there'll be a lot more room, you know, and then maybe we could [do] somethin' other than that." And I said, "Well, look, I got a date at one-thirty, and he said, "At one-thirty in the morning?" I said, "Yeah." I said, "There's a lot of times I go out with guys that late because I been tied up with this case, and I don't have time to go out with people at normal hours anymore." And he said, "Well, we'll, we'll go back. We'll set the alarm. I promise. We'll set the alarm, and my daughter won't know, and I'll get you up, and I'll get you out of the house, and you'll be back in time to do anything you want." And then he said, "But you gotta swear you don't tell anybody." And he repeated that at least ten times over and over, "Donna, please don't tell on me! Please don't tell on me!" And I said—

Billings: What else did he say?

Donna: Oh, "I promise I'll get you a job. I'll do this for you, I'll do that for you." In other words, he promised me and tried to impress me, and he never had any intentions of helpin' me. He didn't give a shit about me!

Donna went on to describe the moment when Slaughter took her to his house. He left her in his car while he went inside to check on his daughter. He returned a moment later and, after explaining that his daughter was still awake, sneaked Donna through the door from the garage and across the hallway to his bedroom. Donna didn't stay long—maybe thirty minutes. But she was there long enough to have sex with the detective, after which she asked him to drive her home.

Donna: The whole time we drove back, "Oh, Donna, please don't tell. I swear I'll get you a job. I'll do this, I'll do that. Please don't tell."

Billings: Did he say why he didn't want you to say anything?

Donna: He had too much to lose. He didn't say specifically what; he just said, "I got a lot to lose." I said, "Yeah? How long you been on the police force?" He said, "Twenty years." I said, "Did you ever, were you ever a uniform cop?" He said, "For a while." Now he told me he stayed on uniform for about—I think it was seven years, he said—and then he became a detective. And then I went to the Pelican. Instead of goin' home, I had him drop me off at the Pelican, 'cause I was pretty upset by then. And I went in. It was two-for-one night, and Jeannie was behind the bar. I said, "Jeannie, give me two white Russians now!" and I drank 'em down. I kept drinkin' and drinkin'.

Billings: Donna, those things that you said to him that night, those truths, or those truthful statements, were said for the first time to him and were never told to anybody else. Is that correct?

Donna: Yes.

Billings: They were significant to the, to the trial itself?

Donna: Yes. Just because I had beer in me, and I was bein' myself. I wasn't bein' somebody that I wasn't. I was bein' Donna LaPredo [maiden name]. I was feelin' good, tipsy, tired. I said, "Donna, you can't fight it. You're tired. Don't even try to bullshit the guy. It's a waste of time." That's when I started talkin', and that's when he started findin' things out. In other words, I was just bein' me instead of bullshittin'.

Before Billings wrapped things up, he asked Donna about her ongoing conversations with Frank Clark. Billings was particularly interested to know how the attorney had reacted after Donna had told him that she'd had sex with Detective Slaughter.

Billings: Did he say anything to the effect, "That will be significant at the trial?" or "We'll bring that up at the trial"?

Donna: Uh, I'm not gonna answer that, because uh, I really am not sure, and I don't want to get myself into any trouble. In other words, I'm not positive that he said, you know, specifically, specifically, "Hey, this is going to help our case!" I can say that, you know, he looked pleased. That's why I was so upset when I saw the article today, 'cause he said that it had nothin' to do with it, the case, which is a lie.

Like Bill, Donna appeared dismayed by Frank Clark's comments to the newspaper. How could her affair with Slaughter be immaterial to the defense? Nevertheless, she'd made hash of the investigation. The star witness was reading the newspaper and communicating with local reporters while detectives were questioning her. More information was leaking every day to the press, and much of it, Bill believed, was likely coming from Donna, who was feeding the media, the police, and the attorneys a constantly changing story. She had admitted to repeatedly lying and deliberately misleading investigators. Then she'd rolled on Detective Slaughter after he'd failed to come through with a job in exchange for her silence.

Detective Charles Slaughter, meanwhile, had been suspended, demoted, and removed from the case—and docked thirty days' pay. Not long after the conclusion of the internal investigation, he retired from the force, his career in shambles, and Sergeant James Bolick stepped in to take his place. Thom Fair, in turn, became the acting lead investigator in the James Dvorak murder case. What Bill didn't know was the extent to which the affair had spooked the prosecution. It was obvious from Billing's interview with Donna that the prosecution was terrified the affair would sink their case. It appeared the charade was beginning to unravel, and Frank Clark presented Bill with a welcome piece of good news. The prosecution had suddenly taken the death penalty off the table. In Bill's mind, the tide was beginning to turn and the prosecution would soon admit they had the wrong man.

CHAPTER 9
AN AGING JURY

Locked in the county jail, cut off from the outside world, Bill felt almost peripheral to his own case. In fact, as the trial approached, he had only a vague understanding of the case the prosecution was building against him. The prosecution, Frank had explained, was going to try to destroy Bill's alibi. They had gathered numerous witnesses who would soon testify they had seen Bill at the Pelican, near the scene of the crime, on the night of the murder.

Then there was the supposed eyewitness. A man by the name of John Douglas Parker had come forward claiming to have picked up a bloody hitchhiker in the early morning hours of August 17 on Highway A1A, near the vicinity of the murder. According to Parker, he'd had oral sex with the stranger, who had inadvertently left a bloodstained orange Surf-It T-shirt in Parker's pickup truck. The police had used Parker's description of the hitchhiker to create a composite sketch, which had shown up in the newspapers as a best-guess rendering of James Dvorak's suspected killer. With short dark hair and a mustache, the man in the sketch hardly resembled Bill. But police said witnesses had seen Bill wearing an orange Surf-It T-shirt at the Pelican on the night of the murder. Moreover, they had supposedly connected Bill to the bloodstained T-shirt with the help of Harass II, the intimidating German shepherd Bill had come face-to-face with on the night of his interrogation.

A week before the trial date, Frank filed a motion asking Judge Stanley Wolfman to ban the evidence associated with the tracking dog, which Clark asserted was incompetently gathered and highly prejudicial. But the judge delayed a ruling either way, stating that he would rule on the motion when the prosecution called the dog handler to testify.

Bill, meanwhile, had just a few meetings with Frank to prepare for the trial. At the last one, just before the trial, he learned that more witnesses had come forward against him, including barmaids at the Pelican and Mark, the bar's bouncer. According to police, the bouncer had given Bill a ride to Donna's home on the night of the murder.

"He gave me a ride," Bill said irritably, "but not the night of the murder. He's got his dates mixed up."

As frustrated as Bill was, he knew Frank Clark wasn't happy either. Bill had long since given him all the information he had, which wasn't much, and Frank clearly had been struggling ever since to cobble together a defense. Bill had an alibi in Charles and Roseanna Rogers, but what if the prosecution threw so much mud against the wall that something stuck?

Monday, November 30, 1981, dawned warm and clear in Brevard County. Just after lunch, Bill was escorted from the county jail to the courthouse through the "time tunnel," a ground-level pedestrian tunnel that traversed the back parking lot, connecting the back of the jail to the back of the courthouse. As wide as a two-lane road, the tunnel was dotted with numerous tiny windows through which light streamed into the tan-colored passageway. All of the windows were above head level, though, which meant Bill couldn't see outside as he walked.

Bill was taken to the holding pen and shackled to other prisoners awaiting hearings. But he didn't stay there long.

He was called out a few minutes later and taken back through the time tunnel, back to the jail, where he was informed he was about to receive a haircut. Frank showed up in the jail's office a few minutes later to explain.

"You can't go into the courtroom looking sloppy," the attorney said. "You have to look neat."

"But I don't want a haircut," Bill protested, eyeing the huge pair of shears in the bailiff's right hand. As soon as this farce of a trial was over, he'd be returning to the real world. The last thing he wanted was a bad haircut.

Frank, though, was adamant, and Bill reflexively scrunched up his shoulders as the bailiff, taking his cues from Frank, went to work with the shears.

Frank had been insisting that Bill get a haircut for several days now, and Bill had dutifully relayed his attorney's request to the guards, who in turn had told him he couldn't get a haircut because there was no place in the jail to cut inmates' hair. He would later learn this was not true.

For the moment, all Bill could do was hold still while the bailiff cut Bill's hair along a straight line. His hair was cut dry, without the benefit of a shampooing. Not that any shampoo was available in his cell. Bill had been washing his hair with bar soap whenever he took a shower. As Bill watched all the hair below his chin line fall in clumps to the floor, he wondered at the wisdom of changing his appearance right before the trial. He remembered the artist's sketch of the suspected killer: the perpetrator had sported short hair and a mustache. Everyone knew Bill grew his hair past his shoulders—and had never had a mustache, since he could hardly grow any facial hair. Why make him look *more* like the killer?

A couple minutes later, Bill was the owner of a hacksaw haircut.

"Listen," Frank said, no doubt hoping to reassure Bill, "the prosecution didn't want to agree to this. It will be easier for them to assassinate your character if they can portray you as a long-haired, pot-smoking kid."

In fact, Frank told Bill, the start of jury selection had been delayed by thirty minutes while the two sides argued over the haircut.

"You can't go in there looking sloppy," he repeated.

Bill understood Frank's fears. It was obvious the prosecution hoped to depict him as a vagrant beach bum. Nevertheless, the haircut seemed like an ill-advised move, and he began to wonder about his attorney. Whose side was he on? Bill had no choice but to put his faith in the justice system, which he believed in wholeheartedly. Yes, he was scared. But he was also mad—and confident. He knew he was innocent and couldn't be found guilty since there couldn't possibly be any evidence against him. All he had to do, he told himself, was get on the stand in his own defense and tell the truth. He would surely be acquitted after that.

The county courthouse, a classical revival structure with four enormous white columns out front, boasted a sprawling profile. Cameramen from all the local TV stations and newspapers were huddled on the steps out front, but Bill never saw them as he and Frank emerged from the time tunnel. This time, rather than go to the holding pen, Bill walked with his attorney straight into the courtroom. The journey was made more laborious by the heavy sandbag strapped to Bill's right ankle and hidden from view. Dressed in a blue jacket with a light blue shirt peeking out from underneath, Bill took a seat at the defense table, from where he was expected to silently watch the jury selection. Working its way through his system was a dose of Sinequan, an antidepressant doctors had prescribed for Bill to help combat his nerves. The drug had a subduing effect, but Bill was far from calm.

Directly in front of him, and perched above an imposing square podium, sat Judge Wolfman. Balding slightly, with a smattering of dark hair in back, he wore a black robe that looked almost ghoulish in the bright glare of the courtroom. On Bill's right was the aging jury pool, most of whom had been eyeballing him from the moment he'd entered. Every one of them looked older than Bill's parents. To Bill's left was the prosecution. All that was missing, Bill thought as he took in the courtroom for the first time, was an upper balcony like the one in the film *To Kill a Mockingbird*.

It was 2:30 p.m.

Judge Wolfman, having already made sure the room was cooled down to his liking, slammed his gavel on the desk and called the court to order. As jury selection began, Bill got his first glimpse of the prosecution team, led by assistant state attorney Karen Thompson. She was of average height, with light brown hair and a clear, makeup-free complexion. Bill's impression, from the moment she spoke, was that she evinced an air of superiority, as though she couldn't possibly be wrong about anything. It was clear she was the alpha on her team, never mind her gender.

Assisting Thompson was Michael Hunt, also an assistant state attorney. He struck Bill as a perpetually angry man. Bill imagined Hunt as the kid who had spent most of his youth being bullied; someone who had a chip on his shoulder. What Bill could not imagine, however, was how they could put together a case.

Thompson and Hunt belonged to an ambitious but relatively young group of prosecutors working out of the Brevard County state attorney's office. Thompson and Hunt, would likely benefit from working on big cases like Bill's to help them climb the professional ladder.

The prosecution tossed a few jurors as they worked their way through the jury pool. Frank, too, dismissed a few after interviewing them but foolishly used up all of his strikes too early, before he had sized up the entire group. For his part, Bill couldn't help withering a bit under the collective stare of the prospective jury members. It wasn't just that they were much older than him. None appeared friendly.

After two and a half hours, the attorneys had whittled the group down to eight men and four women. The jury was then excused for five minutes while the prosecution informed the judge that Donna was a possible flight risk because Bill had intimidated her, warning her that she better get her act together. This was true, Frank countered, in so far as Bill, fed up with Donna's endlessly changing story, had simply told her it was time to tell the truth. But the prosecution was obviously trying to convince the judge that Bill was a dangerous and violent young man. Frank, doing his best to counter such a portrayal, pointed out that Donna had made upward of twenty-five wildly conflicting statements to the state attorney's office, to the investigators, and to the grand jury. Her statements weren't just "confused," Frank argued. She was weaving a complex web of deception.

After the jury was called back in, Judge Wolfman informed the jury members that they would not be officially impaneled until the following morning. Neither would they be sequestered. Before dismissing them for the day, the judge instructed them to avoid reading any newspaper articles about the trial in the interim, lest anyone be exposed to the numerous stories concerning the murder. But would they listen? And would the prosecution's witnesses also be told not to watch the news or read the papers?

Bill hadn't been reading the news, but some of the morning headlines, such as WITNESS SAYS MURDERER HAS BLOODY HANDS and WITNESS: SUSPECT WAS AT MURDER SITE, had nevertheless made their way to him during his conversations with Frank and his family. His reaction each time was one of anger but also disbelief. Had he already been convicted in the court of public opinion? He was innocent, which meant people were lying to the press. But who? And why?

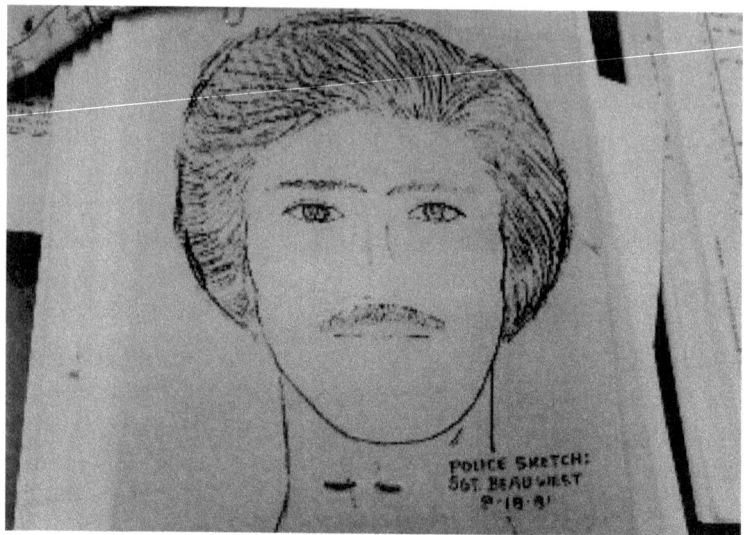

Artist sketch of suspect above. William Dillon arrest photo below.
Brevard County, Florida sheriff's department 1981

CHAPTER 10

TALL TALE

Judge Wolfman's gavel banged against his wood podium at precisely 9:35 the next morning, signaling the beginning of the second day of the trial and the first day of testimony. After impaneling the jury and giving the jury members their preliminary instructions, he turned the proceedings over to Michael Hunt, the assistant prosecutor.

Bill, drowsy from the sedatives but still agitated, watched from the defense table as Hunt began his opening remarks. Hunt outlined the case and what the prosecution expected the evidence to show. He then offered a motive for the crime: William Dillon had come to the beach looking for money, and only after robbing James Dvorak did he beat the man to death. Hunt described Bill as destitute and as someone who spent most of his time with Donna Parrish, also moneyless. After telling the jury that Bill and Donna had met on August 2, Hunt claimed that the two had been together at the apartment of Glenn Zeller and Matt and Joe Bocci on Sunday, August 16, the night of the murder.

"They arrived there in late afternoon of that date," Hunt told the jury. "Neither of them had any money at that time, we expect the evidence to show. The defendant was wearing, at that time, clothes that he would be wearing at the time of the killing. He had on blue jeans over baggies with flip-flops or thongs, if you will, and most importantly, a yellow T-shirt which had the insignia on the pocket that said, 'Surf-It, Ocean Promotions,' and on the back it had the same words: 'Surf-It.'"

Bill cocked his head in surprise. Had Hunt just called the T-shirt yellow? During questioning, Bill had told detectives that he owned a yellow T-shirt with the Pelican's logo on it. The detectives had been probing for information about Bill's wardrobe, hoping to get him to admit he owned an orange Surf-It T-shirt. And of course, later, when Frank had told Bill about the bloody Surf-It T-shirt, he had indeed referred to the T-shirt, a key piece of evidence, as orange. But now the prosecution was calling it yellow.

"Neither Donna nor the defendant at this time had any money," Hunt continued. "They were to part company only to meet later at the Pelican Lounge in Indian Harbour Beach, which is close to Canova Beach. When the defendant arrived at the Pelican shortly after Donna, or sometime after Donna, he was wearing the same yellow Surf-It T-shirt. He was still without money.

"The defendant and Donna left the Pelican Lounge around midnight and returned, once again, to the Bocci's and Mr. Zeller's apartment. They met Tracey Herman and her young baby who had just flown in that night from Texas, arriving in Melbourne shortly before midnight on August 16.

"The defendant left there once again around twelve-thirty in the morning and returned to the Pelican, where once again neither had any money. In fact, they didn't have any money, and there was an argument between Donna Parrish and the defendant as to the lack of money, that the defendant did not have any, and Donna was upset about this. They had an argument, and they parted ways, going separate ways around 1:00 a.m. Donna went south, and the defendant went towards Canova Beach.

"Jim Dvorak at this time was parked in his car at the beach, and the defendant, who left the Pelican looking for money, came across Jim Dvorak. They had occasion to go back into the woods, a little wooded area with underbrush, palmettos, where the victim's clothes were removed. A struggle began shortly thereafter in an effort by the defendant to obtain money that he needed so badly, in other words, to rob Jim Dvorak. But Jim fought back, not willing to give up what was his. He was not willing to pass so easily in this effort by the defendant to get the money. And he was to die in an effort to keep what was his. His nude body was discovered the following morning around eight-thirty, nine o'clock. His head and face were badly beaten.

"The evidence will show that once the defendant accomplished his deed that evening, or that morning early, he left the area and he went down the beach and went north on the beach. He was carrying his yellow Surf-It T-shirt. We will show that throughout the struggle the defendant lost his shoes, his flip-flops, in his efforts to get away. He left them there."

Bill shook his head in bewilderment. There was no truth to this tall tale. What evidence was Hunt talking about? Bill knew there was no evidence.

Hunt, after carefully describing John Douglas Parker's encounter with a bloody hitchhiker he had picked up, told the jury that the hitchhiker had left his yellow Surf-It T-shirt behind in Parker's truck.

"During this time," Hunt explained, "Donna had returned once again to the Pelican Bar. She stayed there for a short period of time, then went to her mother's house, where she was to stay until the defendant arrived sometime later. While Donna was there, the defendant came to the house dressed only in baggies. He had no shirt and no shoes and no jeans over the baggies. The flip-flops were not there. His hair was darkened and damp and matted. He was perspiring. He was very tired and depressed at that time.

"He went to the bathroom of Donna's house, or her mother's house, there in Indian Harbour Beach. They stayed there at the house for some time and returned, once again, to the Pelican Lounge."

By now, Bill was fuming. It was clear Hunt was working from Donna's testimony. Frank had been right. So had Donna's friend Joanne Stinchcomb. Donna couldn't be trusted. She had turned on Bill and fed the police and the prosecution false information.

Hunt continued with his opening statement, claiming that Bill had been seen that night by two barmaids, both of whom had corroborated the prosecution's contention that Bill had been broke that night. Sometime after two o'clock in the morning, Hunt explained, Donna and Bill had once again gotten into an argument. Donna had left the Pelican and returned to her mother's house. Bill had followed her there, after closing time, thanks to a ride from Mark Muirhead, the Pelican's bouncer. Their car had been followed by Deputy Sheriff George McGee, who had watched Bill get out of the car.

"Donna and the defendant went later—they did a lot of traveling that night—went later to Sambo's in Satellite Beach," Hunt said. "The defendant, once again, had money, which he used to pay for his meal and coffee for Donna. As they left Sambo's, they were seen by Joe Bocci and Glen Zeller. And that was the morning of August 17, 1981, somewhere after three o'clock.

"A search of the crime scene revealed the clothing of the victim, as well as a matching pair of blue and black, with some white mixed in, flip-flops, thongs," Hunt continued. "With the assistance of John Douglas Parker, the gentleman who had given the person a ride in his truck, they were able to locate the shirt, the yellow Surf-It T-shirt, which had been left in his truck the night of his murder. They went to a shopping center, where it was obtained from a trash can where Mr. Parker had deposited it. Using this yellow Surf-It T-shirt, we will confirm the defendant's presence at the scene of the murder.

"Keep in mind, ladies and gentlemen, that we only have to prove the charge that is alleged. And listen to the court's instructions at the end of all the evidence as to what that charge is. But throughout the trial, remember that we do not have to prove premeditation. I believe that was mentioned briefly in *voir dire* and, perhaps, by the court. So don't expect any evidence on that, because the defendant did not intend to go over there and kill anyone; he wanted money. And the charge is, as the court has told you, first-degree felony murder, which the court will explain.

"And we will use several witnesses throughout the trial who have unique evidence, evidence unique to themselves, something that only they know. Some evidence may seem unimportant, but I ask you that you consider all the evidence together. It may be necessary to put on some evidence somewhat out of order. But look not at the minute details but the overall picture, and look at the totality of the evidence and keep it in the proper perspective.

"And, ladies and gentlemen, through the testimony that we will hear from this witness stand and from the physical exhibits that we will introduce into evidence, the state will prove that the defendant during the commission of a robbery at Canova Beach on the morning of August 17, 1981, went a little beyond the robbery and took the life of Jim Dvorak. Thank you."

Hunt returned to his seat and Bill, seething with emotion, could do nothing but glower in disbelief. Hunt's opening statement had been laughably untrue, but there was nothing funny about what was at stake. If the prosecution succeeded in convincing the jury that its case was based on fact, not fiction, Bill could spend the rest of his life in prison.

CHAPTER 11
NO EVIDENCE

After Michael Hunt finished his opening statement for the prosecution, Frank Clark took his turn addressing the jury.

Bill, watching from his front-row seat, pinned his hopes on his attorney to set the record straight.

"Members of the jury," Clark began, "the state has the burden, of course, of proving Mr. Dillon guilty beyond and to the exclusion of every reasonable doubt of what is called felony first-degree murder. And they're going to have to prove that Mr. Dvorak is dead. There's no particular problem there. They're going to have to prove that Mr. Dillon was in the process of robbing him and that during that robbery that he killed Joseph [sic.] Dvorak. That's the state's burden, beyond and to the exclusion of every reasonable doubt. Proof of robbery, proof of death, proof that William Dillon killed him.

"Now, the state's evidence is nearly all circumstantial—"

Hunt shot to his feet. "I'm going to object to Mr. Clark's argument of the case. I think he's getting into argument."

"I don't think that's argument, your Honor," Clark countered.

"I'll permit him to continue," Judge Wolfman said, "but do not give the law of the case."

"All right, sir," Clark said. He returned his attention to the jury. "In other words, they cannot actually put William Dillon at the scene of the crime at the time that this man died or anywhere near the time. They can put him at the Pelican, possibly, by one or two witnesses. That's several hundred yards away. There's a very good reason why they can't put him at the scene of the crime at the time the man died, and that's the simple reason that he wasn't there; he was somewhere else. There will be testimony from a Mr. and Mrs. Charles Rogers—her name is Rosanna Rogers—they're presently living in Columbus, Georgia. They will appear here and testify before you that from nine o'clock on Sunday evening, the sixteenth day of August, 1981, until eight o'clock the next morning, William Dillon and Donna Parrish spent the entire night in that apartment and did not leave, in Cocoa Beach, fifteen miles away from the death scene.

"Their memory is refreshed by things that happened, such as Mr. Rogers will testify that on that afternoon he made a beef roast with all the trimmings, or all the fixings, and potatoes and vegetables and things, and it was in a crock pot, and that when he met William Dillon and his girlfriend, Donna, they were down on the beach in front of the motel, which his wife managed, and that a conversation ensued, following which Donna and Bill went to a phone booth and tried to get a ride home by calling friends. They weren't able to raise anybody, and so the motel, being full, Mr. and Mrs. Rogers asked, told them they could stay the night.

"They fed Bill Dillon and Donna Parrish the warmed-over beef roast. Mr. Rogers is a sport-racing fan, automobile racing fan, and he has a very clear recollection that that afternoon he had watched the race up in Brooklyn, Michigan. There was a stock car race that was run by Richard Petty. And there will be more evidence supporting that that will be presented to you. There is no doubt in his mind that that couple spent the entire night there and did not leave the apartment ever.

"Mrs. Rogers will testify that she slept on a couch in the living room and that there was only one access in and out of the apartment—and that was the front door. That was the manager's apartment. Then they had eighteen units in addition on a two-story level located in the south part of Cocoa Beach. She will testify that she did not go to sleep until three o'clock, that William Dillon and Donna Parrish went back into one of the two bedrooms where they had twin beds and slept in one twin bed and her husband slept in the other twin bed. She will testify she went to sleep about three o'clock and dozed fitfully and that if Mr. Dillon would have had to come out of the apartment, she would have awakened. She slept very lightly.

"But the main point is she was there and she saw him in bed at three o'clock. And she got up twice during the night to go to the bathroom, and she saw the opened door in the bedroom where the three people were sleeping, and Bill Dillon and Donna Parrish were lying there in the exact same position as she saw them in there at two o'clock. Then she awakened them at eight o'clock the next morning, and because it was a Monday morning—that's another reason she remembers it—because she had a lot of checkouts and a lot of laundry to do, and to clean seventeen rooms. So that is going to be the testimony of Mr. and Mrs. Charles Rogers.

"Now you're gonna be snowed under with things like that. Matt and Joseph Bocci and Matt Bocci's girlfriend, Tracey Herman, are going to testify that William Dillon and Donna Parrish spent Sunday night in their apartment in Satellite Beach, that Tracey remembers it was a Sunday, August the sixteenth, because she flew in from Houston, Texas, that day on Eastern Airlines and Matt Bocci picked her up at the airport between ten-thirty and eleven-fifteen that Sunday night. And when they got home Bill Dillon and Donna Parrish were there. Now that's in Satellite Beach. That's five miles away from the death scene. They're gonna further testify that Tracey Herman had a little baby and that she went to bed about twelve-thirty and left Bill Dillon and Donna Parrish asleep on the floor, that she got up at five-thirty to feed her baby, and in the process—the floor plan of the apartment is such that you have to walk through the living room from the bedroom to get into the kitchen—and Bill and Donna Parrish were still sleeping.

"Now some magical movement's gonna whisk them out of that apartment, I suppose, and down to Canova Beach long enough to kill somebody and then back again. It's a little bit on the ridiculous side."

"Your Honor," Hunt interrupted, "I'm gonna object and ask to strike—"

"Mr. Clark," Judge Wolfman said in a slightly irritated tone, "would you not give the final argument?"

"Yes, sir," Frank said before resuming his opening remarks. "Also, the state has this advantage: they have taken samples of every conceivable material at that death scene. I'm speaking of debris. I'm speaking of clothing. I'm speaking of saliva. I'm speaking of head hair. I'm speaking of pubic hair. I'm speaking of blood samples. And they took them from William Michael Dillon. They ran exhaustive tests at the Sanford Crime Laboratory and at the FBI Crime Laboratory in Washington, DC, and they were unable to match one hair. They took twenty-five hairs from his head, twenty-five hairs from his pubic area, blood and saliva, and they could not match one single thing on that crime scene or to the body of Joseph [sic] Dvorak. Not one. So there is some evidence for you to consider.

"They talked about a man named John Douglas Parker who picked up a man who had a bloody body, bare chest, and that the next day he found a bloody yellow Surf-It T-shirt in the floor of his truck, of his pickup truck.

He also gave the police a description of this man, because he turned on the dome light when he picked him up. The man had lost his car, and they spent several fruitless minutes searching up and down A1A going into subdivisions to find out if his car would have been there. Finally, the man is dropped off in the A Frame.

"So he gives the police, this John Douglas Parker, he gives the police a description of the man. He's less than six feet, or he's six feet. Mr. Dillon's six-feet-four. He has the man wearing a mustache, a thick mustache, and the hair is—he describes the hair. So a composite photograph was drawn based on that description given by Mr. Parker to the authorities, and a sketch was made, and it has a thick mustache, there's no doubt about it. The evidence from the defense will show that Mr. Dillon has never had a mustache in his life, that he is totally incapable of growing one. And as if that weren't enough, his sister Debbie Dillon will testify that while she was at the parents' home Saturday afternoon, August fifteenth, that he shaved.

"So there you have it. Donna Parrish, the evidence will show, has made many, many statements to authorities and to other people, and all of them are conflicting, and that's for you to decide just how much credibility, if any, to give her testimony. We think that the evidence falls far short of that type, that quantity, and that quality of evidence that would justify conviction of William Dillon. Thank you very much for your attention."

CHAPTER 12

THE HALF-BLIND EYEWITNESS

With the opening statements out of the way, the prosecution went about introducing its first few witnesses, and Frank Clark cross-examined each in turn. Phillip Stafford, an acquaintance of James Dvorak and the last to see him alive, spoke on the witness stand about identifying the body. Medical examiner Dr. Nongnooch Dunn gave expert testimony on the cause of death: blunt force trauma to the victim's head, face, and skull. She described the brutal injuries in vivid detail. Five more witnesses followed, and Bill watched silently as the story of Dvorak's murder unfolded, from the moment his body was discovered by a construction worker to the next few hours as first responders from the Melbourne Police Department and the county sheriff's office began to investigate the scene. Several items had been collected at the site of the murder, including clothing, a pack of Benson & Hedges cigarettes, and vegetation and soil samples. By all accounts, the murderer had left a grisly trail in his wake.

When the prosecution invited John Douglas Parker to the stand, Bill leaned forward to catch his first glimpse of the man. Here was the eyewitness who had supposedly picked up the murderer just minutes after the crime had taken place.

Parker, older and the owner of a slender frame, had sandy brown hair, a thick mustache, and rugged facial features. After settling in at the witness stand, he recounted to Karen Thompson what he had been doing on Monday, August 17, at 1:30 a.m.

"Why did you go to Canova Beach?" Thompson asked.

"Well," Parker answered, "I frequently went there. I have a camper, and I frequently go to camp at Canova Beach."

"Okay. Was anybody with you when you went there?"

"No."

"Would you describe that camper for me that you drove there?"

"It's a '75 Chevrolet pickup with a topper."

"Okay. What color is it?"

"It's blue and white."

After asking Parker to state the pickup truck's license plate number, Thompson inquired about where he parked.

"In the public parking area at the curb facing the east," Parker answered.

"And can you give us an estimate as to how far you were from the beach itself, approximately?"

"Well, I was at the curb. There is a drop-off there of perhaps fifteen feet and steps and a railing leading down to the beach area."

"Okay," Thompson said, "and where were you located in relation to the steps?"

"I was parked very close to the steps, within a few feet."

"Okay. Were you to the north of the steps or the south of the steps?"

"The south."

"Did you see something unusual there that night?"

"Yes."

"Okay. What did you see?"

"I saw a young man come from the right and ascend the steps about halfway, stop, throw out one arm, utter an exclamation, and sit down."

Thompson, after confirming Parker had been in his truck and parked about twenty-five to thirty feet away, asked him what the man had exclaimed.

"Not really other than exclamatory," Parker said. "It was, 'Oh God,' or, 'Oh damn'—something to that effect."

After a few more questions, Parker revealed that the man had been wearing a pair of tan shorts and, though shirtless, had been carrying what looked like a shirt in his right hand. After sitting for a minute or two, he had climbed the rest of the steps and headed toward Highway A1A, just a block away. Parker had watched him for a moment and then had driven onto the highway, where he had spotted the young man on the other side of the road waving what had appeared to be a large cloth or something similar. Parker had made a U-turn and pulled over to ask the man what was wrong.

"He said something to the effect that he couldn't find his car," Parker explained. "He was looking for his car, which was a, as I recall, a blue Dodge Dart."

"That's what he told you he was looking for?" Thompson asked.

"Yes."

"Okay. Now when he got into the car, were you able to get a good look at him?"

"Yes," Parker answered. "As he—he mentioned wanting to go to the A Frame Tavern, approximately two or three miles from that location north, to look for the car and wanted to know if I would take him there. And I said, 'I rarely pick up hitchhikers, but I will take you up there.' And the door was open, the light was on, and I could see him."

"All right," Thompson said. "Did you observe anything unusual about him at that time?"

"When he got into the truck, I switched the dome light on and left it on, and after a short time I noticed some blood smears on his upper leg, which was bare, and also his, some on the, the short pants that he was wearing."

"Okay. Anyplace else?"

"Not that I recall."

"Did you notice anything other than the blood on him that was unusual?"

"He appeared to be sweaty, clammy—his bare skin."

"Did you say anything to him about the fact that he was sweaty and bloody?"

"I asked him, I said, 'You've got blood on you. How or where did you get it?' And he said, 'I was in a fight at the A Frame.'"

"Did he give you his name at any time?"

"He gave me the name of Jim."

After exchanging names, Parker explained to the jury, he propositioned the hitchhiker. They left the highway to search for the stranger's car but ended up parking in a secluded area between two houses. Parker then performed oral sex on the man.

Bill, who had been listening attentively to Parker's testimony, leaned back in his seat, shocked. It was surreal enough to hear this man he'd never met before talking about an event that supposedly involved him. But it was far worse to know that many in the jury were probably imagining Bill as the man Parker was describing: a blood-covered hitchhiker eager to engage in sex acts with a total stranger.

Thompson continued with her line of questioning. "Would you give us a physical description of the man that came into your truck that night, please, as best you can recall?"

"Well, I recall his height as six feet, six-feet-one, maximum weight of one-seventy-five, dark brown hair, dark brown mustache, otherwise clean shaven, no sign of a beard or ever having shaved there."

"Now," Thompson said, "was this a white male, black male that we're talking about?"

"White."

"And approximate age?"

"I later estimated his age to the police as twenty-one to twenty-seven years old."

"And did you notice anything that you also told the police—perhaps about his skin color or any features that you noted?"

"His features were very regular. Clean-cut. I gave a drawing, a description for the police artists."

After Parker described the man's skin tone as "white" and "light olive," Thompson asked about the hitchhiker's mustache.

"Was it a full mustache," she asked, "or a medium mustache or a thin mustache or what?"

"Medium," Parker answered. "Not bushy or full but noticeable because of the dark brown color and the contrast with his skin."

Parker went on to describe dropping the man off at the A Frame Bar. The man retrieved a pack of Marlboro cigarettes from the floor of the truck and then got out. Parker and the hitchhiker had spent a total of forty-five minutes together. The next morning Parker found the bloody

Surf-It T-shirt on the truck floor, and he tossed it into a trash can while at a Publix grocery store plaza. He was at a restaurant when he heard about the murder later that same day. After talking it over with the restaurant owner, he agreed he should contact the police and tell them about the bloody hitchhiker. Just before nine o'clock that night, he took the police to the plaza, and they retrieved the bloody Surf-It T-shirt from the trash. Thompson asked Parker to identify several photos of the shirt, the trash bag, and his truck. Parker then successfully identified the Surf-It T-shirt itself, and for the first time Bill got a good look at the shirt, now being displayed to the jury as Exhibit AU.

"Mr. Parker?" Thompson continued.

"Yes."

"Do you see the man that you picked up on the beach on August 17, 1981—"

"I think so," Parker interrupted.

"—who left that shirt in your truck here in the courtroom today?"

"I believe I do."

"Would you point him out for the jury, please?"

Parker pointed at Bill, whose face burned with disbelief and anger.

"Indicating this gentleman underneath my outstretched left hand?" Thompson asked for clarification.

"Yes," Parker answered.

"Thank you," Thompson said. "No further questions. Your Honor, may the record reflect that the witness has identified the defendant, Mr. Dillon?"

"Yes, it may," Judge Wolfman declared.

Frank Clark stood up to cross-examine Parker. "Mr. Parker," he began, "you said that you believed you do, and you appeared to be a little bit hesitant. You're really not all that sure, are you?"

"I'm not a thousand percent sure," Parker answered.

"Well, are you even six hundred and twenty-eight percent sure?"

When Parker didn't answer, Frank tried a different tack. "You described this man as six feet or six feet one. Are you aware that Mr. Dillon is six feet, four inches tall?"

"No, sir."

Frank, after confirming that it was Parker who had performed oral sex on the hitchhiker and not the other way around, asked about the hitchhiker's hair.

"Now I think you testified that this man's hair was close to his head, close-cropped to his head." Frank motioned to Bill's new haircut. "Do you consider that hair to be close cropped?"

"No," Parker answered, "the hair as I recall it was much shorter."

As Frank continued with his questions, Bill lamented once more that he'd been forced to have his hair cut. True, it was much longer than the hair Parker had described. But it would have been even longer, Bill thought, had Frank not insisted he get it cut just before the start of the trial.

Frank, though, did a decent job of exposing other discrepancies between Bill and Parker's description of the hitchhiker, chief among them Bill's lack of a thick mustache, which was how Parker had first described it to the police. He also asked Parker if there had been anything unusual about the hitchhiker's penis, and Parker had answered in the affirmative, that the man's penis had been unusually narrow at the tip.

On recross-examination, in what should have been a stunning moment, Frank Clark exposed a handicap that would gravely diminish the key eyewitness testimony.

"Did you ever make a comment to the agent or one of them that you were half-blind, do you recall?" Frank asked.

"I am half-blind legally," Parker answered.

"Okay, all right," Frank said. "No further questions."

The prosecution appeared ready for the embarrassing question.

"With the light on in your truck," Thompson asked while conducting a further redirect examination, "were you able to get a good look at the person that was in it?"

"Yes," Parker answered, "for several minutes he was close to my good eye, which is my right eye. I have a cornea scar in this eye."

"Thank you. Nothing further."

As Parker left the witness stand, Bill wanted to scream at the jury, the judge, his attorney—anyone who would listen. Where was the outrage? The key eyewitness in a case that could send Bill to prison for life had just admitted he was half-blind! How could he be allowed to identify Bill as the bloody hitchhiker he'd picked up on the night of the murder? Bill glanced at the jury, and after briefly studying a few members, could tell they hadn't been the least bit affected by Parker's admission. He then turned his attention to Judge Wolfman. He, too, seemed unconcerned. How could any judge allow such suspect testimony to be given in his courtroom?

Reality was now assaulting Bill with a jolt of clarity, as his memory returned to the night that Detective Slaughter instructed him to change his appearance by holding his long hair out of sight as he stood sideways in front of the one-way window.

"They had to know this man couldn't see well," he whispered to Frank. They had to know they could trick him. They *know* I'm innocent; they're trying to frame me!"

Bill was disgusted. Frank lowered his eyes and stared at the floor. He had nothing to say.

Following Parker's testimony, a handful of investigators took the stand, including Dennis Croft, a criminologist with the Brevard County Sheriff's Office. After identifying several items he'd found at the scene, he told the court he'd been unable to dust Parker's pickup truck for fingerprints due to the vinyl and shag carpeting that covered most of the interior of the vehicle. All told, however, investigators had managed to collect from the crime scene numerous hairs, pubic hairs, and blood samples and send them to the FBI's Sanford Crime Lab in Washington, DC.

"And did any of those reports link Mr. Dillon's hair, blood, pubic—head hair or blood to any of the material found at the scene?" Frank asked.

Thompson shot to her feet. "Objection, your Honor."

"What grounds?" Judge Wolfman asked.

"On the grounds that this witness is not competent to answer that question. He's not the crime lab technician."

"Sustained."

"Okay," Frank said. "Well, did you see these reports as they came back?"

"Objection," Thompson said. "Hearsay."

"Sustained."

Once again, Bill was mystified by what was happening. It seemed that the expert witnesses called forth by the prosecution weren't being allowed to say what they knew about the evidence. Clearly Thompson didn't want Croft to concede that none of the samples taken from the scene of the crime had been traced back to Bill.

At 4:30 p.m., after a dozen witnesses had given testimony, Thompson advised the judge that her next two witnesses were going to be lengthy.

"How long is each of these witnesses, do you anticipate?" Judge Wolfman asked.

"One is Ms. Parrish," Hunt answered, "and—"

"That will be long," the judge said with a huff.

"The other is our, sort of, cleanup officer," Thompson explained. "Tie up the details. We really need to go through all this evidence with him. The jury's tired, and they're falling asleep. I'm tired, too."

"I just don't want this thing dragging on till Friday or Saturday," Judge Wolfman said.

Dragging on? Bill thought angrily. Here he was fighting for his life, and the judge didn't want to be inconvenienced by a trial that might last more than a few days.

"Things are going a little faster than we had anticipated, actually," Thompson said.

"What do you anticipate for tomorrow?" Judge Wolfman asked.

"We anticipate Thom Fair, Donna Parrish, and several other witnesses," Thompson answered.

"Does that wrap up your case?"

"Except for the other evidence we've discussed," Hunt said.

"The hearing," Thompson added.

"About the dog," Frank chimed in.

"We can wrap up probably everything except the dog tomorrow," Thompson said.

Since the prior afternoon's jury selection, Bill had felt Judge Wolfman favored the prosecution. Embittered, in a rush—he didn't seem interested in administering a fair trial, just a quick one. It was almost as if Bill and his attorney were obligated to prove his innocence—as opposed to the prosecution proving his guilt.

Bill heaved a heavy sigh. He doubted things could get any worse.

CHAPTER 13
ACE IN THE HOLE

After a restless night of tossing and turning in his cell, Bill awoke Wednesday morning, December 2, feeling tired and on edge. Along with sleeping fitfully the past few days, he'd been unable to eat much of anything. The trial had already begun to chip away at his faith in the judicial system. After hearing the prosecution's lies and the incredible testimony from witnesses, both his heart and soul were beginning to ache.

Judge Wolfman brought his gavel down on his desk at 9:25 a.m. Frank Clark had added three names to the witness list at the last minute. One, a dog handler by the name of Sonny Brannon, would act as a rebuttal witness to John Preston, assuming the judge allowed the prosecution to introduce Preston's testimony. The other two were also listed as rebuttal witnesses, this time to rebut Donna Parrish.

Although the prosecution objected to all three witnesses, Judge Wolfman didn't appear ready to rule out any of the three from taking the stand. Donna's testimony, though, was causing the most consternation among all three parties. No one was sure who she was testifying for or against.

"I was taken completely by surprise," Frank explained to the judge while discussing Donna's listing as a witness for the prosecution, "and I think I had some right to rely on her representations, considering the fact that she was his avowed girlfriend and that she heard the tape, a half-hour tape of Charles and Rosanna Rogers, in my office, which tape puts Donna Parrish and Bill Dillon in the Ocean Star Motel from nine o'clock Sunday night until eight o'clock the next morning. She listened to the tape and at the end of it said, 'That's exactly the way it was.'"

"Your Honor," Thompson protested, "Mr. Clark has been aware that even at the time of her grand jury testimony that she said they were at the Bocci's that night and she's repeated that statement and several other statements as well."

Donna's changing statements had the prosecution *and* defense confused. It seemed, every time she opened her mouth, she switched sides, and it was obvious neither side was confident she was firmly in their camp.

"I ask the court to defer ruling until I can call these impeachment witnesses, if they're necessary," Clark said. "It may be that she admits it."

"That's correct," Judge Wolfman said. "The court will defer ruling on those two witnesses, will allow the testimony of Brannon, if that's the purpose of the testimony."

It appeared a delicate compromise had been reached. But when Michael Hunt declared his wish to interview Brannon ahead of his testimony, something that might not be possible until the following day, Judge Wolfman's impatience showed once again.

"I'm hoping this case is gonna move faster than that," the judge said, "and I'm requesting that you move the case faster than that. You're saying that your testimony's gonna go through tomorrow afternoon?"

"Mr. Preston is our last proposed witness," Hunt answered, "and that's why we say tomorrow afternoon perhaps."

"I would hope that you would be able to push your case," Judge Wolfman replied, "but it would appear to me that, from what I've seen up to this point, that you can, perhaps, move it to a faster degree."

Bill grimaced. Once again the judge seemed far more concerned about presiding over a fast trial than a fair one. But with that last detail out of the way, the proceedings resumed.

Detective Thom Fair, a short man with dark, curly hair and a mustache, was the first to take the witness stand. Although Bill felt he bore a passing resemblance to actor Gabe Kaplan from the popular television show *Welcome Back, Kotter*, his demeanor veered sharply from the affable Mr. Kaplan. On the day of his arrest, when Bill had told Detective Fair he hadn't committed murder, Fair had responded tersely, "Well, we believe you did, Dillon." Now he was on the witness stand, ready to make his case stick.

As a homicide investigator with the Brevard County Sheriff's Department, Fair had been on the job approximately thirty-one months. After telling the court he had been to the crime scene somewhere between half a dozen and a dozen times, he described being present at the scene when various items of evidence had been found, including the pack of cigarettes, a pair of shorts with underwear in them, and what he characterized as a variety of trace evidence. He had searched the scene for a murder weapon but had been unable to identify one. The weather had been overcast that day, with intermittent rain, he told the court, and it had rained hard the night before.

Thompson questioned Fair about the first time the defendant came into contact with any policemen about the case. "On the twenty-second day of August, 1981, at approximately 1:30 a.m. at Canova Beach," Fair responded.

Bill flinched in his seat. "Frank, he got the time wrong! I was never there at that hour."

"Hush, it doesn't matter," Frank said, intently looking at his notes.

Thompson showed Fair state's exhibit fourteen, the bloody Surf-It T-shirt, and continued questioning the witness. "Okay. And was the shirt at the crime scene at that time?"

"No, ma'am, it was at the Sanford Regional Crime Laboratory in Sanford, Florida," Fair explained.

"Okay. In other words, the shirt was at the crime lab before Mr. Dillon was talked to by anyone from your office?"

"That's correct."

"So," Thompson inquired, "did the defendant have any opportunity to come in contact with the shirt from the time *he* left it in Mr. Parker's truck to the time it came back from the lab?"

Bill, although groggy from the sedatives, sat bolt upright in his chair. He began to see where things were going, but did Frank? Frank looked up from his notes and objected. The objection was sustained, but the jury was getting an earful.

During his cross-examination, Frank Clark established the fact that Detective Slaughter had handled the yellow Surf-It T-shirt himself, a vital piece of information that the prosecution didn't want the jury to hear. He then questioned Fair regarding a revised statement he'd made about Bill's hands. Fair had first noted that he hadn't seen anything wrong with Bill's hands, only to later indicate that he had seen scratches on Bill's knuckles.

"You saw what you thought to be healed scratches?" Frank asked.

"No, sir, I did not say that. I saw small white lines lighter than the tan of Mr. Dillon's hands, which could have been healed scratches. They were in the knuckle area."

"Right, and you have no idea how long, if they were, in fact scratches, that they had been healed."

"No, sir, I do not."

"Could have been a year, could have been six months?"

"Yes, sir."

"Okay. Did you ever take any photographs of William Dillon's hands?"

"Yes, sir."

"Okay, and what did you do with those photographs?"

"They were insufficient to demonstrate the scratches in question. I have them in the case file."

"Even though you took them at close range, did you not?"

"It was a Polaroid camera," Fair answered, qualifying his statement. "Yes, sir."

While describing the scene of the crime, Fair explained that blood had been spattered in a wide area approximately twelve feet in diameter and four feet high.

"So in all probability, Mr. Fair, would it be a fair assumption to say whoever administered those blows was certainly sprayed with some blood, that it was all over the bushes and foliage?"

"I would think so."

"Unless he used a twenty-foot plank or something."

"Yes, sir."

Frank, after asking about all the pieces of evidence that had been collected at the scene, as well as the evidence that had been vacuumed from Mr. Parker's truck, moved in for the kill. "Now were all those—were all those bits of evidence collected and examined under microscopes and doing whatever they do to them?"

"Objection, your Honor," Thompson interrupted. "This is outside the scope of this witness's knowledge. He doesn't know—"

"He can answer that," Judge Wolfman said. "I'll permit the question and the answer, if you know it."

"Thank you," Frank said. He turned again to Detective Fair. "Do you know if those various items of—how many were there, seventy or eighty all together?"

"I believe sixty-nine."

"All right, sir. And did those, any of those items examined include head hairs from William Dillon?"

"Yes, sir."

"And did they include pubic hairs from William Dillon?"

"Yes, sir."

"And did they include a sample of blood from William Dillon?"

"Yes, sir."

"And did those samples come back from the Sanford Crime Lab?"

"Yes, sir."

"And did they also come back from the Federal Bureau of Investigation?"

"Yes, sir."

"And did you have access to those reports and did you read them?"

"Yes, sir."

"Okay, and isn't it a fact that every one of them was negative as to any—"

"Objection!" Thompson interrupted.

"—evidence of William Dillon?"

"Sustained," Judge Wolfman said.

"Your Honor," Frank responded, "at this time I'd make a demand on the state for those reports and their exculpatory—"

Now it was Hunt doing the interrupting. "Your Honor, may we do this outside the presence of the jury or at the bench or in chambers?"

Bill knew his attorney had an ace in the hole—if Frank could just get the jury to see the forensic lab reports that had excluded Bill from *any* connection with the evidence. But it was obvious the prosecution was going to run their best game of interference and try to block the crime scene lab results altogether.

The judge granted Hunt's request to discuss the matter outside the jury's hearing.

"May it please the court," Frank began as soon as the jury had left the courtroom, "the reason for that last question is that these reports, of which there are several, are exculpatory in nature, and I have talked to the prosecution, both—"

"Are they not contained in the pleadings," Judge Wolfman asked, "fifty-eight items, which are listed as additional discovery?"

"Yes, your Honor," Hunt said, "the pleadings will reflect that there is an extensive list, as the court has just observed, of fifty-eight items of physical evidence. Subsequent to that, every report was disclosed to the defendant in a timely fashion as soon as it was received. He has made no demand for any report from the FBI or anyone else. They've all been available. I may have made—I may have made copies of a couple—I was in the office a couple of times. I made copies a couple of times. But every report was disclosed to him as soon as it was received, on the day it was received."

"That's true, your Honor," Frank said.

"And the court file will reflect that," Hunt said, "and I resent the fact that he is accusing the state in front of the jury of withholding evidence."

"I'm not," Frank insisted. "I just thought their copies would be better files of all, your Honor. But, secondly, and most importantly, the state attorney advised me, Mr. Hunt, that the two witnesses who conducted the serology examination on the blood and the one who did the hair would be made available to the defense."

"They are, your Honor," Hunt said.

"To testify on behalf of the *defense*, your Honor," Frank clarified.

"They're available," Thompson said flatly.

"I thought that rather than do that," Frank said, "if this witness has seen these reports, he could identify to them and I could offer them into evidence out of turn."

Thompson objected to moving the reports into evidence, but she agreed to let Frank call in the lab witnesses, as long as the state could cross-examine them.

Bill understood that the forensic evidence didn't link him to the crime, which was why Frank, instead of the prosecution, was trying to put the reports' findings in front of the jury. What Bill didn't realize was that Frank had just tipped his hand to Thompson and Hunt.

"Your Honor," Frank said, "I told the state last week that *I* intended to call them because *they're* obviously *not* gonna call them. They've subpoenaed them, and they said that they'd be available to me, and I announced last week I wanted them here."

Judge Wolfman asked Hunt to make the arrangements to have the laboratory personnel testify.

Hunt agreed, but he was already trying to cast doubt on the validity of the laboratory test results. "Your Honor, before the jury comes back, there's a matter that's going to be at issue tomorrow. I'm having someone notify the two witnesses that are going to be here, be here tomorrow as requested. However, no chain of custody will have been laid at that time, and I'll leave that up to Mr. Clark."

It was obvious Karen Thompson and Michael Hunt did not want the laboratory evidence test reports to be admitted at all. In fact, their goal was to suppress the lab evidence in its entirety. The prosecution's whole case depended on witnesses who would swear, under oath, that Bill Dillon was the owner of the Surf-It T-shirt and had been seen wearing it on the sixteenth of August. Any forensic evidence that might contradict that theory had to be suppressed in some way by the state, lest the jury see room for reasonable doubt. The state's strategy, to challenge the chain of custody of the evidence, would allow them to present their case—that the T-shirt belonged to Bill and had been worn by Bill on the night of the murder—without having to use lab results to prove it! If they could convince the court that the items sent to the crime labs had been mishandled, they could get the results thrown out but could continue with their theory using circumstantial evidence and witness testimony to prove their conjecture. The prosecution had been so confident that their strategy would work that they had even told the crime lab technicians that they wouldn't be needed to testify. Now Thompson and Hunt found themselves with their backs against the wall. The *defense* was going to call the lab experts to testify. The prosecution's only hope was to convince the judge and jury that the evidence, which had been solely in the state's own control, was tainted.

CHAPTER 14

BRILLIANT THEATER

Bill steeled himself as Donna took the stand. His fateful two-week fling was with a woman who had toyed with the police and attorneys and who was now smiling, laughing, and appeared to be enjoying the heady glow of the spotlight. Never mind the fact that Bill's fate rested in her hands. He still had no idea what she was going to say, but he tried to take solace in Frank's contention that no one would find her a credible witness. She'd made too many conflicting statements to too many people.

After being sworn in, Donna testified that she had met Bill on August 2, and that on the afternoon of August 16 she was with Bill at Matt Bocci's apartment with Matt and his brother Joe. She had an argument with Bill, she told Michael Hunt, who was doing the examining for the prosecution, and she left the apartment and went to her mother's house. At the time, Bill was wearing blue jeans, flip-flops, and a light yellow T-shirt with some kind of surf shop logo on it. Beneath his jeans, he wore a pair of baggy shorts. Donna eventually returned to Matt Bocci's apartment, but Bill had left. When Donna went to the Pelican Lounge, Bill wasn't there either. But he eventually showed up around midnight, at which time he was still dressed in the same outfit. His flip-flops, Donna told Hunt, were blue, with black on the worn bottoms and multicolored stripes on the top.

Bill felt a sinking sensation as Donna spoke. She knew she and Bill had spent the night of August 16 at the Ocean Star Motel, so why was she spinning this tale? Where was she going with this?

Hunt showed Donna a pair of flip-flops and asked her whether she recognized them. She answered in the affirmative, noting that they were worn down like the flip-flops Bill had worn on August 16. Hunt then asked to move the flip-flops into evidence as the state's next numbered exhibit.

Frank Clark objected. The flip-flops lacked the multicolored stripes Donna had just described. But Judge Wolfman overruled him.

Hunt then showed Donna the infamous orange—now called yellow—Surf-It T-shirt, which Donna said she recognized as Bill's and the one he'd worn on the night of the murder. Another piece of evidence was officially entered into the record.

From there, Donna resumed her sprawling narrative. Bill showed up at the Pelican around midnight, she told Hunt. Bill and Donna then returned to Matt Bocci's apartment, where they met Matt's girlfriend, Tracey Herman. After buying a pack of cigarettes across the street, the couple returned once again to the Pelican. Donna wanted a drink, but Bill couldn't afford to buy her one. Tired of being broke all the time, she threw a temper tantrum and left, with Bill close on her heels. The two argued. Later that night, by now early morning, Bill showed up at her mother's house wearing only shorts and shoes. He was covered in sweat.

"I said, 'Where is your shirt?'" Donna told Hunt. "And he just kind of stood there, and I said, 'Where is your shirt?' I always had to ask to him over and over, you know, 'cause he doesn't like to talk to me too much; he thinks I ask him too many things. And he said, 'I left it in someone's truck.'"

"Did you see anything about Billy's hair that you observed at that time?" Hunt asked.

"Just looked messy," she answered, "and right here"—she pointed toward her forehead—"it was kind of sweaty."

"How about the rest of his body?" Hunt asked. "Did you observe that?"

"Yeah, you know, he looked like he was really—he had run or something. He was all perspiring."

"What did you do after you went outside and saw him there?"

"I did my usual nagging, like, you know, a wife or a mother would do or something like that."

Donna continued with her story, explaining that they stayed at her mother's house for about fifteen minutes before once again leaving for the Pelican. On the way, Donna realized Bill couldn't get in the way he was dressed. She had loaned him her brother's light yellow jacket, but that still wasn't sufficient to get into the Pelican.

"Well, we were almost at the Pelican," she explained, "and he said that he wanted to—I'm not really sure why we went over there—but we went over to the beach."

"And had you been over to that beach before that night?" Hunt asked.

"I need a few minutes to think," Donna said. "I'm starting to get really nervous."

"Take your time," Hunt said.

Bill felt his blood boil. He couldn't hold his tongue any longer.

"I'll write you a dialogue," he said sarcastically, speaking directly to Donna who seemed to be having trouble remembering what she was supposed to say.

It was a foolish move—and surely one that wouldn't endear him to Judge Wolfman or the jury. But Bill had finally run out of patience. Why was she doing this? Was this her fifteen minutes of fame? First she'd had sex with Detective Slaughter. Now she was spewing wholesale untruths from the witness stand. Was she trying to get back at Bill because he had tried to break things off with her? Bill couldn't say. All he knew was that she was messing with his life. She held his future in the palm of her hand—and didn't seem to care.

"Could you repeat the question?" Donna asked as Bill glared at her.

"Yes," Hunt said. "Had you been to the beach that you're talking about before on that evening, before the time that you and the defendant went there?"

Donna fidgeted nervously. She was clearly flustered. "I can't think. I'm starting to get a block or something."

Hunt, though, wasn't ready to give up on his star witness. He continued to gently coax answers from her, and Donna, after recovering just enough to soldier on, explained that she had followed Bill to Canova Beach to apologize to him for yelling at him earlier. But after spotting him talking to someone, she hadn't been able to find him.

"Okay, Donna, what time was this?" Hunt asked. "Was this before you went back to your mother's and the defendant arrived there in shorts, or was this after?"

"Yes."

"Which one?"

"Oh, yes—I mean, I'm sorry, this was—all right. I went back there looking for him and I didn't find him."

"Okay, what point, Donna?"

"Around twelve—I mean, after one."

"Was this before you went back to your mother's?"

"Yes."

"And before you had seen the defendant arrive in shorts?"

Donna backtracked to explain that she had gone to the beach before Bill had arrived. She didn't find him there but noticed a blue and black Charger in the parking lot, a car she had seen Bill approach earlier.

"Where did you go specifically to look for him?"

"It's gonna sound strange, but I don't know," Donna said shakily. "I need to have five minutes. I don't feel too good."

Hunt pressed on. "Is there something about what you did at the beach that bothers you or concerns you?"

"Yes."

"Okay."

"I just need . . . I don't feel like I'm being much good up here if I can't—"

Hunt turned to Judge Wolfman. "Your Honor, may we take—"

"Okay," the judge said. "The court will take about a, well, the morning recess. So we'll take about ten minutes at this time."

Donna, laughing and smiling when she had taken the stand, left looking shaky. It was tough to gauge how the jury viewed her testimony so far. Were they buying it? Likewise, Bill had no idea where Donna would take things after the break. In any case, one thing seemed apparent: she'd already put on quite a performance.

Bill could tell Frank wasn't thrilled with the break. It was obvious the attorney didn't want to give Donna a chance to regroup and go over her story with the prosecution. But Frank wasn't the only one unhappy.

Before resuming, Judge Wolfman put Bill and his attorney on notice that any further outbursts were unacceptable. If Bill wanted to stay in the courtroom, he would have to keep a lid on his emotions.

"No trying to stare down a witness," the judge ordered.

Donna, having recovered somewhat, resumed her narrative from the witness stand. She described walking south from the parking lot at Canova Beach, down the nearby path, to continue looking for Bill. It was then that she spotted someone lying on the ground on the left-hand side of the path. He was covered in blood, and she couldn't see his face. She hurried home to her mother's house, and shortly afterward Bill arrived all covered in sweat and wearing only his shorts.

Earlier, Donna had told Hunt that she had repeatedly asked Bill what had happened to his shirt, nagging him in a motherly way. But for this new version of the story, the repeated questions about Bill's attire didn't earn a mention. Instead, Donna explained that she had been extremely frightened—too frightened, in fact, to say anything about what she had just witnessed. She followed Bill back to the wooded trail.

"What did you observe him do at that time?" Hunt asked.

Donna began to cry. "Excuse me," she said. "I saw him putting on one leg of the jeans and the other one—you know, he was putting them on."

"What jeans?"

"The jeans he borrowed from Matt," she said between sobs. "They were real tight."

"How far was he away from the body when he was doing this?"

"From about where I'm sitting to Mr. Woodson?" Donna said in an unsure voice and nodded to the judge. "Judge Woodson? I'm sorry."

"That far, from you to the judge? Judge Wolfman, by the way."

Donna nodded. "I'm sorry. I wasn't sure."

"Did you say anything to the defendant as you were there at that time?"

"Uh huh."

"What did you say to him?"

"I just tried to find out, you know, if there was any involvement on his part, and he told me to shut my face."

Donna, continuing with her detailed account of the evening placing Bill not only at the scene of the crime but standing over the body, told Hunt that Bill found a pair of flip-flops in the parking lot—she wasn't sure exactly where—and was thus able to meet the Pelican's dress code. Once at the bar, she ordered a White Russian, instructing Maggie, the bartender, to "make it a strong one." Bill paid for it—and several other drinks. Donna didn't know where he'd found the money. Upset, she slammed her drink down and went home to her mother's house. There, she told the courtroom, she wrote a poem in her journal entitled "Why Billy Why?"

Bill fumed in his seat as the prosecution made a huge deal about the poem, in order to make it sound as though Donna's poem was about her reaction to seeing a dead body in the woods. In fact, the poem was about Bill not wanting to see Donna anymore but that meaning was conveniently twisted.

Donna told Hunt she called the Pelican looking for Bill and asked him to stop by her mother's house. Bill, without wheels, asked for a ride from Mark Muirhead, the bouncer at the Pelican. The two were followed by a sheriff's deputy named McGee.

"Did you tell the deputy what you had seen at the beach?" Hunt asked.

Donna shook her head no. "I should have."

"Why didn't you?"

"Like I said: I didn't want—I don't know. I don't know why I do a lot of things."

Bill couldn't believe his ears. Mark had indeed driven him to Donna's house but on a totally different night, and the two were never followed by a deputy. This was pure fiction.

Donna continued with her story, saying that after Bill arrived at her mother's house, they went to Sambo's and Bill paid the tab. Donna said she remembered that a friend of Bill's named Joe passed them as they were exiting the restaurant. They then returned to the Bocci brothers' apartment, where they fell asleep. Bill was wearing a pair of blue jeans, brown flip-flops, and the jacket. The next day, Donna told the court, she and Bill went to Buccaneer Beach, and there she penned an entry in her diary as a way to remember Bill if they broke up.

"He said my dates were wrong," Donna told the court. "He said, 'Boy, LaPredo, you fucked up, didn't you?' Excuse me, but that's what he said. And then he said, 'I think you should change the dates.' I said, 'Yeah, I guess you're right,' took a black pen, and I scratched out the dates and went down each one."

"Did you scratch out just the dates or the day of the week?" Hunt asked.

"I think . . . I'm pretty sure just the dates. And I put arrows, 'cause it was really confusing. I was confused reading it myself."

"Did the defendant say why he wanted you to change the dates?"

"I don't know. He just said, 'Never know.'"

"He said what?"

"'You never know.'"

And just like that, Michael Hunt had scored another point for the prosecution. Donna had now effectively insinuated that Bill had tampered with the dates they had been at the Rogerses' in order to have an alibi on the night of the murder when in fact the reverse was true. Through the entire trial, the prosecution used tactic after tactic to tamper with the date the two were at the Rogerses' apartment.

Hunt asked Donna if, at some point, she'd ever told the police about what she'd seen at the beach before Bill was arrested.

Yes, she answered, she'd stopped a police officer and told him her boyfriend was acting weird, but she hadn't gone into detail. In fact, she told Hunt that at one point Bill had accidentally pushed her, and she had fallen into a wall and hurt her face.

"He didn't mean it," she explained. "We were both kind of, you know—he tried to grab me and tell me he was sorry and everything, and I ran away." Donna added that Bill had been depressed, even suicidal.

"Now, Donna, during the weekend that you've described to us—during the sixteenth and seventeenth of August—did you at any time spend—there's been times you've mentioned about the diary—spend time with Rosanna and Charles?"

"Yes."

"Do you remember when that was?"

"Well, I was totally convinced at first—let me explain—that we were together, you know, in that hotel, Rosanna and Charlie and Billy and I. But as days went by, I started figuring, you know, I started, you know, just—yeah, Saturday, the fifteenth."

"When?"

"Saturday the fifteenth."

"Of what month?"

"August."

"And how did you first meet Charlie?"

"I—well, Billy and I—wanted to be alone, and we didn't have any place to go, so we went down to the beach on a blanket, and you know, we did what normal couples do when they can be alone."

As Hunt continued with his line of questioning, Donna was more than happy to offer up lurid details of what she claimed had taken place.

"What was Charlie doing when you first saw him?" the prosecuting attorney asked.

"Standing right in front of the blanket looking at the ocean doing something perverted."

"What was that?"

"I'm trying to think of a nice way to say it. He was masturbating."

There was no truth to Donna's outrageous claim, and her stories became even more sensational as time went on. Charles had been standing beside a lieutenant colonel on a deck overlooking the beach when he had first spotted Bill and Donna. But in Bill's mind, it was clear that the prosecution had settled on character assassination as a strategy to discredit Charles Rogers. She went on to assert that after Charles had invited her and Bill to stay at their apartment, things had gotten a little risqué and some partner-swapping had ensued.

"Was it difficult for you to relate this story to people?" Hunt asked.

"Yes," Donna answered.

"Why was that?"

"It was my boyfriend, and I was very protective of him. I didn't want him—you know, I had a feeling all along he was gonna end up going away. They had told me if he messed up he would go to jail."

"Objection," Frank said. "Move to strike that as hearsay, your Honor."

"Sustained," Judge Wolfman said, "and the Jury will disregard the last comment."

"Is it easy for you to sit here and relate this to this courtroom today?" Hunt asked.

"No," Donna answered solemnly.

"Why is that?"

"Well, when you see someone laying there dead and you don't tell anybody about it, you don't feel too good, do you?"

~ ❖ ~

Bill breathed a sigh of relief when Frank Clark finally stood to cross-examine Donna. Did Frank have the patience and stamina needed to untangle Donna's web of confusing and conflicting testimony? Her narrative had thus far been strong on emotion but weak on coherence. Frank's job would be to expose the latter to the jury. Unfortunately, he'd have to do it in a hurry. Judge Wolfman denied Frank's request for an early lunch break, which would have made it possible to question Donna without interruption over the course of the afternoon session. Instead, Frank would have to pack in as many questions as he could before lunch. Once again, the judge seemed more intent on maintaining a fast pace than running a fair trial.

Frank began by trying to get a bead on the sequence of events, according to Donna, as well as Bill's varying outfits on the night of the murder. He did manage to get Donna to admit that Bill had never worn a mustache—at least not during the time she'd known him, including August 16. He also compared several of Donna's prior statements with the testimony she'd just given, forcing Donna to explain away the many discrepancies.

"Do you recall coming to my office on several occasions and talking to myself and my wife, who identifies as Lael Clark?" Frank asked.

"Yes," Donna answered.

"And do you recall on several occasions telling me in the presence of my wife that you were going to repudiate and recant and withdraw all of your previous statements and that you were going to tell it like it was and tell the truth? Do you remember telling me that?"

"Your Honor," Hunt said, intervening, "I'm gonna object and ask to approach the bench."

Out of hearing of the jury, Hunt argued that Frank was positioning himself as a witness in the case.

Judge Wolfman ruled that Frank could not become a witness, but his wife could.

With the matter decided, Donna answered Frank's question in front of the jury. "First of all," she said, "I've been to your office twice, and second of all, I did tell you the first time that I was going to—first or second time—that I was gonna repudiate, or whatever that word is."

"Uh huh," Frank said.

"I'm not denying it."

"But you did say it, make that statement."

"Yes."

"All right. Did you have occasion, also in my office, to hear in the presence of Lael M. Clark, my wife and secretary, a tape purportedly made whereby in Columbus, Georgia, I interviewed Charles and Rosanna Rogers? Do you recall playing that tape back, that half-hour tape?"

"Oh, yes."

"And did that tape, in fact, state that you and Bill Dillon spent the night—"

Hunt objected once more. "I'm gonna object to what the tape—your Honor—"

"—of August sixteenth?" Frank asked, finishing his question.

"Sustained," Judge Wolfman ruled.

"Okay," Frank said. "Well, did you recognize the voices of Charles and Rosanna Rogers as being their voices?"

"Yes."

"And isn't it a fact that you turned to Mrs. Clark after the tape was made and said, 'That's exactly the way it was, and that's the day it was on'? Do you remember making that statement to her?"

"I remember saying that's exactly the way it was," Donna said, "but that's where you got to get the point across that somebody's got their dates wrong and I'm not the one. 'cause I know what I'm saying, okay?"

"I'm sure you do," Frank said caustically.

"And you shouldn't assume," Donna shot back. "It makes an ass out of you and me, and I really feel like you're trying to make me look like a really stupid person, and I'm not."

"Mr. Clark," Judge Wolfman said, "I think this might be a convenient time for a lunch break."

Frank nodded resignedly. Bill knew he had hoped to question Donna without interruption, which was why he had lobbied to take the lunch break before he started. Now Donna would have a chance to regroup with the prosecution team. Hunt and Thompson, no doubt, would spend the break coaching Donna to help her get her story straight.

~❖~

After the break, Frank homed in on one of the many contradictions in Donna's story, which had Bill buying her drinks at roughly the same time that Mark Muirhead, the bouncer at the Pelican, drove Bill to Donna's home. Frank then asked Donna about a nine-page statement she'd made under oath on August 26.

"Ms. Parrish," Frank began, "you testified to this jury that on the fifteenth of August, a Saturday, you spent the night in the apartment of George [sic] and Rosanna Rogers at the Ocean Star Motel in Cocoa Beach. Your statement on page three of your August twenty-sixth statement says you spent the night alone with Linda Plumlee in a different apartment in the Ocean Star Motel. Which is correct? You couldn't have spent the night, the same night, with both sets of people."

"I know," Donna said. "Saturday, August fifteenth—I stated before the grand jury that I was with Linda and George, and Billy was not there."

"Right," Frank said.

"And that I had gone to bed early that night because I was really tired," Donna added. "Went to bed at eight-thirty."

"All right. Now why, then, did you testify before this jury this morning that you spent that same Saturday night, the fifteenth of August, with George [sic] and Rosanna Rogers with Bill?"

"Because I've had three months to sit down and think about what I know, and it's finally clear to me what I know."

"You're saying your memory improves with time. Is that what you're saying?"

"No, my memory's fine. I just—I had to decide whether I wanted to tell the truth or protect my ex-lover."

"I see. Well, then, in other words, you do admit that at times during the course of this investigation you have not told the truth, right?"

"I'm not ashamed of that. I do admit it."

"And you were under oath at that time that you didn't tell the truth, weren't you?"

"Yes, I was."

"So you have lied under oath on different occasions," Frank said in an exasperated tone. "We can establish that."

Frank, still trying to make heads or tails out of the sequence of events from Donna's latest version of the truth, wasn't letting up. He was going after her relentlessly for changing her testimony.

But Donna, too, was frustrated. "Confusing me isn't gonna help this problem right now because time is important," she said.

"Well," Frank replied, "you said in one case that you bought the drinks, you drank the drinks after Mark Muirhead brought him home, and that's three-eleven; the Pelican's closed."

"Yes."

"How do you explain that?"

"Error in judgment."

"You couldn't be mistaken about being at the death scene, though, could you?"

"No. No, I couldn't."

"Even though you talked to any number of police investigators for three months and you never mentioned it once."

"I had to make a final decision," Donna said dramatically. "And I did: Billy or justice."

So this was how Donna—or the prosecution team coaching her—had decided to play it, Bill thought. Her inconsistencies and contradictions were merely the byproduct of an internal struggle between the truth, on the one hand, and her devotion to him, on the other. He glanced from Donna, flustered and upset, to the jury. Would the jury members buy her convoluted testimony? Would her tears and emotional outbursts play on their sympathies? Bill now knew her as an admitted liar. But the jury, he feared, might view her as a tortured woman finally turning her boyfriend over to the law in the name of justice.

Frank, meanwhile, kept hammering away. First the flip-flops were multicolored, he pointed out. Now they were brown. Donna's testimony had changed the moment she had seen the state's exhibit of a pair of worn brown flip-flops. But each time he tried to expose Donna's tangled web of contradictions, the prosecution would step in and Michael Hunt, reframing whatever issue was at hand, would manage to get an emotionally charged revision from Donna.

Someone must have gotten to Donna. Someone must have frightened her into giving bogus testimony, Bill thought. Or perhaps, in her emotional condition, she had been susceptible to strong persuasion. Frank had told Bill that detectives had taken a blood sample from Donna as forensic evidence, which likely was orchestrated to scare her. Frank spoke as well of a friend of Donna's who had come forward claiming Donna had been offered something in exchange for her testimony against Bill. Bill knew Donna was not happy that he had tried to distance himself from her shortly after they had begun dating. But to put him at the scene of a murder, standing over a dead body—that was something he would have never believed her capable of doing. This couldn't be just because she felt jilted. More had to be going on behind the scenes.

Frank asked Donna about Joanne Stinchcomb. "Did you ever mention to her that the prosecution had been putting a lot of pressure on you or the sheriff's department or somebody to change your testimony back to where it was with the grand jury?"

"No, I never said that to her. I won't say—"

"Did you ever say that some authorities—we don't know who—offered you somewhere between two and five thousand dollars and a new identity to get you out of town and so forth?"

"No."

"That was never said?"

"That's right. That was never said."

"And you never said to Jo Ann Stinchcomb that that's a lot of money when she asked you, 'You really wouldn't do that, would you?' Do you recall that conversation?"

"I recall it, but where she got her information I'd like to know, because I don't even talk like that. I don't say two, five, and I don't, you know—I know what I said."

"Well, to save time, can we simplify it? Did you ever volunteer any information to her that you would in any way be rewarded by changing your testimony again back to where it was before the grand jury? Did you say you were gonna be rewarded in any way?"

"I'm not really sure. I don't understand what you're trying to get at. Are you talking about me as a character, as a person, or are you talking just about state's evidence?"

"I'm talking about, were you ever promised anything of value to go back and change your testimony, which you've changed three or four times?"

"No."

"You were never offered anything of value by anyone?"

"No."

Frank returned to the Surf-It T-shirt. Donna had given conflicting testimony, saying earlier that the first time she had seen the bloody T-shirt was on September 26, when Thom Fair had questioned her.

"On September twenty-sixth," Frank began, "when Agent Fair first showed you the shirt, did you say, 'I know Billy has a shirt like that'?"

"The first time he showed it to me I said, 'No, that's not his shirt.' And then after, about three or four hours later, I said, 'Yes, that's his shirt.'"

"Were you under oath the first time?"

"No, I wasn't. I had just been brought in."

"And later, you were under oath?"

"I'm not sure. In other words, I'm confused again."

"Well, do you recall this question and this answer? Question: 'When you were at the Pelican earlier before you left him,' meaning Dillon, 'and you went to your mother's house, was he wearing a different shirt, or was he wearing that same shirt, or do you remember?' Answer: 'I really, honestly don't remember, but I can say that that shirt they found with blood on it is his shirt.' Do you remember that question and that answer, giving it?"

"Yes, I remember giving it."

"Now my question is: if you did not see the shirt for the first time until September 26, 1981, twenty-three days later, how could you tell an investigator or the grand jury that that shirt with the blood on it was Bill Dillon's shirt?"

"That's a matter of emotions, love relationship, and the law. I mean, you're asking me to sit here and—when I was in love with him, and at first, I didn't want him to get into trouble, so I did everything in my power to cover for him, and then I had to, you know—"

"Well, were you in love with him on September the third when you told the grand jury—"

"I still am, but that's beside the point."

"Let me finish my question."

"Yeah, you know, just because I love him doesn't mean that a guy's supposed to die. There's, you know, right and wrong."

"Did you love him on September third—let me finish my question—when you testified before the grand jury that a bloody T-shirt that you had never seen or been shown belonged to William Dillon when you didn't see it until September 26, 1981?"

Hunt, clearly tiring of Frank's badgering, stepped in to defend his witness. "Your Honor, I'm gonna object—unless she understands the question and she can answer it. But I think the question is vague and ambiguous."

"It's painfully clear, your Honor," Frank insisted.

"Argumentative and also repetitive," Hunt shot back.

"It's repetitive," Judge Wolfman ruled, "but I don't know if the witness understands the question or the predicate for the question."

"I don't understand it," Donna said.

"Ms. Parrish," the judge said, "was it your testimony that the first time you saw the shirt was on—"

"September twenty-sixth," Donna cut in.

"—September twenty-sixth?"

Donna nodded her head.

"The question is," the judge continued, "how could you tell the grand jury then on September third about the bloody shirt?"

"Oh, I don't know. I'm still really confused."

"That's the question that Mr. Clark is asking."

Donna tried to answer the question. "In other words, you know, you got to understand here I don't think—I think you think this is some kind of circus or something, I'm having a joy ride, and it's not. Because my butt's on the line just as much as, you know, anybody else's. I'm trying to help. I'm trying to tell the truth."

"Ms. Parrish, just answer the questions," Judge Wolfman said.

"Well, I need specifics. I don't understand still."

"Is it your answer, then, that you don't understand the question?" a mystified Frank asked.

"Yes."

"Well," Frank said, shaking his head, "I can't phrase it any better."

Donna's declaration—that *her* butt was on the line—raised huge red flags. She hadn't been charged with anything, but Bill suspected that Donna was feeling pressure to lie. Who was pressuring her to frame him? Bill could only hope the jury would pick up on the remark.

Frank, plowing ahead, tried to pinpoint whether or not Donna had, in fact, returned to the Pelican on the evening of August 16. Then he returned to a previous line of questioning. "Were you ever threatened with prosecution by any member of the law enforcement agency in Brevard County or elsewhere if you didn't shape up and testify the way they wanted you to?" he asked. "Weren't you told that you were gonna be named an accessory after the fact for murder?"

"Yes."

"Weren't you also threatened with perjury if you didn't shape up and testify as you had in front of the grand jury?"

"Objection to the form," Hunt said. "Yes, your Honor, he can ask her if she was ever threatened, but not in the manner he put it."

"Sustained," Judge Wolfman said.

Frank reframed his question. "Were you told you would be prosecuted for your perjury if you didn't return to your original grand jury testimony?"

"Same objection," Hunt interjected.

This time the judge found in Frank's favor. "Overruled."

"Would you repeat the question?" Donna asked.

"Yes," Frank replied. "Were you told or informed by any member of any law enforcement agency in Brevard County that if you did not return to your incriminating grand jury testimony given on September third that you would be prosecuted for perjury? Yes or no?"

"I can't really say yes or no. I was told that if I didn't tell the truth I could be charged with perjury."

"Did they tell you how many years you might draw?"

"No."

"They didn't. They didn't mention jail—"

"I looked it up," Donna explained.

"Okay. How many years was it?"

"I don't remember. I just—I don't really want to think about it. It's not a pleasant thought."

"Did you tell the grand jury that you did not spend the night at the Bocci's apartment on Sunday, August 16, 1981, on the floor? Do you remember testifying to that?"

"No, I don't."

"All right, let me turn you to page thirty-one of the, of your grand jury testimony. Start with line four and read down to the bottom of the page."

Hunt asked to approach the bench. In lieu of going over the entire grand jury testimony, he moved to enter it into evidence to let the court determine which sections were relevant.

That was fine with Frank, who went a step further: he wanted all of Donna's statements admitted into evidence so the jury members could see for themselves how much of Donna's testimony conflicted with itself.

Hunt, clearly hoping the jury wouldn't have the patience to slog through so much discordant testimony, agreed.

Frank, for his part, was obviously betting that the jury would be responsible enough to take the time to comb through the documents with utmost scrutiny. The job would be voluminous.

Judge Wolfman agreed but once again expressed concern about time. "If this jury gets out," he said, "they'll be out for a week."

"So be it," Frank replied and continued questioning the witness.

In his redirect, Michael Hunt gave Donna a chance to save herself. "Why did you first not admit that that yellow Surf-It T-shirt belonged to the defendant?"

"I didn't want to have to believe that, you know, you know, there's a possibility it was Billy's," Donna answered, "because he was my boyfriend. I really, you know, didn't want to say that. I said no, but I knew, you know."

"Does it bother you being right here in front of him today?"

"No, not anymore."

"Did it earlier?"

"Yes, I mean, when you sit there in front of someone that you used to go out with, it does bother you."

Hunt continued to try to tie up several loose ends. "At the time you saw him, the first time, just describe briefly—we won't go through everything again—how was he dressed the first time you saw him in your mother's driveway that day?"

"No shirt," Donna answered. "Pair of shorts. No shoes. Half dry. Half sweaty. Tired. Depressed."

"At that time did the defendant say anything to you about his condition or where he had been or what he had done other than what you have related—"

"No."

"—about the shirt."

"No, he just said that, you know, he left his shirt in someone's truck, pick-up truck, and that, you know—we didn't really talk about anything specific."

Donna had once again linked Bill to the bloody Surf-It T-shirt and to John Douglas Parker's pickup truck.

Clearly satisfied that Donna had delivered what the prosecution needed for a probable conviction, Hunt tried to clear up any suspicion that Donna might have been forced to testify against Bill. "Did you testify today as to what I or anyone else wanted to hear?"

"No."

"Did anyone force you to say anything today?"

"It's not a matter of force," Donna answered. "It's a matter of a person can only walk around so long holding things in, and their emotional stability, you know, holding it in, really did a lot to me, you know, health-wise."

"What did it do to you?"

"Well, I've lost twelve pounds in a week. I don't eat. I don't sleep. I don't have any friends hardly because they're mad at me."

"Before you told Thom Fair that you had seen the body, did that create any emotional or physical problems for you?"

"Yes, first of all, my family was affected and then put pressure on me because I had to decide between—"

"Objection to continuation of this testimony," Frank said. "Goes beyond direct, and it has no bearing on this case, your Honor."

Judge Wolfman tried to clarify Frank's objection. "Goes beyond—"

"The scope of cross-examination," Frank explained.

"Overruled," the judge said.

Hunt continued on. "Did you have any physical difficulty before you related this to police? Just a continuation of what you were telling us."

"Yes, I started—people actually came right out and said what they felt about me, and they didn't like me anymore, you know. I had no friends. I was lonely. Had to move into an apartment and live by myself. People harass me. I was threatened."

"Was this a result of—"

"Yes."

"—of what you knew but had not related?"

"Your Honor," Frank objected, "now he's leading the witness. Ms. Parrish is not on trial."

"Sustained," Judge Wolfman ruled.

The damage had been done. With help from Hunt, Donna had found a way to explain away her conflicting testimony. Indeed, she had successfully framed her actions in a positive light. She was the loyal girlfriend, conflicted in her heart, who had finally turned in her boyfriend after no longer being able to live with the consequences of lying to the authorities. It was brilliant theater. And the jury appeared spellbound by her performance.

CHAPTER 15
INCONCEIVABLE

If Donna's emotionally charged testimony had been incoherent at times, the nine witnesses who followed her in rapid succession Wednesday afternoon managed, bit by bit, to bolster her narrative—despite diverging on crucial points. By now it was clear to Bill that everyone was tired: the attorneys, the judge, certainly the jury. The attorneys no longer quibbled over details. Instead, each witness was hurried on and off the stand.

Matt Bocci, the first to take the stand after Donna, had curly brown hair. At eighteen years old, he was a year younger than his brother Joe but the owner of a larger frame. He and Joe dealt marijuana to many in the neighborhood, including Bill, who had bought from them in the past. The prosecution likely knew as much, Bill mused, since it was common knowledge among pretty much everybody who knew the Bocci brothers. But Matt wasn't on trial. On the witness stand, he looked like any upstanding citizen doing his civic duty and testifying before the court.

Karen Thompson began her examination by asking Matt who was living with him in his apartment on August 16.

"Glen Zeller, my brother Joseph Bocci, and my fiancé flew in that night, Tracey Lorraine Herman," Matt answered.

"What time that night did Tracey fly in?"

"It was ten-thirty."

"Did Tracey have anyone with her?" Thompson asked.

"Yeah, our little girl."

"What's her name?"

"Heather."

"Where did she fly in to?"

"Melbourne Airport."

Matt went on to tell the jury that Bill and Donna had been waiting at the apartment when Matt and his family had returned from the airport. Bill had been wearing a yellow Surf-It T-shirt. When Matt had gone to bed at 12:30 a.m., Bill and Donna had been bedding down as well on an improvised mattress in the living room, and they were still there when Matt had roused early the next morning to go to work. Matt added that Bill had been asked by several people at a party whether he was the murderer.

Matt's older brother Joe testified next. Joe had straight dark hair and a more athletic build.

"I live with Matt and Tracey and Glen Zeller," he told the court.

"Okay. Who did you live with on August the sixteenth?" Thompson asked.

"Same people."

"Okay. Was Tracey already there?"

Joe mulled over the question. "I don't know. The sixteenth—was that Saturday?" he asked tellingly.

"No," Thompson emphasized. "The sixteenth was Sunday."

"Tracey lived there," Joe replied. "She moved back Sunday."

"Okay. Now you recall that Tracey did return on a Sunday?"

"Yeah, it was a Sunday."

"How do you know?"

"I don't know. That's just the day she came back."

After stumbling on the date, Joe continued with his testimony. Unlike Matt, Joe testified that the apartment had been empty when he and Matt had returned from the airport with Matt's family. According to Joe's version of events, he had spotted Donna and Bill later, somewhere between two and four that morning, at Sambo's, which meant they hadn't gone to sleep at the same time as Matt, after all—or at least hadn't stayed in bed long. Joe and Glenn Zeller had been leaving the restaurant just as Bill and Donna had been entering. A few days after the murder, Joe told the jury that Matt's fiancée, Tracey Lorraine Herman, had asked Bill in front of several people at a party whether he was the killer. Bill's sarcastic comeback in the affirmative had been heard by several of the partygoers.

Tracey took the stand next. From what little Bill knew of her, he believed she resented Joe for letting people sleep at the apartment. It was likely she had viewed Bill in a negative light even before he had become a murder suspect.

After inquiring about her current living situation, Thompson asked Tracey where she had been living on the night of the murder.

"Satellite Beach," Tracey answered.

"Okay. And where was that residence located?"

Tracey gave the address and then added, "Behind Sambo's on A1A."

"About how far is it from Sambo's?"

"It's right behind. It's the parking lot and then the apartments."

Just as Joe had before her, Tracey appeared unsure at first while pinpointing the date of her flight. But with Thompson carefully framing the questions, Tracey testified that she had met Bill and Donna for the first time on August 16 after flying home. They had been at the apartment when she had arrived at 10:45 p.m., she said, echoing Matt's testimony but contradicting Joe's. Bill had been wearing a yellow Surf-It T-shirt, and the next morning, Tracey had noticed small scratches on his knuckles. She, too, had heard Bill joke at the party that he was the killer, although she denied having asked him about it, despite what Joe had just testified to minutes earlier.

During cross-examination, Frank pointed out that Tracey had originally told police that she really didn't remember Bill's shirt. Bill could only watch as Tracey claimed to have heard about the murder when two police officers had come to the Bocci apartment looking for Bill—*before* the party. But no one had seen Bill after he himself had given the police the Bocci brothers' names, for he'd been arrested the very next day. Tracey also claimed to have knowledge, gleaned directly from Bill, about the lie detector test Bill had taken, despite the fact that he'd never left police custody after the test and therefore, couldn't have told her about it. In short, Tracey's timeline was impossible. But Frank, perhaps too tired to catch the myriad discrepancies, didn't have the presence of mind to call her on it. Nor did he demand that the prosecution submit proof of the date of Tracey's flight. If she'd truly flown home on August 16, it would have been easy to produce a plane ticket, a baggage stub, the manifest from the airline, or a record of some kind. Confirming that date was the key to cementing Bill's alibi, but it hit Bill that Frank was not on his game.

Maggie McDonald appeared next on the witness stand. She was an attractive girl: tall and slender, with curly dark hair. Bill thought that Maggie had always been nice to him and had even smoked weed with him right outside the bar.

"What was your occupation last August?" Thompson asked.

"I was a bartender at the Pelican Lounge," Maggie answered.

Maggie testified that she remembered Bill coming into the bar on August 16. The first time she had seen him, she said, he had been shirtless. The comment was hard to believe, considering the Pelican had a strict dress code that required shirts and shoes. A short while later, she added, he had been wearing a light jacket. While there, he had bought several drinks, including a White Russian for Donna. Not normally a tipper, Bill had made sure to tip Maggie that night, she told the jury, indicating he had money at the time. Frank's cross-examination included questions about Donna, who, Maggie said, had once worked at the Pelican before being fired.

Genevieve Tisdale, another bartender at the Pelican, testified next. She was polite, had long blond hair, and, like Maggie, had smoked weed with Bill outside the bar. She testified that she remembered seeing Bill at the bar on August 16 because that was the night the band Close Call had played. Bill had been wearing a yellow Surf-It T-shirt, Genevieve claimed.

While cross-examining her, Frank asked Genevieve whether she had ever evicted Donna from the Pelican.

"No," Genevieve answered, "I evicted her from my part of the bar where I was working. I asked her not to sit there one night."

"Why did you ask her not to sit there?" Thompson asked on redirect.

"Because she got on my nerves," Genevieve stated flatly.

"Okay, thank you." Thompson returned to the prosecution's table. "No further questions."

Frank, though, wasn't finished. "Was that because she talked so much?"

"Yeah, possible," Genevieve answered.

Up next was Mark Muirhead, a doorman at the Pelican. Mark said he had driven Bill home on the night of the murder and remembered being followed by George McGee, a deputy sheriff with the county sheriff's office. Donna had been waiting for Bill when they had reached the house. After dropping off Bill, Mark had stepped out of the car to talk to Deputy McGee.

The deputy corroborated Mark's version of events when he took the stand next, telling the jury that Mark had made several moving violations while driving Bill home, including speeding and briefly going the wrong way on Highway A1A. Deputy McGee had warned Mark about his noisy muffler but hadn't issued a citation. While there, he had noticed Donna emerge from the garage. Bill, he said, had been wearing a shirt from the Pelican.

The last two witnesses to take the stand seemed weaker. Stacy Lee, a pretty, underage seventeen-year-old who threw a party at her folks' home when they were gone, claimed Bill had bragged at the party that he had beaten up someone on the beach. However, during Frank Clark's cross-examination, Stacy admitted she had been drinking the night of Bill's alleged remark and that her parents would not have been pleased to know what had been going on in their house while they were away. Frank insinuated that Brevard County was using that fact as leverage to hold over her head.

Brian Kersey, the final witness of the day, was a young kid from the neighborhood. Unbeknownst to the jury, he had been in some legal trouble. Having recently violated his probation, he was awaiting a new sentence. He testified that he had seen the composite sketch in the newspaper after the murder and had noticed a resemblance to Bill.

Frank needed less than a minute to expose the foolishness of Brian's testimony.

"Mr. Kersey, you say that the picture resembled Dillon except for the hair, the moustache, and the cheeks, right?"

"Yes, sir," Brian answered.

Frank paused for effect. "There's not much else, is there?"

"No, not really," the teenager admitted.

"Okay," Frank said. "Nothing further. Thank you."

Bill felt his shoulders sag as he was escorted back through the time tunnel to his cell. After three days of sitting through testimony, he could feel exhaustion gnawing at his bones. Everyone, it seemed, had their dates wrong: Donna, the Bocci brothers, Matt's fiancée, the bartenders and the doorman at the Pelican—even a deputy sheriff. But Bill still had faith that the jury would find in his favor. The alternative—that he might soon be convicted of a murder he hadn't committed—was inconceivable.

CHAPTER 16
WITNESS FOR THE DEFENSE

Bill awoke Thursday morning to another hangover. Since being prescribed Sinequan for his anxiety, he'd grown accustomed to waking each day feeling groggy and listless. The medicine was supposed to help him sleep and was administered by a nurse each evening after dinner, with either the nurse or the accompanying guard inspecting his mouth afterward to make sure he'd swallowed the blue capsule. But instead of calming him, the Sinequan exacerbated his agitated state, all while making him feel tired, hazy, and even nauseous. After repeated complaints that the drug was too strong, his dose was cut in half.

Bill was also applying an ointment twice daily to treat a head-to-toe rash, which the doctor had diagnosed as the result of acute anxiety. The rash had cleared up slightly since his diagnosis—and since he'd begun the treatment, which had also included an initial oatmeal bath. But the cause of the rash remained. Every day spent in custody was another day spent fighting for his freedom. As the weight of the fight became more onerous, he began convening with God in his cell each night, trying to grapple with the reality of his predicament, and struggling to understand why God was permitting it.

Unbeknownst to Bill, he was experiencing the legal equivalent of a marathon, and he was about to enter the race's toughest, most grueling stretch: a twelve-plus-hour day that would push everyone involved to the limits of their endurance.

Thursday morning's court session began just after nine o'clock, with Roseanna Rogers appearing as the day's first witness. Roseanna and Charles, who had recently moved to Georgia and had therefore been flown in for their testimony, represented the defense's best chance to provide an alternative narrative for what had occurred in the early hours of August 17. But since the couple would be testifying "out of turn," *before* the prosecution had rested its case, Bill feared that Karen Thompson and Michael Hunt would then have plenty of opportunity to discredit his main alibi. Bill was told there was no other way. Charles and Roseanna had a tight schedule and could only fly out at that particular time.

As Bill watched Roseanna take the stand, he felt a resurgence of confidence. He was certain she would put an end to the confusion over where he had been on the night of the murder. Roseanna, attractive and several years younger than Charles, was a hardworking, upstanding citizen. She had been kind and hospitable to Donna and Bill, two perfect strangers on the day Charles had brought them to their motel apartment. Like Charles, she had no reason to lie or cover for Bill, who, as he recalled the events leading up to his arrest, hadn't even been able to remember the couple's surname the first time he was questioned by the police.

After Judge Wolfman explained to the jury that Roseanna and Charles would be testifying out of turn, Frank Clark began his direct examination.

Roseanna, clearly nervous to be testifying in a murder case, explained her role as the manager of the Ocean Star Motel in Cocoa Beach, and then described the night she and her husband hosted Bill and Donna. Not long after Charles met Donna and Bill down on the beach, Roseanna told the court, he invited the young couple into their apartment because they had nowhere to stay for the night. Charles offered Bill and Donna several servings of the roast he had cooked in a crock-pot earlier in the day, and after eating, the four stayed up late into the evening while Charles and Roseanna's ten-year-old son slept in one of the two bedrooms. Eventually the adults went to sleep, too, with Charles taking one twin bed and Donna and Bill taking the other in the master bedroom. Roseanna slept on the couch in the living room, just a few feet from the apartment's only exit. When questioned whether or not it would have been possible for someone to come and go from the apartment during the night without her noticing, she answered that she was a very light sleeper. Moreover, her poodle, which had a habit of barking at anyone who came to the door or moved around at night, slept nearby.

"What time do you recall getting up in the morning?" Frank asked.

"I had to open the office at eight o'clock a.m.," Roseanna answered nervously. "I was up at seven."

"And what did you do as regards William Dillon and Donna Parrish? Were they still sleeping?"

"Yes, they were sound asleep. I had to wake them up on several occasions and finally just told them they had to get out. My husband's boss was coming in that day."

Frank homed in on the central question. "Was that Monday?"

"Yeah, Monday, the seventeenth," Roseanna replied, "and I had to prepare the room for him."

"All right. Now what did your husband do for entertainment and diversion that Sunday afternoon, if you recall?"

"He was listening to the Michigan 400 race."

"And is that an automobile stock car race?"

"Stock car race, uh-huh."

"And is your husband a stock car buff?"

"Yes, he's a sports fan."

"Does he ever miss a race?"

"No."

"That he can help?"

"That he can help."

Roseanna explained that Charles's boss arrived early that Monday and stayed with them for over a week.

"Now," Frank began, "do you have any other reason other than the dinner you served that evening, the fact that there was an automobile race on Sunday that Charles listened to, and the fact that Jack Clark was coming in the next day, Mr. Rogers's boss—do you have any other reason to remember that it was, in fact, Sunday, August 16, 1981?"

"Our anniversary was the next day," Roseanna answered, "and I wouldn't forget that."

"Monday. You were married Monday, August seventeenth?"

"Seventeenth, uh-huh."

"Where?"

"In Virginia Beach."

"Now after this happening, did you later learn that a man had been found dead in Canova Beach?"

"Yes."

"And did you discuss this matter with your husband?"

"Yes, I did."

"And did you at that time recall that Donna Parrish and Bill Dillon had stayed there the entire night of August sixteenth?"

"Yes."

"Did you contact or were you contacted by authorities?"

"Yes, I was."

"Who contacted you?"

"The sheriff's department. He was sending two detectives over to the house to question me."

"All right. And did, in fact, two detectives come over?"

"Yes, a man and a woman."

Roseanna testified that the deputies identified Bill as the suspect in the case, but they didn't show her any pictures of him. She told the deputies that Bill and Donna had stayed with her and her husband the entire night. She later found out that Bill had been indicted by the grand jury for the murder of James Dvorak. At that point, the sheriff's department contacted Charles, who talked to Detective Slaughter.

"And did Charles in your presence reiterate what he already told detectives?" Frank asked.

"Yes," Roseanna answered.

"Did he want to be heard on the matter?"

"Yes, he did."

Karen Thompson objected to the question.

"Please don't lead your witness," Judge Wolfman instructed Frank.

"All right," Frank said.

"Don't ask her hearsay testimony," the judge added.

"Yes, sir." Frank returned his attention to Roseanna. "Well, at some time after the night that Donna and Bill stayed there, Sunday, August sixteenth, did you receive a phone call from Donna Parrish?"

"Yes," Roseanna answered. "I received a call from Donna."

"And what was the gist of that conversation?"

"She told me that they were trying to convince her that it was Saturday night."

Thompson intervened once again. "Objection, your Honor."

"Sustained," Judge Wolfman ruled. He frowned at Frank. "Mr. Clark, please do not ask for hearsay testimony."

"All right."

"Thank you," the judge said.

"What night did you tell Donna it was?" Frank asked, resuming his questions.

"Sunday night," Roseanna answered.

"There was no doubt in your mind?"

"No doubt in my mind."

"Okay. What was Donna's reaction to that?"

"She told me to stick to the story."

Thompson shot to her feet again. "Objection again, your Honor. Hearsay."

"Sustained."

Frank kept on point. "No doubt in your mind, is there, Mrs. Rogers, that—"

"No doubt in my mind it was Sunday, August sixteenth." Roseanna pointed to Bill. "That right there is the boy that was with Donna Parrish."

When Thompson's turn came to cross-examine Roseanna, she remarked to Roseanna how hard it must have been to take care of seventeen units at the Ocean Star Motel, which required Roseanna to do all the laundry and be on call virtually twenty-four hours a day. Then, with the pleasantries out of the way, the attorney went negative in an attempt to smear Roseanna's character and thus her credibility.

"And when you and your husband went to bed," Thompson asked, "it was sometime after two o'clock in the morning?"

"Yeah."

"And Mrs. Rogers, did you have sex with Bill Dillon that night?"

"No."

Thompson, cocking her head to the side, didn't bother to hide the condescension in her voice. "You're under oath, Mrs. Rogers."

"Yes," Roseanna said, affirming that she understood she was obligated to tell the truth.

"Did you have sex with him?"

"No."

"Did your husband have sex play with Donna Parrish?"

"No."

"You sure about that?"

"Yes, I'm positive," Roseanna insisted. "I'm a very jealous woman."

Unsuccessful in her attempt to squeeze an admission from the witness, Thompson tried another angle. She asked Roseanna about when she had learned of the murder. "The first you really started to pay attention to it was when the two deputies came over, right?"

"Yes, yes."

"Would that have been Steve Kindrick and Chris Barringer?"

"I believe so. I remember Chris. That was the lady, the blond-headed lady."

"Okay. And up 'til that time, you knew a murder had happened but you hadn't been following it closely."

"No, I hadn't."

"Now what day was that when they came?"

"It was on Tuesday morning, very early, two o'clock in the morning. They called me very late, and I thought it was a prank call. I was ready to hang up until he said it was the sheriff's department."

"Do you remember the date?"

"It was the following Tuesday, I believe."

"Okay. The calendar date—do you know?"

"No, I don't."

"It was, in fact, about ten days after the actual murder had occurred, wasn't it?"

"I guess."

"Somewhere around there?"

"Yeah."

"It was over a week, anyway."

Roseanna nodded.

Bill frowned. It was obvious Thompson was trying to make it look like Roseanna's memory was suspect.

"And they asked you if a couple named Bill and Donna had spent the night with you that night?" Thompson asked, continuing her line of questioning.

"Yes."

"And you told them the truth: that they had spent the night with you."

"Yes, uh-huh."

"And they told you which night the murder had happened so you would know."

"They asked me if they were there August the sixteenth, and I said Sunday night. I looked on the calendar to make sure, because I knew it was Sunday."

"But they were the ones who told you the calendar day."

"Yes."

"Okay. Then as soon as they left, you and your husband talked about it."

"Yes."

"You told Mr. Clark."

"Uh-huh."

"Okay. I guess that's natural. It's not every day detectives come to your home and talk about a murder."

"No."

"Do you remember what you had for supper that night?"

"Which night?" Roseanna asked.

"The night the detectives came."

"No, I don't, to be honest. I don't."

"How about the night after Bill and Donna were there?" Thompson asked. "Do you remember what you had for supper?"

"Leftovers."

"Leftover roast?"

"Uh-huh."

"How about the night after that?"

"I believe it was pork chops. I fixed them. Also in the crockpot."

"How about the night after that?"

"I don't know. I really don't."

"And when you were talking with Charles, Charles told you he remembered the date because of that NASCAR race he'd listened to on the radio?"

"Yes, yes, and also our anniversary is August the seventeenth, so that pinpointed it, you know? A date I know."

As soon as Karen had finished, Frank began a redirect. "Mrs. Rogers, on Sunday, the sixteenth of August, when Bill Dillon was at your apartment, yours and Charles's apartment, did he have a mustache at that time?"

"No, he didn't."

"Did his upper lip look exactly as it does now?"

"Yes."

"And was his hairstyle any differently—"

"It looked like it had a little bit more body to it."

"On that Sunday?"

"Yes."

Roseanna's testimony had clearly helped the defense. She had placed Bill at her apartment on the night of the murder, and she had described him as mustacheless and with slightly thicker hair. Now it was Charles's turn to take the stand.

Charles, a highly decorated navy veteran, boasted a military record that included a Presidential Unit Citation, Meritorious Unit Commendations, five Good Conduct Medals, a Vietnam Service Medal, a National Defense Service Medal, and a Vietnam Campaign Ribbon. But Frank's attempts to bring those commendations and medals to the attention of the jury were blocked by Thompson, who objected each time Frank tried to explore Charles's impressive service record. Bill knew Frank was merely trying to show that Charles was a man of proven honor and integrity—that is, a highly trustworthy witness. But Wolfman was having none of it and sustained every one of Thompson's objections.

Frank did succeed in having Charles sketch the layout of the Ocean Star Motel apartment where he and his wife had been living on the night of the murder. The sketch revealed how difficult—just shy of impossible, in fact—it would have been for Bill to leave the apartment undetected. To access the only exterior door, Bill would have had to sneak right past Roseanna and her poodle without being heard. With the drawing finished, Frank offered it into evidence. He then quizzed Charles about his activities on Sunday, August 16, and Charles explained that he had listened to the Michigan 400 on the radio that day and could still remember who had won it—Richard Petty—and when—five o'clock. When he had met Bill, Charles said, the young man had been without a mustache and had sported longer hair. Charles told the court that he had actually met Donna the day before when Donna had supposedly been visiting her parents. In fact, she had been visiting the Plumlees and had lied in describing them as her parents in the hopes of being able to stay with them for free.

"But Bill Dillon wasn't there when you first saw Donna, right?" Frank asked.

"No," Charles answered.

"Would you describe Donna to the jury?"

"Well, she was kind of small, short."

"Skinny?"

"Skinny? Yeah. Loud."

"Loud, okay."

Charles recounted the evening of August 16 from his perspective. Donna, who had been fighting with her supposed parents upstairs, had been kicked out and was thus without a place to stay—or so she claimed, anyway. Since the girl and her boyfriend were stranded at the motel, which was fully booked, with no place to stay and nothing to eat, Charles and Roseanna had offered up their apartment for the night. The group ate pot roast and watched TV, Charles told the court, and eventually everyone went to bed, with Charles hitting the sack last at five minutes after two in the morning.

After the police began investigating the murder, Charles said he spoke with Detective Slaughter.

"What did you tell him?" Frank asked.

"He told me he [Bill] definitely left our house, and I said, 'No, sir.'"

"Mr. Rogers," Judge Wolfman said and shook his head no.

Charles, Bill knew, was not supposed to testify to what anyone else had said, which would be considered hearsay, and was to limit his comments to what he had said or witnessed himself.

"Okay," Charles said.

"What did you tell him?" Frank asked, repeating the question.

"I told him he didn't leave the house."

"Sunday, August sixteenth, the entire night."

"Yes, sir."

Along with being adamant that he was telling the truth, Charles was clearly miffed at the police for ignoring him, and it showed in his demeanor. It was also obvious that Judge Wolfman didn't appreciate Charles's attitude or his forcefulness on the stand. Bill, though, was glad someone was finally standing up for the truth.

In a replay of her cross-examination of Roseanna, Thompson began by flattering Charles. "Mr. Rogers, I've decided I was rude to you when I interrupted your recitation of your service record. Did you have a good service record?"

"Yes, ma'am," Charles answered.

"Good—an honorable discharge and all that."

"Five or six of them."

Thompson then began to explore Charles's line of work in the food industry, how hard he labored at his job, and so on. She then inquired about the night Bill and Donna spent the night.

Charles explained that he'd felt sorry for the young couple.

"So you invited them in," Thompson said. "You fed them a pot roast."

"Right."

"I was gonna ask you where do you find a man who cooks," she said, "but I'll withdraw that as not being relevant." She only needed a second to shift gears. "And then later on the four of you sat around, drank some beers?"

"Right."

"And the four of you get into a little mate-swapping that night?"

"No, ma'am. I have enough trouble just handling my own."

When Thompson saw she wasn't going to make any headway smearing the witness, she tried a few different tacks before asking about the murder. "Did you follow the story of the murder in the papers real closely?"

"No," Charles answered, "just . . . after he was indicted, I called again to the—"

"In fact, you really didn't pay any attention to the murder until the deputies came in."

"Right."

"Is that the only time that deputies in your lifetime have ever come to talk to you about a murder?"

"I believe so."

"I guess that kind of sticks in your mind."

"Sure, at two o'clock in the morning."

"Have a pretty good memory for dates and times, I think you told Mr. Clark. Do you recall telling Mr. Clark in that interview on the thirty-first in Georgia that you were sure that Bobby Alison won that race?"

"No, I don't think I said he might have won it. I might have said Bobby, but I don't think so."

"Are you sure about that?"

Bill felt his jaw harden. Now Thompson was trying to trip up Charles and make *him* look forgetful. After all, if he couldn't remember who had won the race, who was to say he even had the date right?

"Yes, I'm sure," Charles said. "It's on the tape. It's Richard Petty."

"Are you as sure about that as you are the night that Bill Dillon spent the night with you?"

"Yes, ma'am. Just like I told you, I said on the tape that Richard Petty won the race. He could not have won the race, but on the tape I told Mr. Clark that he did. We discussed it a little bit."

During redirect, Frank asked Charles about Bill's outfit. "Was Bill Dillon wearing the same clothes when you got up Monday, August seventeenth, at six or six-thirty? Was he wearing the same clothes then, sleeping on the bed, as he wore the night before when he ate dinner in the house and then went to bed?"

"Yes, sir," Charles answered.

It was a crucial point, and one Bill hoped the jury understood. To murder James Dvorak at Canova Beach, Bill would have had to slip out of the apartment undetected, change clothes and put on a Surf-It T-shirt, commit the murder, entertain a homosexual tryst while hitchhiking, leave the bloody Surf-It T-shirt in a stranger's pickup truck, clean off all the blood from his body, change back into his other outfit, and hurry back to Cocoa Beach, fifteen miles away, where he would have to get back into bed without waking a soul—all in an hour to an hour and a half and without the use of a vehicle.

After Charles left the stand, Judge Wolfman ordered a quick recess at 10:15 a.m. Court was back in session twenty minutes later, and the next person to testify was Glenn Zeller, the Bocci brothers' friend and roommate. Like Matt and Joe Bocci before him, Glenn placed Bill at their apartment on the night of the murder. He echoed Joe's testimony and claimed he had spotted Bill and Donna at Sambo's in the early morning hours of August 17.

Detective Thom Fair took the stand next, and after the attorneys argued at the bench, out of the jury's hearing, Fair was allowed to testify that Donna had told him she'd seen Bill standing over a dead body on the beach. With damaging testimony piling up against Bill, he couldn't begin to imagine how bad things could get if the judge actually allowed dog handler John Preston to testify. Unbeknownst to Bill, Preston was as good on the stand as any actor delivering an Oscar-winning performance. But this performance could mean life in prison or death for Bill.

As soon as Fair was excused, so was the jury. Judge Wolfman was finally ready to decide whether or not to allow testimony from John Preston, the dog handler. Frank Clark was strongly protesting the admission of what he believed to be unreliable evidence. In order to make a final decision, the judge would hear proffered testimony—testimony given out of the jury's hearing—from Preston; from E. R. "Sonny" Brannon, who was Frank Clark's expert-witness dog handler; and from Bill.

Preston was the first up. As Brevard County's go-to dog handler, he was highly respected in the law enforcement field, from low-ranking detectives to John Dean Moxley, the chief prosecutor for the state attorney's office. Preston and his dog Harass II had carved out a stellar reputation as expert man-trailers and scent-trackers. Preston's services were so in demand, that he'd worked cases all over the country, connecting suspects' scents to those found at crime scenes. He had famously claimed that his dog, which suspiciously only responded to commands in German, had *never* been wrong and could even track a scent under water. His fantastical claims included being able to track a scent that was eight years old. By all appearances, John Preston had trained a wonder dog. His expert services commanded $300 a day, a handsome sum in 1981.

Frank, though, was highly skeptical of Preston's capabilities, particularly where the murder of James Dvorak was concerned. He had submitted a motion to suppress both the dog handler's testimony and the results of Preston and Harass II's supposed tracking of Bill. According to the prosecution, Preston and his dog had tracked Bill's scent at the scene of the crime and had also found Bill's scent on the bloody Surf-It T-shirt. But Preston's so-called tests, which purportedly linked the wadded-up piece of paper that Bill had signed at the police station to (a) Bill's scent trail from the parking lot to the judge's chambers in the courthouse, and (b) the bloody Surf-It T-shirt, seemed dubious at best.

As usual, Judge Wolfman was concerned first and foremost with time. "Are we gonna be able to cover that and the motion by twelve-thirty?" he asked.

Hunt spoke up first. "I think the motion is gonna take a little longer than what the court—"

"I'm not gonna hear a lot of testimony," the judge snapped. "It will be very simple. I think you can stipulate to what the facts are, and then if you're talking about experts, let's hear the experts."

With one eye on the clock and the other on his gavel, Judge Wolfman listened as Preston described how he'd handled the case. First investigators had presented the bloody Surf-It T-shirt to Preston and Harass II to use as a reference. Next the tracker and his dog had visited the scene of the crime. Preston had then offered investigators a second test to confirm the results of the first one. After telling investigators to get a piece of paper from the suspect, Preston had suggested they go back to the courthouse and compare six pieces of paper, including the paper Bill had crumpled up, to the T-shirt already in evidence. Once back at the courthouse, Preston claimed that Harass II had "alerted on" the piece of paper in question three out of three times. Convinced he'd found a match, Preston had suggested they bring the suspect in, walk him through the parking lot to the courthouse, and let Harass II follow his scent. According to Preston, Harass II had done exactly that and had made a positive ID of Bill while he sat in the judge's chambers with Detective Charles Slaughter.

During his cross-examination, Frank insinuated that the crime scene had been stale by the time Preston and Harass II had arrived. Indeed, in the eight and a half days between the murder and the tracking, a major tropical storm, Dennis, had blown through and countless investigators had trampled the murder site. Moreover, any number of detectives, including Detective Slaughter, had walked through the courthouse parking lot along with Bill Dillon. Even if Harass II was as good as Preston said he was, it was quite possible the dog had tracked Slaughter's scent. After all, Slaughter had likely been in contact with the T-shirt, the piece of paper, the crime scene, and the courthouse parking lot.

To further bolster his argument, Frank invited Sonny Brannon to testify after the lunch break. A former Brevard County deputy sheriff, Brannon had amassed nineteen years in the law enforcement field and had extensive experience with tracking dogs. His background as a tracker stretched as far back as 1967, and he had trained thousands of dogs for different branches of the armed forces. Duke, his training dog, was a police dog.

Brannon testified that the conditions in which Harass II had tracked Bill were not suitable for a good track. More than a week had passed between the crime and the tracking. The crime scene had been located next to the Atlantic, which was a source of several corrosive effects, from high humidity to salty winds. And multiple people had handled the evidence and visited the crime site. But during cross-examination, Hunt did his best to make Brannon look like the local hick ill-versed in the modern techniques of dog tracking. The prosecutor pointed out that L. Wilson Davis, the author of *Go Find!*, proposed theories that backed Preston's claims. He also tried to embarrass Brannon by exposing Brannon's ignorance of the term *sebum*, an oily skin byproduct that causes odor when it breaks down, and of the Schutzhund Three FH, a German tracking dog.[2]

By the time the two trackers had finished testifying, it was obvious they differed on several important points.

Bill, whose only job so far had been to sit silently at the defense table, was asked to take the stand for the first time to deliver proffered testimony. True, the jury had been excused and would not hear his testimony, but he still felt a fair amount of trepidation as he made his way to the stand.

Bill began his testimony by describing the circumstances around the paper test, when Detective Barringer had asked him to thoroughly crumple the form he had signed, and the tracking at the courthouse, when he

---

[2] According to Preston, Harass II could track sebum and owned the honorary designation of Schutzhund Three FH.

had been forced to wait in a squad car in the parking lot for approximately twenty minutes before being escorted inside to the judge's chambers. Frank's line of questioning exposed the underhanded nature of both tests, which had been conducted without an attorney present and without Bill's full understanding, either of the tests or of what was at stake.

During his cross-examination, while describing the moment when Bill had reacted to Preston's supposedly successful tracking of him in the courthouse, Hunt tried to put words into Bill's mouth. "Didn't you tell him at that time that in response to his question, 'What do you think the jury's gonna do?' Didn't you respond, 'I guess they'll find me guilty?'"

"No, sir."

"Never said that."

Bill wasn't about to be railroaded. "No. Guilty of something I didn't do?"

After Bill had finished giving his testimony, much of it in clear opposition to Hunt's portrayal of events, Frank began to argue previous cases. "I have found no case, and I have read all of them, that said that eight to nine to ten days, when the tracking was not in, from the crime scene to the suspect and where the crime area was trampled from twenty-five to forty people, where it had rained heavily—there is not one case of record that I know that matches this factual situation and where the court has ruled that such evidence is admissible." The defense attorney then framed the issue in stark terms. "It's dangerous, scary testimony. It's difficult to rebut and to cross-examine. It's almost impossible. Because the handler, of course, is secure in the knowledge that his dog couldn't possibly be wrong."

Judge Wolfman, though, seemed unmoved. "We don't have a factual conflict," he said. "We have a conflict in experts."

Hunt, meanwhile, argued that case law was on the prosecution's side, citing numerous cases in which dog-tracking evidence had been admitted. Moreover, all of the impediments to a good tracking claimed by the defense—the long delay between the crime and the tracking, the hurricane, the numerous people at the crime scene—had been overcome at one time or another in the past by Harass II, according to Preston.

Clark, though, stuck to his guns. "I do not see any case where eight and a half days is a reasonable time, and especially where the tracking was never done from the scene of the crime to the defendant, which is the case in every case I read on this entire point. There never was."

"There's no case that you're saying is on what we have been describing this afternoon as an I.D.?" Judge Wolfman asked.

"As a what?"

"Identification."

"Right, yeah."

"The dog identifying an accused."

"Right," Frank said. "From the scene."

"Other than the scene."

"Right, other than the scene."

"You say there's no case in all of these where that was done?" the judge asked.

"No," Frank answered, "this is a unique factual situation. I find no authority for that at all. Every case I read was from the scene or from the place where the scene was tracked by the officers, virtually, and then picked up there, unbroken."

"How do you reconcile the state's expert who says that ID identification by dogs have been accepted in multiple courts throughout the country?"

"Well, they may have, your Honor, but all we have to go on are the appellate courts, and I don't find any appellate courts affirming and approving an eight and a half day old scent."

"That's the point I was talking about," Judge Wolfman replied. "I'm talking about identification by a dog other than from the scene. It's not tracking from the scene; it's simply identifying."

The debate dragged on until Frank finally exposed the underlying problem: whether the shirt used to scent the dog even belonged to the defendant. "Well," he said, "I think we're building a premise on top of a supposition to get this into evidence because, to me, the testimony is very fragmentary and probably insufficient to the jury on whether he was wearing that shirt that night and whether he owned it. There's been conflicting testimony, and I don't think we should assume, for the sake of this motion, that the shirt was his and he was wearing it that night."

"That's the point they're trying to establish," the judge said.

"I think it would be very prejudicial to him at this stage."

Bill, who only minutes earlier had been on the witness stand, waited anxiously for the judge's decision. Neither expert had been able to agree on the basic principles of dog-scenting and man-trailing. It came down to one expert's word against another's. The state's position was that John Preston and Harass II had identified their killer, and they had the evidence and experts to prove it. Bill, on the other hand, knew that the state had no physical evidence to point toward him as a suspect or even as a person of interest. To Bill's mind, Preston was either a liar or completely incompetent. Without John Preston and his dog, the state had no way to connect Bill to the shirt and the shirt to the crime scene. *More importantly*, Bill wondered, *how do you cross-examine a dog?*

"The court may be setting some possible law in the state of Florida," the judge finally announced, "but the court is going to allow the testimony of both experts, meaning we have the testimony of the expert the state has available, and if you want to present your expert, he'll be available, your expert. Then we're really getting to the weight of the evidence as we do in any other type of expert testimony."

Judge Stanley Wolfman's decision to allow the testimony of John Preston into his courtroom was a blow to the defense. Frank told him not to worry, but Bill couldn't help but be concerned about Preston's reputation as a first-rate tracker. At the same time, he was confident that Sonny Brannon was a far more qualified expert. Brannon spoke with more common sense. He was more believable. Surely the jury would believe him over Preston. Or would they?

CHAPTER 17

A CAREFULLY ORCHESTRATED TRAP

After Judge Wolfman denied Frank's motion to suppress Preston's testimony, he ordered a short recess. Less than twenty minutes later, at 2:27 p.m., the bailiff escorted the jury back into the courtroom and the trial resumed.

Sergeant Steven Kindrick of the Brevard County Sheriff's Department took the stand next. Short, stout, and balding, he had a football player's physique. He had been with Detective Christine Barringer when four sheriff's agents had picked up Bill at his parents' home and brought him in for questioning on the evening of September 25.

"When you arrived at the Melbourne Sheriff's Department," Hunt asked, "where did you park?"

"At the very north end of the courthouse," Kindrick answered.

"And at that time were other vehicles in the parking area?"

"Yes, sir."

"How many, approximately?"

"The parking lot was full. Twenty."

"These sheriff's vehicles and others?"

"Yes, sir, that's correct."

"This was at night, and the courthouse isn't open at that time."

"They were—probably eight or nine of them would have been marked cars parked up toward the sheriff's office. The others were unmarked cars or employees' cars."

"Did you see Agent Charles Slaughter at the courthouse that night?"

"Yes, sir, I did."

"Where did you see him?"

"He was at the entrance going into the courthouse itself, the north entrance."

"How far approximately was he from your vehicle when you pulled up with the defendant?"

"Sixty feet."

"Did he ever approach your vehicle that night before what Preston did?"

"No, sir. He came out of the courthouse, but he only went ten or fifteen feet."

"What did you do upon arrival at the courthouse with the defendant?"

"I directed the defendant to go to Agent Slaughter."

"And what did you do?"

"I went inside the sheriff's office."

"Did the defendant for some time sit in the car?"

"From his house over to the courthouse."

"How about at the courthouse upon arrival?"

"Just a minute or two."

"And was he alone in the car?"

"No, sir."

Bill shook his head in disbelief. He had been left alone in the sheriff's car in the parking lot for a minimum of twenty minutes that night. Kindrick certainly had to know that since he'd been there.

"Who else was present?" Hunt asked.

"Agent Barringer and myself," Kindrick answered.

"Agent Slaughter ever approach the car until the time the defendant got out?"

"No, sir."

It was obvious Hunt was trying to pave the way for Preston's testimony.

"Did he come out and get the defendant?"

"No," Kindrick answered, contradicting what Bill knew had happened that night.

"How did the defendant get from the car to the courthouse?"

"I directed him to go to Mr. Slaughter."

"And did he do that?"

"Yes, sir."

Bill felt powerless as Kindrick continued to deliver his version of what had transpired.

"And did you observe a yellow Surf-It T-shirt that evening?"

"Yes, sir, I did."

"Who was in possession of that?"

"Agent Tamillo."

"Was anyone else present once you arrived in the parking lot?"

"No, sir."

"Did subsequently someone go out to the parking lot?"

"Slaughter. Sergeant Slaughter. When I say into the parking lot, he didn't actually come into the parking lot. There was no one in the parking lot at the time. I radioed ahead and told them I was arriving, and Slaughter went out the door."

"Met you at the front door there?"

"He came out the north door of the courthouse itself."

"And that was some sixty-five feet from where your car was?"

"Approximately, yes, sir."

"Now before the test with the dog did Agent Slaughter ever approach your vehicle?"

"No, sir."

"Okay. Did you see Mr. Preston's dog?"

"Yes, sir."

"Did you ever try to make it come to you or obey your command in any way?"

"No, sir."

"Did—were you present when the dog did whatever he did inside the courthouse?"

"That's—yes, sir, I did."

"Thank you. No further questions at this time."

Frank Clark stood to cross-examine the witness. "Sergeant Kindrick," he began, "you say you picked up Mr. Dillon the night of the twenty-fifth. Was that around eleven-fifteen p.m. or thereabouts?"

"Yes, sir, that would be correct."

"Prior to that time, do you have any personal knowledge that Mr. Dillon wadded up a piece of paper and threw it away, which was later retrieved?"

"No, sir, I didn't."

"You didn't know of any paper test that was done that night?"

"I know of one being done, but I wasn't involved in that part of it."

"I see. Mr. Dillon was there at the request and the direction of the sheriff's department, was he not?"

"Yes, sir, he was."

"Okay, and he was—was he a suspect in the murder case at that time you asked him or procured him to come to the courthouse?"

"Yes, sir, he was."

"And did you give him any precautionary warnings of any nature whatsoever, such as the Miranda warning, that he was, in fact, a suspect in a murder case?"

"No, sir, I didn't."

"Did you do anything that led him to believe that he may be a suspect?"

"I advised him that we wanted to talk to him about it."

"But you never gave him a copy and read him his Miranda rights, did you?"

"Not at that time, no, sir."

Frank turned to Judge Wolfman. "Your Honor, we move to strike this testimony."

"Denied," the judge said flatly.

"Sir?"

Bill had been driven to the sheriff's department in a patrol car, left in the locked car for twenty minutes, thoroughly questioned, subjected to tests designed to incriminate him—all while being considered the prime suspect in a murder investigation. But he'd never been read his rights, which was why Frank was asking the judge to strike everything Kindrick had just said as inadmissible.

"Denied," the judge said, this time more emphatically.

"Nothing further," Frank said in dismay.

Hunt offered a brief redirect. "Was he free to leave?"

"Yes, sir, he was," Kindrick answered.

"Okay. No further questions, your Honor."

Detective Christine Barringer, had applied a soft touch during Bill's initial interrogation, at times suggesting answers to her own questions and guiding him to remember when he was confused. The proverbial "good cop" in the good cop/bad cop routine, she had expertly presented herself as just wanting to be helpful. Now under oath, she was bringing her considerable skills to the witness stand.

Hunt, attempting to frame the crumpled paper test at the Satellite Beach Police Department in a positive light for the jury, asked Barringer to recall the incident. "Did anyone else handle that piece of paper in your presence?"

"No, sir."

"What did the defendant do with the piece of paper after you touched it and handled it?"

"After I was talking with him, he wadded it up and threw it away in the wastepaper basket."

"And did the defendant later leave the room or wherever you were when this was occurring?"

"Yes."

"What did you do after the defendant left the room?"

"I retrieved the wadded-up piece of paper."

"How did you do that?"

"Out of the trash can and put it into the plastic bag."

"And was that the same piece of paper you observed the defendant wad up and put in the trash can?"

"Yes, it was."

"And what did you do with the plastic bag containing the paper after that?"

"I kept it in my possession."

"And where did you keep it?"

"In the trunk of my patrol car."

"Did anyone else have contact with that paper?"

"No."

"Where did you take that paper, that wadded-up piece of paper in the plastic bag?"

"It remained in the trunk of my patrol car."

"And where did you go in your patrol car?"

"To the Melbourne Sheriff's Office."

"And what was the purpose of going there?"

"To meet with the other investigators."

"For what purpose?"

"To have a discussion about, you know, the day's events and the case that we were working on."

"Was there any test performed the evening of the twenty-fifth of August, 1981, concerning the piece of paper you obtained?"

"Yes, after, in the evening."

"And up until the time that test was performed did anyone have any contact at all with that wadded-up piece of paper?"

"No."

"Where did it stay?"

"It stayed in my possession."

Hunt, after showing the piece of paper to the detective, tried to have it entered into evidence. But Frank objected based on no foundation, and this time Judge Wolfman sustained his objection.

Hunt then continued with his line of questioning, slowly building a narrative for the events behind the so-called paper lineup. According to Barringer, the piece of paper was put into a lineup with four other similar pieces of paper on the hallway floor of the Melbourne courthouse, where John Preston's dog scented on it. Barringer was careful to point out that Detective Slaughter had never touched the piece of paper in question. Neither had she, she asserted, since she'd saved it from the trash can with a pair of forceps, or metal tweezers. A few hours after the paper test, Barringer said, she and Kindrick retrieved Bill at his parents' home and drove him in Kindrick's unmarked patrol car back to the Melbourne police office.

When Barringer also testified that Bill walked alone from the patrol car to the courthouse entrance, all Bill could do was shake his head in dismay. It was an absurd notion—that the police would leave Bill in a locked patrol car for twenty minutes and then let him walk unaccompanied into the courthouse. Had they forgotten that the patrol car had lacked handles on the inside and thus someone would have had to let him out?

When pressed by Frank during cross-examination as to how she'd come up with the idea of keeping the paper in the first place, Barringer repeatedly danced around the issue.

"Are you telling us that you weren't instructed by Mr. Preston or someone else to have him handle a piece of paper and then retrieve it?" Frank asked. "You were never given those instructions?"

"No," Barringer answered.

"And are you saying that you handed him back the paper after he first threw it in the trash and said, 'No, you have to crumple it up'? Did that happen?"

"Didn't."

Frank stroked his chin thoughtfully. "Well, who got the bright idea, then, of retrieving this with a pair of forceps or tweezers?"

"I did."

"And what was the basis of that? Did it suddenly come to you that that might be a good piece of evidence?"

"That thought occurred to me, yes."

"And for what reason would that be a good piece of evidence?"

"Any number of things."

"You already knew that Mr. Preston was in the area and wanting something from Mr. Dillon, didn't you? Isn't that the reason, honestly now, that you retrieved that crumpled-up piece of paper?"

"I can't say that, no, because of the interview I was conducting earlier that evening with him."

Frank pressed on. "Well, he never filled out this confrontation form, did he?"

"Yes, he did."

"He filled it out, and then you said, 'It's not necessary,' and he threw it in the wastebasket, didn't he?"

"That's correct."

"But he didn't crumple it up the first time, did he?"

Barringer dodged the question. "He threw it away."

"Isn't it a fact that the paper was brought back to him and told—he was told he would have to crumple it up?"

"No, sir."

"Are you saying that on the first and only time he crumpled that up, crumpled it up with his hands and then placed it in the wastebasket—is that your testimony?"

Once again, Barringer was elusive with her answer. "I told him it wasn't necessary, yes."

"So he crumpled it up and threw it away. He wasn't instructed to crumple it."

"I told him it wasn't necessary. We didn't need it at that time, and he could throw it away."

Frank, unwilling to let Barringer slither free, continued to hammer away at her. "Did you tell him to crumple it up?"

"No, I told him to throw it away. I didn't need it."

"He crumpled it voluntarily."

"Yes, sir."

"And up until that time, you had no intention of saving that particular piece as evidence, did you, before he crumpled it?"

"No."

"And it came to you at that exact moment in time. Was it sort of a blinding flash or revelation that that could be a key piece of evidence?"

"No."

"When did it come to you?"

"After I received a telephone call from Agent Fair during the middle of my—"

"I see. Did Agent Fair tell you he wanted a crumpled-up piece of paper from Mr. Dillon?"

"I don't remember."

Like Kindrick before her, Barringer admitted that Dillon had never been read his rights before the interview that resulted in the crumpled-up piece of paper or even after being picked up at his parents' house. But when Frank moved to suppress her testimony, Judge Wolfman once again denied the request.

Bill, still mystified that police personnel were so brazenly shameless on the witness stand, slowly began to understand that the whole paper test had been a carefully orchestrated trap. Preston, his services in high demand, had clearly been brought in to participate ahead of time—well before Bill had even been read his Miranda rights. Since Bill had never worn the infamous Surf-It T-shirt, if Preston's dog had been tracking *anyone* at all, it had been tracking Detective Slaughter, who had handled the T-shirt and had escorted Bill into the courthouse. It was also possible the dog had tracked Parker, the half-blind eyewitness who had indeed touched the T-shirt while retrieving it from the back of his pickup truck and who had been brought in to identify Bill from behind the smoked-glass window in the door leading to the judge's chambers before the dog had arrived.

John Preston had thick, dark, wavy hair, brushed neatly to the side, and was of average weight and height. He was clean-cut and spoke in a deep voice, which only added to his authoritative air. As he took the witness stand, a hush fell over the courtroom. Here was the man of the hour, the man who had expertly tracked the crime scene after Hurricane Dennis had washed it clean, the man who had followed Bill's scent from the bloody Surf-It T-shirt to the crumpled-up piece of paper to Bill himself.

Unlike Charles Rogers, John Preston was given ample opportunity to tout his credentials. He was an expert witness, after all. The jury sat silently as Hunt tossed one softball question after another to Preston in an effort to bolster his credentials. Preston, the owner of Preston's Kennels in Galeton, Pennsylvania, spoke at length about his background, his experience in man-trailing, and his qualifications as a national expert on the subject. Though retired from the Pennsylvania State Police, he told the court, he was a deputy sheriff with commissions in several counties and had retainer contracts with federal agencies nationwide, including the US Postal Service. He was, in short, the go-to guy when it came to tracking a scent.

"How long have you been doing nationwide man-trailing?" Hunt asked while quizzing Preston about his résumé.

"Since about 1976," Preston answered.

"How many states have you done man-trailing in?"

"You want me to name them?"

"First how many," Hunt clarified, "and then you can name some of them."

"Well," Preston said in a confident tone, "excluding Pennsylvania, Ohio, New York, New Jersey, Maryland, Virginia, North and South Carolina, Tennessee, then on out to Missouri, Kansas, Indiana, California, New Mexico, Alaska, Puerto Rico, and a few more, probably, that I haven't named."

Bill sank in his seat. The response was confusing, but the dog handler deftly made it sound like there were precious few places he hadn't worked.

Hunt eventually worked his way to Preston's experience as an expert witness in court, and once again, Preston rattled off a long list of states where he and his dog's skills had helped settle cases. Preston waxed eloquently about his close relationship with his dog, among other details associated with his work. When asked about weather factors, how long a scent could be tracked, and so forth, he answered in a way that made it clear Harass II was a highly capable tracker. Harass II, in fact, was a highly qualified dog, a dog that had earned the equivalent of a master's degree in its field, according to Preston. The dog handler then explained how he was involved in the current case before the court, how he and Harass II had worked the crime scene, scented on the Surf-It T-shirt, and so forth, all the way up to his tracking of Bill across the courthouse parking lot to the judge's chambers.

"Upon going in that door," Preston explained, "I was confronted with a small office, probably twelve feet square. The dog upon going in the door was immediately confronted with the edge of the desk, at which he turned right and went to a subject sitting, which was behind the door from me as I was coming in behind the dog. And the individual sat with his hands on his lap. The dog went over, put his head under his hands, pushed his hands up away from his body, and sat there and looked him in the eyes."

"Do you see that suspect," Hunt asked, "that person in the courtroom today?"

"Yes."

"Can you point him out for the jury, please?"

"Sitting at the defense table."

"Which one?"

"With the blue shirt, blue jacket on."

Hunt turned to the judge. "May the record reflect that he has identified the defendant." He then returned his attention to Preston. "At that point, Mr. Preston, when you went in the room, was anyone else present?"

"Yes, sir."

"Who was that?"

"Sergeant Slaughter."

"And did the dog make any effort to go to Mr. Slaughter?"

"None whatsoever."

"Did the defendant you've identified today make any gestures or anything to the dog prior to the dog going up and doing what you've just described?"

"I would not say he made any gestures toward him. I think he may have had a little concern or apprehension about what the dog was gonna do when he came up to him and moved his hands apart."

"Not knowing whether he was gonna bite him or lick him?"

"He sat very still. His eyes were quite big."

"And, Mr. Preston, assume that the, that I was the person whose scent the dog was following. If a dog came up to me and I snapped my fingers, would the dog come to me or obey my command over yours?"

"If you made an overt gesture toward the dog while he was tracking you, he may come to you, but it would not be in a friendly manner."

"Whose command would he listen to: a stranger's or yours?"

"He listens to my command to the exclusive point that if my wife tells him to do something he'll look at me before he does it."

"I may have omitted one point, Mr. Preston. What was used to scent the dog for the scenario you just described, going through the courthouse and stopping at the defendant?"

"The shirt."

"The same one?"

"Yes."

"Thank you." Hunt turned to Judge Wolfman. "No further questions at this time, your Honor."

Frank, after a short break, cross-examined Preston, but nothing could compare to Preston identifying Bill as the person Harass II had tracked. Moreover, for every hole Frank tried to poke in Preston's testimony, the dog handler got a chance during Hunt's redirect to reframe the debate in terms favorable to the prosecution. Knowing the truth, Bill didn't find Preston's charade the least bit credible, but he couldn't be sure the jury was equally skeptical. After all, it's not every man who is both scientist and magician, but John Preston would have the world believe he was, and the jury seemed thoroughly entranced.

After Preston left the stand, two more witnesses for the prosecution followed in rapid succession: John D. Wilmer and Thom Fair, who had already testified earlier that morning as well as the day before. Wilmer, a homicide agent, answered questions from Hunt regarding how the evidence had been handled. He also described how Preston and Harass II had worked the case.

Fair, meanwhile, gave his take on Preston's tracking in the parking lot and in the courthouse. When Hunt changed subjects and asked Fair about McGee's traffic stop in the early morning hours of August 17, Frank protested, pointing out that the best evidence was the police log. Fair asserted that he had checked the log, but tellingly, the log itself was never offered into evidence for proof. If McGee had indeed stopped Mark Muirhead, and if indeed there was a log of said traffic stop, the prosecution never produced the log as evidence.

As the afternoon drew to a close, Bill sensed the police log wasn't the only matter that would be left unresolved. The parade of witnesses, seemingly unending, continued with Roger Dale Chapman, a former frequent resident of the Brevard County Jail.

Chapman, after being duly sworn in as a witness for the state, took the stand. Unbeknownst to Bill at the time, prosecutor Michael Hunt was already well acquainted with Chapman, who, though himself a serial offender, had testified on behalf of the state multiple times, including several times for Michael Hunt. Well before the start of the trial, when Frank had first told Bill that Chapman had "snitched," Bill had been unable to put a face to the name. Who was this mysterious jailhouse snitch? Now here he was on the witness stand. Skinny, rangy—he had a backwoodsy appearance but only looked vaguely familiar. Had Bill actually met him in prison? Bill thought it was possible, perhaps even likely, but he could not recall any interaction between them at all.

"Do you recall the incident that you're here to testify about?" Hunt asked.

"Yes, sir," Chapman answered.

"And do you recall the date?"

"Yes, sir."

"What was that?"

"It was the twenty-seventh."

"Of what month?"

"Of August. August twenty-seventh."

"Of 1981?"

"Yes, sir."

"On that date did you, or time prior to there, meet William Michael Dillon?"

"Yes, sir."

"Do you see Mr. Dillon in the courtroom right now?"

"Yes, sir."

"Can you point him out and describe what he's wearing?"

Bill tried to control his emotions as Chapman pointed at him.

"Right there."

"And what is he wearing?"

"A light blue shirt and blue vest."

"May the record reflect he's identified the defendant," Hunt said. "Where did you have occasion to meet the defendant?"

"In the Brevard County Jail."

"And on August twenty-seventh did you have occasion to have a conversation with the defendant?"

"Yes, sir."

"And where was that?"

"It was in the jail."

"And can you relate to the court and jury what that conversation was?"

"It was about what he got arrested for."

"Did he say at that time what he was doing—not doing in jail, but what he was doing before entering jail? Where he was from?"

"He said he didn't have a job and he was just loafing around."

"Did he say anything about the case, particularly when it's supposed to have occurred or anything pertaining to what he was there for?"

"Yeah, he was charged with beating somebody to death."

"Did he say when that was to have occurred?"

"I can't recall the date."

"All right. Did he mention a date?"

"I don't think he—just said what they picked him up for."

"And was anyone else present in the cell where you were with the defendant?"

"I think there was somebody in there, but I think they was laying on the bed asleep."

"Was there anyone in the immediate vicinity with you and the defendant when this statement was made on the twenty-seventh?"

"There was a couple of people around, but they was just all—everybody was just talking."

Bill felt a sinking sensation as he listened to Chapman speak. This was pure fiction.

"Did you have a subsequent conversation with the defendant?" Hunt asked.

"Yes, sir," Chapman answered.

"When was that?"

"Twenty-eighth."

"And where were you at that time?"

"Just sitting in the bullpen."

"What is the bullpen?"

"That's where everybody eats at."

"Okay. And where were you and the defendant seated specifically in that bullpen area, as you say, at the time you had a conversation with him?"

"We was at the tables where we eat, at the second table."

"Was anyone else at the table with you?"

"Yes, sir."

"How big a table is this?"

Chapman pointed toward the table in front of Bill and Frank. "It's bigger than that table there."

"The one where Mr. Clark and the defendant are sitting?"

"Yes, sir."

"And what were you all doing during or prior to this conversation?"

"Just sitting there talking."

"And how loud was the defendant talking?"

"We wasn't talking loud."

"Were there other people present in the bullpen?"

"They was watching TV."

"And what do you recall the defendant saying at that time on August twenty-eighth?"

"He said he was at a party, him and his girlfriend, and he was drinking. And they all got drunk, and they went down to a beach. And he was walking along the beach, and he asked a guy, he said, 'Do you have any money I can bum from you?' And the guy said, 'Get out of my face.' And when the guy passed him, he said, he asked him, he said, 'Could I have a cigarette, could I bum a cigarette off of you?' The guy turned around, gave him a cigarette. That's when he said he punched him, sucker-punched him."

"How?"

"Sucker-punched him."

"What else, if anything, did he say about that?"

"He said then they got on the ground, they rolled, he got up into an upright position, and he grabbed the guy and started punching him in the face."

"Did he say what happened after that?"

"He said he got up and left."

"Did he say where he went?"

"No, sir."

"Did he say anything specifically about how he kept this man on the ground?"

"Yeah. He motioned with his hand—with his left hand, that is—held him either on his throat or his chest, and punched him."

"Which hand?"

"His left hand. He held him."

"Which hand did he indicate to you he punched him with?"

"His right hand."

"Did he say anything pertaining to what he did after he punched this man in the face after he was on the ground?"

"He said he got up and left, and he had blood on his T-shirt and on his fist, and he cleaned up."

"Did he mention what his purpose was in doing this?"

"Money, I reckon."

Frank intervened. "Objection to that, and move to strike."

"Sustained," Judge Wolfman ruled.

Disbelief. Anger. Powerlessness. Bill fought off an onslaught of emotions as he listened to Chapman spin one lie after another. Everything he'd just said was utter fabrication. Even the underlying premise of Chapman's story—that Bill could tell another inmate something so damning without anyone else overhearing it—was a lie. Anything Bill could have told Chapman would have been overheard by multiple witnesses, for the bullpen had been far too crowded to allow for private conversations. If there was any truth to Chapman's testimony, Bill knew, other inmates would be able to corroborate it. In any case, not even Chapman's timeline withstood scrutiny. Bill had been moved from the bullpen to a single cell on the morning of August 27 and had been unable to speak with any other prisoners. But

Chapman was claiming he had spoken with Bill on August 27 and then again the next day.

"Did he mention anything that led you to that conclusion or opinion?" Hunt asked.

"Well, first off, he said, you know, that was the first thing he asked him for was money, if he could borrow some money, bum some money off him."

"Move to strike that as not responsive to the question," Frank interjected.

"Your Honor," Hunt replied, "I believe it was."

"The response to the question," Judge Wolfman said, "but I want to advise the jury we are striking the answer which said, 'I reckon.' That's an opinion. Can't give that."

Hunt continued with his line of questioning. "Did the defendant say whether or not he was ever struck?"

"He said he was hit but it didn't faze him none," Chapman answered.

"Did the defendant say where this altercation took place?"

"He said on the beach."

"And did he at any point relate that as the reason for his being in jail at that time?"

Chapman appeared confused by the question. "Excuse me now?"

"Did he ever relate the incident you just described to his purpose in being in jail?"

"Yes, sir, he did."

"Objection," Frank said, once again intervening, "that's leading, your Honor."

"Sustained," Judge Wolfman said.

Hunt continued. "What did he say about the incident that—first of all, what did he say he was in jail for?"

"For battery and murder, or robbery and murder."

"And on the twenty-eighth did he say anything about that pertaining to the events you just described?"

"Yeah, that's when he said that he was walking on the beach and he was drunk."

"Do you recall where he said he went after this event?"

"No, sir."

"Did the defendant say how many times he did anything to the man?"

"He said he just punched him, you know, more than once—seven, eight times, ten times."

"Did he indicate the age of this person?"

"It was an older fellow."

"Thank you," Hunt said. "No further questions at this time."

It was Frank's turn to cross-examine Chapman. "You can't recall the date that this incident was supposed to have happened, is that correct?"

"No, sir," Chapman answered.

"Okay. Now you voluntarily called the sheriff's department or someone connected with the sheriff's department after the conversation, didn't you?"

"Excuse me now?"

"You voluntarily, on your own, contacted somebody from the sheriff's department to tell them about this, did you not?"

"Yes, sir."

"Okay. And isn't it a fact that the first thing you said to them is, quote, 'I've got good news for you,' end quote."

"Yes, sir."

"You said that to them. Did Mr. Dillon also tell you during the course of this alleged conversation what he was charged with but he was innocent and they couldn't prove it because he was somewhere else that night, that he had an alibi?"

"Objection, your Honor," Hunt said. "A self-serving statement, and the witness can't be cross-examined on self-serving statements. I have some cases, your Honor. May we approach the bench?"

Judge Wolfman nodded. "Yes, approach the bench."

The attorneys argued case law out of the hearing of the jury, and Judge Wolfman, after taking a few moments to review the relevant cases, ruled that since Frank had already asked about part of the conversation Chapman had allegedly had with Bill, he was allowed to ask about any other part of the conversation, as well.

Frank, free to continue, resumed his line of questioning. "Mr. Chapman, I'll ask you the last question again. You said you had two conversations with Mr. Dillon, right?"

"Yes, sir."

"Two separate days?"

"Yes, sir."

"During one of those conversations, did he tell you that he was wrongfully accused or words to that effect and that he was somewhere else and he had witnesses to prove it?"

"Yes, sir."

"He told you that, okay. You said that he said it happened on the beach. Did he say what beach?"

"Melbourne or Satellite Beach."

"He said Melbourne or Satellite Beach. You know where Melbourne Beach is, don't you?"

"Yes, sir."

"And do you know where Canova Beach is?"

"No, sir."

"You don't know where Canova Beach is."

"No, sir. I've heard of it."

"Do you know where the Pelican Bar is—a rock and roll bar?"

"Yes, sir."

"Well, that's Canova Beach."

"Yes, sir."

"Well, that's Canova Beach. Now how far is Canova Beach from Melbourne Beach? Five miles?"

"Could be five, three miles."

"Okay. Did he describe to you the size and weight of the man he allegedly punched?"

"No, sir."

"Did he say where and when he went and cleaned up?"

"No, sir."

"And you weren't curious?"

"Yes, sir. I was curious. He didn't say nothing."

"Why didn't you ask him?"

"He didn't say nothing."

"He never said he took any money from the victim, did he?"

"No, sir."

"Ever. Did you say that you couldn't remember when you were taped and sworn by a sheriff's deputy, Agent Thom Fair and Dan Wilmer? Did you say you couldn't remember about some part of the conversation, the first conversation?"

Chapman appeared puzzled by the question. "Now what do you mean by that?"

"Well, did you during part of the interview with Thom Fair, Agent Thom Fair, and Agent Dan Wilmer in answer to one of their questions, did you say, 'I can't remember,' during the first—"

"Your Honor, I object," Hunt said, stepping in for his client. "This is improper impeachment and—"

"Sustained," Judge Wolfman said.

Clark tried another angle. "He did not say there was any weapon used other than his fist, is that correct?"

"Yes, sir."

"Did he—you see any scars or marks on his fists at the time he was talking to you?"

"Not no scars."

"Okay, now you were in there at that time on a charge of rape, weren't you?"

Hunt, not surprisingly, protested. "Objection, your Honor. It's irrelevant. Move to strike."

"We have a right to develop this," Frank shot back.

Once again, the attorneys approached the bench, and once again, Frank was allowed to continue.

"Now," he said, "you were in the Brevard County Jail on a charge of rape at that time, were you not?"

"Yes, sir."

Frank went on to present the facts surrounding Roger Dale Chapman's bond reduction hearing, which had taken place only *after* he had related to Thom Fair the story of Bill's alleged confession.

"Well, at least, Mr. Chapman, we can establish that it was after your statement to Mr. Fair and your agreement to testify—it was only after that that the rape charge was dropped and you were let out of jail. Isn't it a fact?"

"They didn't have no evidence on me."

"Answer the question. Isn't it a fact that the rape charges were dropped and you were released after you made this statement to Mr. Fair and agreed to testify—*after*?"

"Yes, sir."

"All right. Nothing further."

Frank had finally homed in on the inspiration for Chapman's bogus testimony. It was clear to Bill that Chapman, a classic jailhouse snitch, was out to save his own skin. In exchange for his fake testimony, the state had promised him his freedom. It had obviously been an easy choice to throw Bill, a complete stranger, under the bus.

For the first time since the trial had begun, Bill began to sense that none of this—the arrest, Donna's ever-changing story, the police's willful misrepresentation of the facts, the involvement of Preston and his German shepherd—was a mistake. He was convinced that he was being framed. It was hard to accept that it was happening at all, much less understand *why* it was happening. He felt helpless. All he could do was watch as his fate was decided by people like Chapman, a slippery character willing to doom another man to preserve his own freedom.

Hunt took a moment to gather his thoughts and then offered a redirect. "Mr. Chapman, you made a statement—are you familiar with why the case was dropped, the rape case?"

"Yes, sir."

"Why, if you know?"

"Cause the victim had a venereal disease."

"What kind of disease?"

"Objection, your Honor," Frank protested. "Goes beyond the scope, and also it is not the best evidence. Self-serving."

"Overruled," Judge Wolfman said.

"You mean venereal disease?" Hunt asked, continuing.

"Gonorrhea," Chapman said.

"Okay, and subsequent to this happening, had you ever had gonorrhea?"

"No, sir."

"Do you have it now?"

"No, sir."

"And was this gonorrhea had by the defendant at the time of the rape allegedly?"

"Yes, sir."

"No further questions."

Frank stood up to recross-examine Chapman. "How do you know you don't have gonorrhea? Have you been tested in the last six months?"

"Yes, sir."

"When?"

"When I was in Brevard County Jail."

"And they tested you for gonorrhea?"

"Yes, sir."

"Okay. Didn't test you for Syphilis, though, did they?"

"Well, my lawyer had them check me."

Incredibly, no proof was offered into evidence to bolster Chapman's claim. No lab results. No medical records. As had been the case with the missing police log, an assertion was allowed to stand as proof—and Frank didn't speak up in protest.

Bill felt a feverish rage he had never experienced before as he stared at the jailhouse snitch. Chapman had effectively put Bill at the scene of the crime, by his own admission. And Bill, with his blood boiling, could do nothing about it. He wanted to leap from his chair and scream that he was being framed. But his fate, at least for the moment, belonged in other people's hands.

CHAPTER 18

A SMALL BUT WELCOME VICTORY

As Thursday's session dragged into the late afternoon, Bill fought to control his emotions. He was exhausted. Drugged. But he was also beside himself with anger—a shaken and capped bottle of carbonated fury with no way to vent.

After Chapman left the witness stand, Alfred Albright, a special agent for the Florida Department of Law Enforcement (FDLE), testified next. Albright had overseen the lie detector test and told the jury that Bill had admitted to lying to him about his whereabouts after Dvorak's murder. First Bill had claimed the stormy weather had trapped him and Donna inside for a couple of days, but later he'd corrected himself and revealed that they'd gone out for food and whatnot at some point. Albright interpreted that correction as a lie, and seemed to suggest that it pointed toward the possibility that Bill had told other untruths while talking to the police. The prosecution was clearly trying to show Bill as untrustworthy, as someone who had something to hide.

At 5:23 p.m., the court took a short break so Frank could read a transcript he'd never seen while preparing for the case. The trial reconvened at 5:35 p.m., but the convoluted debate that followed between the attorneys and Judge Wolfman occurred out of the jury's hearing. The prosecution, in a move to shield the jury from the fact that their own evidence exonerated Bill, wanted the lab results from the investigation barred from admission. Despite the fact that Brevard County officials had collected, processed, and possessed the evidence before handing it over to the state lab, the FDLE laboratory, the prosecution was now claiming that the chain of custody was somehow tainted. They were, in essence, arguing that they themselves had mishandled the evidence and couldn't be sure it was in fact the right evidence. Frank countered that it had never left their control, that nothing in the way the evidence had been documented proved their grounds, and that it wasn't *his* responsibility to prove that *their* evidence had been properly gathered.

The physical evidence included several items taken from the crime scene: a pair of shorts, a pair of jeans, a club, and a tree branch. It also included the bloody Surf-It T-shirt, as well as blood samples taken from Bill, James Dvorak, John Parker, and Donna. After a prolonged discussion, the prosecution finally, reluctantly, stipulated that the chain of custody was intact. It was a small but welcome victory for the defense. However, Bill and his attorney were now in the dubious position of having to call the crime lab personnel as witnesses for the defense, when customarily they would have been brought in as witnesses for the prosecution. Bill hoped Frank would be able to get the lab techs to clearly state the results of the tests. Confusing scientific explanations might baffle a jury whose members likely knew nothing about forensic laboratory testing. But those lab experts, employed by the state, would in a sense be hostile witnesses, not impartial, objective ones. It was unlikely they would be eager to testify against their employer.

With the matter settled, the prosecution trotted out its final two witnesses, both of whom were making repeat performances: Steven Kindrick and Christine Barringer. Hunt began by questioning Kindrick about an interview with Bill the sergeant had conducted on August 26, just before Bill's arrest. During the interview, Kindrick testified, Bill had been read his rights for the first time, but no attorney had ever been present. Bill had told Kindrick that he had been at the Bocci brothers' apartment on the night of the murder, an admission that seemed to bolster the prosecution's narrative. But the longer Kindrick testified, the clearer it became that Bill hadn't been entirely sure of himself during the interview. Kindrick even admitted to Frank during cross-examination that Bill had been upset and nervous, although the sergeant wouldn't go so far as to say that Bill had been confused.

Barringer, meanwhile, testified that Bill had first claimed he'd been with the Plumlees at the Ocean Star Motel in Cocoa Beach on August 14 and 15. Only later, in subsequent interviews, had he appeared less sure about where he'd stayed, which seemed to suggest that he'd been telling the truth initially.

During cross-examination, Frank tried to frame Bill's conflicting testimony in a more positive way. "I think from your testimony I can conclude two things: that he was confused and he was cooperative. Are both of those statements correct: confused and cooperative?"

"Basically, yes," Barringer answered.

"They are not mutually exclusive or anything," Frank added. "You can be confused and cooperative at the same time. Do you accept that?"

"Yes, sir."

"All right. Did he tell you during that interview that he had been talking to one Daryl Novak, who had told him that he, Daryl, knew who the killer was?"

Hunt intervened. "Objection, your Honor. Hearsay."

"Overruled," Judge Wolfman said.

Frank picked up where he'd left off. "Do you recall the question?"

"I'm sorry," Barringer said. "Could you repeat the question?"

"During the interview," Frank said, "did Mr. Dillon inform you that one Daryl Novak informed him that he had information as to who the killer was?"

Barringer carefully hedged her answer. "Mr. Dillon mentioned Daryl Novak's name, yes."

"Yes," Frank said, "in connection with his somewhat supposed knowledge of who the killer was. Did you follow up that lead?"

"I personally didn't, no."

"Did you put Mr. Novak under oath and question him?"

"No, sir. I did—"

"Well, who interviewed him? Do you know?"

"I'm not sure."

"Well, do you know if he was even interviewed?"

"I'm not sure."

Frank turned from Barringer to Judge Wolfman. "Nothing further."

During redirect, Hunt asked Barringer whether Bill had claimed that Novak was the killer or whether the police had ever considered Novak a suspect in the case. The answer to both questions was no, although Barringer danced around the second one slightly by answering, "Not to my knowledge."

As Barringer left the stand, there was no uproar in the courtroom. Far from being unsettled by the detective's admission that the sheriff's department had neglected to follow up with Daryl Novak, the only person who had expressed knowledge of the crime, the jury, the audience—everyone in attendance—appeared appallingly sedate. How could the police name Bill as the killer when they hadn't even chased down every lead? It seemed nothing—not even a possible lead on the real killer—was going to derail the case against Bill. The state had its man.

More pressing, it appeared, was the matter of whether to press on or call it a night. By a show of hands, the jury decided to stay on late in order to get as much done as possible and thereby shorten the next day's workload. The jury then left for dinner at 6:25 p.m. Bill, too, was escorted from the courtroom to the holding pen for his evening meal. By law, he was entitled to three square meals a day, although at the moment all he could think about was what the state had thus far denied him: a thorough investigation and a fair trial.

By the time Bill returned from dinner, the prosecution had officially rested its case. What few witnesses remained would belong to the defense. Bill also learned that Frank, unaware that his client had left the courtroom along with the jury, had made a motion for judgment of acquittal, contending that the state had presented a lengthy list of confusing and conflicting witness testimony. But Judge Wolfman had denied it without much consideration.

Frank, no doubt running on fumes by now, called his first witness since examining Charles and Roseanna Rogers roughly ten hours earlier.

A forensic serologist at the state crime lab in Sanford, Florida, Keith Paul was a tall, slender man with a markedly timid disposition. It was clear from the start that he was uncomfortable on the stand and would have probably preferred getting a root canal to testifying against the state.

Frank showed the serologist the bloodstained Surf-It T-shirt. "And did you examine the stains on that shirt which appear to be kind of reddish brown or more brown than red, actually? Did you examine those stains?"

"Yes, sir, I did," Paul answered.

"And were—did you determine them to be blood?"

"Yes, sir, I did."

"And were you able to compare the blood samples that were on that shirt with the blood samples which came from a known source, that is to say, William Michael Dillon?"

"I grouped the blood on both items. Yes, sir."

"All right. And did you find any similarity at all between the blood samples on that shirt and the blood of William Michael Dillon?"

"I believe there were a couple of enzyme types that were the same."

"All right."

"But there were other factors that were not the same," Paul added.

"So," Frank said, "your conclusion was that the blood on that shirt, whatever it was, was not the blood of William Michael Dillon?"

"Based on my findings," Paul answered, "it was probably not."

"All right. Now what other things did you compare blood that was—was there blood given to you that was on leaves or flora or fauna or twigs?"

"I believe there was, yes."

"All right. And did any of those articles of blood match the blood of William Michael Dillon?"

"I would have to check my notes," Paul said evasively. "I believe on the leaves I may have only gone as far as determining that it was human blood and was not able to get a blood grouping."

"I see. All right. And were there any items of blood that were brought to you that came from a vehicle or any other thing other than the clothing and other than the body of the deceased and Mr. Dillon? Were those your total sources of blood samples for testing?"

"I believe I got a pair of jeans—"

"Uh, huh."

"—from Mr. Dillon, a pair of cutoff shorts, that shirt, some vegetation, and perhaps a few other clothing items, sticks, and things."

"You say these things came from Mr. Dillon," Frank said. "Were you advised of that?"

Paul hesitated. "I'd have to check my notes and see."

Rather than press the point, Frank tried to home in on the question at hand. "Well," he said, "was there any matching of Mr. Dillon's blood on—let's make it a broad, general question. On everything that you found, no matter what you examined, could you tie in Mr. Dillon's blood type and grouping with the scene or the crime itself?"

"No, sir."

Karen Thompson stepped up to cross-examine the witness. Bill knew the prosecution needed the jury to believe the Surf-It T-shirt was connected to the crime scene. If they couldn't get the lab personnel to testify that his blood was on the shirt, they surely needed to convince the jury that the victim's blood was on the garment. Paul had ambiguously testified that the blood on the T-shirt was "probably" not Bill's; however, he *had* said that some of the enzymes were the same as Bill's. Frank had failed to ask what the significance of that finding was, in light of the blood typing not matching Bill's.

"Mr. Paul," Thompson began, "you run a variety of tests on those items when they come into the lab, don't you?"

"Yes, I do."

"Okay. The blood on the T-shirt—is that consistent with the blood identified to you as Donna Parrish's blood?"

"No, it is not."

"Okay, the blood on the inside pocket of those blue cutoffs that we talked about, of those you compared, whose blood is that consistent with?"

"I believe it was a type O on those cutoffs," Paul answered. "I would have to check my notes to make sure about the enzyme—"

"Okay. Would you check the enzymes?"

Paul took a moment to review his notes. "Okay. The blood on the cutoffs was consistent with Dvorak's blood."

"All right," Thompson said. "Now, as to the T-shirt, what types of tests did you run on that?"

Keith Paul explained that his normal procedure was to test for an ABO typing, after determining whether the blood was human or animal. Next, he ran six different enzyme tests.

"Okay," Thompson said. "Now would being in a plastic bag for ten or twelve hours in ninety-degree heat cause any problems with typing the blood?"

"Heat," Paul said. "All the work that we do—we're working with biological specimens, and heat can destroy some of the proteins. When I'm talking about an ABO blood-grouping system, I do what's called a forward and reverse grouping, and the heat could destroy a reverse grouping."

"Okay. In fact, doesn't the Sanford Crime Lab specifically request that evidence with blood on it not be packaged in plastic bags in order to avoid decomposition?"

"Yes, that's in our evidence manual."

"Okay. Couldn't degradation or decomposition cause the test results to give an indeterminate or inconclusive reading?"

"They could be indeterminate, yes."

"Okay. Now normally when you do a blood typing, you said you run both a forward and a reverse grouping. Is that true?"

"That's true."

"Okay. And if a particular blood sample with type—did you test to what the blood type was on his shirt?"

"I don't know if I did or not."

"Let's just use this as an example," Thompson suggested. "If a particular blood sample were type A—"

"Yes."

"—what results would you expect from the forward grouping?"

"I would expect to find A."

"Okay. And what results would you expect to find from the reverse grouping?"

"Anti-B," Paul answered. "Would you like me to explain that?"

"I don't think it's necessary."

"Okay."

"On the samples from this shirt, then," Thompson continued, "when you were trying to determine the blood type, did you run a forward grouping?"

"Yes, I did."

"And did you get the results that you expected from that?"

"Well, I got type A."

"And did you run a reverse grouping?"

"Yes, I did."

"And did you get the results that you'd expect from type A blood from that?"

"I got no results. There was no reverse grouping."

"Okay. Then can you conclusively state that blood on that shirt is type A?"

"Not type A blood," Paul answered.

Thompson shifted gears slightly. "Now, did you run enzyme tests, as well?"

"Yes, I did."

"Isn't it true that all of the enzymes that you were able to identify in the blood on this T-shirt matched the enzymes that you identified in one of the blood samples?"

"Yes. The enzymes that did work on the shirt were consistent with one of the blood samples," Paul answered.

"Which one?"

"Dvorak's."

"Thank you," Thompson said and returned to the prosecution's table.

Bill glanced warily at the jury. The prosecution's whole case was tied to the bloody Surf-It T-shirt, which was the one piece of physical evidence that supposedly could tie him to the crime. The lab results hadn't positively linked the shirt to either Bill or the victim, but had all the talk about enzymes confused the jury? Since the blood group typings were exclusionary regarding Bill and at best inconclusive regarding James Dvorak, confusing the jury with complex talk about enzymes was a strategy that might work in the prosecution's favor. What the jury had heard was that there were enzymes in the blood evidence that were consistent with the enzymes in both Dvorak's and Bill's blood. No other explanation regarding the meaning of that finding was offered. No information regarding the frequency of those enzymes within the general population was discussed.

Bill's frustrations continued to mount. His blood type was O+, and James Dvorak's had been type O. Bill had told Frank emphatically that he had type O+ blood and that it would be absolutely critical to emphasize the A typing lab result. But Frank, like most lay people, had a limited understanding of the topic and hadn't thought to dig deeper into the fact that the shirt had produced a forward A typing. Frank seemed content that Keith Paul had been unable to tie Bill's blood type to the evidence. On the other hand, Thompson, perhaps sensing Frank had missed an opportunity, had been smart enough to muddy the water with all of her questions about enzymes, regardless of their relevance. The jury would be able to review the laboratory test results during deliberations, but those results would be lumped in among a burdensome mountain of other exhibits, all of which would need to be sorted through.

Steven Drexler, a crime laboratory analyst from the FDLE, took the stand next. As a microanalyst and specialist in hair analysis, he had been given samples—including head and pubic hair from Bill—to examine. Drexler testified that one of the hairs belonging to the evidence was Caucasian in origin and "had the same microscopic characteristics as the head hair represented as from Parker."

"In the debris from the T-shirt," Frank said, "you found no hairs whatsoever, either pubic or head, that you could say were similar to Mr. Dillon's. Is that correct?"

"That is correct," Drexler answered.

He then explained that he had also examined debris from one pair of cutoff jeans, vacuum sweepings from the pickup truck, fingernail scrapings from both the right and left hands of the victim, four loose hairs collected from the body of the victim, a wooden club, a white shirt, and all of the standards that had been submitted for basis of comparison.

"And on any of those things, including the club," Frank said, "did you find any examples of hair, either pubic or head hair, that were in harmony with that of William Michael Dillon, the defendant?"

"No, sir, I did not."

If Paul's testimony had offered some ambiguity, Drexler's seemed clear-cut. Frank, though, managed to help the prosecution when he asked whether it was typical to find the hair of a suspect on the clothing of the victim. Drexler, perhaps relieved that he'd been given a chance to score one for the prosecution, answered that it was not typical and only happened occasionally. Drexler left the stand.

Sonny Brannon, the last person to testify for the evening, was called as a rebuttal witness. He had already offered proffered testimony out of earshot of the jury, but now he was Bill's only hope to counter the bald-faced lies of the celebrated dog handler. Although he was more soft-spoken than Preston, the man whose testimony he was on the stand to refute, he struck Bill as more factual in his delivery—and more believable as a result.

Frank began his examination by asking Brannon about his qualifications and experience, pausing briefly to request that Preston sit away from the prosecution team so he couldn't coach them. Frank was then free to proceed with his questions, most of which exposed the shaky ground upon which Preston's tracking had been based. On cross-examination, in a virtual replay of his questioning during the proffered testimony, Hunt tried to make Brannon look ignorant in his field. But Brannon held his own.

Finally, during his redirect, Frank tried to hammer home his contention that Preston's so-called tracking of Bill was faulty on several levels. Hunt repeatedly objected to Frank's questions based on form, and Judge Wolfman repeatedly sustained those objections.

But eventually Frank managed to ask a question in the proper form. "Mr. Brannon," he began, "assuming for the purpose of this question that certain facts are as follows: that a T-shirt, a bloody T-shirt was located in a trash bin approximately a mile to a mile and a half from Canova Beach, and assuming further that that T-shirt was recovered and handled by one or more people after it was recovered, and then assuming eight and a half days later the tracking dog and its handler were taken to the area about three hundred and thirty-five feet north of where the crime was committed, and that at that time the dog was scented with the T-shirt which was found in a trash bin handled by others and told—the handler was told to start tracking in a southerly direction. Would that be normal procedure, in your opinion?"

"Not in my opinion," Brannon answered. "No, sir."

"All right, sir. And what would be wrong with those set of facts that would violate whatever you would do?"

"Well, the first thing would be having other people's human scent on the article. The second thing is they are telling me to try to find an area that that scent belongs to. You could hunt all day and not find the same scent because the scent that you're trying to pick up would be the person that handled it last. He could be right next to you. He could be walking along with you. The dog is gonna smell him, so naturally he's gonna have a harder time picking up the scent on the ground somewhere else because the man is next to you."

The implication was clear: for all anyone knew, Harass II had tracked Sergeant Slaughter, or even John Parker, not Bill Dillon.

Court adjourned that night at 9:30. After a long and trying day, Bill was escorted back through the time tunnel to the holding pen. More than a dozen people had testified over a twelve-hour stretch, including several who had taken the stand twice. Bill, too, had given proffered testimony. It was difficult to gauge whose testimony would stick with the jury the most. Chapman's? Preston's? Brannon's? The lab experts'? Frank had committed a handful of critical errors, but he'd also asked some tough, penetrating questions, poking holes in the prosecution's contentions in the process. The bloody Surf-It T-shirt, it seemed to Bill, was the lynchpin of the prosecution's case. But tonight, two lab experts had stated that nothing on the shirt—no blood, no hair—could be traced to Bill. Would that be enough to create reasonable doubt?

Bill and his attorney had one more day to make their case.

CHAPTER 19
ASKED AND ANSWERED

Bill awoke the next morning, Friday, December 4, with his feet hanging over the edge of his bunk. The landscape of his life had changed, and for three months, his home had been the same 6 ft. x 8 ft. isolation cell. During that time he'd slept without sheets and with only a blanket to cover him. His tiny bed, as puny as it was, took up half his cell, but at six feet long, it couldn't contain his lanky frame. His feet almost touched the metal toilet at the end of his bunk. Nearby and bolted into the wall was a matching sink.

Bill lived his life without windows. Food came through a slot in the steel door—or was slid beneath the bars. Each meal was served on a paper plate with a plastic fork and spoon. No knives. To occupy his mind, Bill had begun to read voraciously since the prison trustee who ran the jail library had turned him on to Westerns. But today, for the fifth straight day, Bill would leave his cell and spend most of his waking hours in court, where his future was being decided by a brusque, impatient judge and a somewhat geriatric jury.

Friday's session convened at 9:35 a.m. Bill's stepfather, Joe Dillon Sr., was the first to take the stand. He told the jury that he and his wife had been out of town on the weekend of the murder, but he was certain Bill couldn't grow a mustache and that Bill's limited wardrobe did not include a yellow Surf-It T-shirt.

While cross-examining Mr. Dillon, Michael Hunt tried to portray Bill as a vagrant. Bill's dad was infuriated. "My son is no bum!" he would later say to the press.

The prosecuting attorney then asserted that Bill's scent had been found on the yellow Surf-It T-shirt. Frank was quick to object, pointing out that such a contention was very much open to debate, as Sonny Brannon had already testified.

"Sustained," Judge Wolfman ruled.

Moments later, and just twenty-five minutes into the session, the judge had to order a short morning recess while the court waited on Donna Parrish to return to the stand. This time she would be testifying for the defense—sort of. No one seemed quite sure the role she would be playing. Hunt, however, was adamant that Frank not be allowed to impeach his own witness. As a result, when Donna appeared on the stand at 10:15 a.m., Hunt and Judge Wolfman kept Frank on a short leash. Hunt then used his cross-examination to ask Donna about the moment when she confessed to Thom Fair that she'd seen Bill standing over the dead body of James Dvorak, once again giving her an opportunity to portray herself as Bill's loyal girlfriend, torn between standing by her man and telling the truth.

"I was trying to—I was afraid to tell them," Donna said. "And then finally Thom Fair yelled at me and I started crying, and I said, 'I have a confession,' and they gave me my rights and they told me—"

"Thom Fair advised you of your rights," Hunt said.

"He advised me of my rights, and I told him everything."

"Right in my office."

"Right in your office."

"Downstairs. We're on the fifth floor."

"Right."

"And did you then tell me that you had not been able to sleep because of what you were holding?"

"Yes," Donna said ruefully. "I couldn't turn off the light 'cause every time I closed my eyes I'd see, you know, certain things."

"You would see the body."

"Yeah, and it was scaring me 'cause I was afraid, you know. I was just scared. I still can't sleep with the light off."

Once again, Donna had put on an impressive performance. Bill no longer knew how to react, but the jury appeared moved by her hysteria.

Debbie Dillon, Bill's sister, testified next. She told the jury she'd been housesitting at their parents' house on Sunday, August 16, having traveled there from her home in Orlando. She had invited Bill over for pork chops that day, but when Donna had shown up in a red convertible, he'd left with her. Debbie was sure of her dates and was able to corroborate that Bill had been in Cocoa Beach on the night of the murder.

Another short recess followed as the prosecution protested Frank's next witness: Joanne Stinchcomb. Hunt was certain Frank wanted Joanne on the witness stand to impeach Donna's testimony, and he was right. But Judge Wolfman allowed the young woman to appear. Joanne told the jury that she'd been friends with Donna for thirteen years and that Donna had told her she had been offered $5,000 and a new identity to testify against Bill.

Hunt, during his cross-examination, asked Joanne whether Donna had bought a new car or flown to Hawaii. When Joanne pointed out that Donna had bought several new outfits, Hunt countered that Donna had worn the same outfit at court during each of her appearances. He then went on the offensive and, in an attempt to make Joanne's testimony appear self-serving, asked her whether Bill had promised to be with *her* as soon as he got out of jail.

"No, sir," Joanne answered timidly.

Judge Wolfman asked the witness to speak up.

"No, sir," she said, this time more forcefully.

"That's not correct," Hunt said.

Bill didn't know where Hunt was coming from with that question, but it surely appeared as if Hunt was trying to imply that Bill had been manipulating the young woman.

Joanne didn't respond.

"But if he does get out of this," Hunt continued, "you have plans to get together with him, don't you?"

"No, sir."

Finally, after sitting mute all week while his name was dragged through the mud by countless witnesses, William Michael Dillon went before the jury, ready to tell his side of the story. For three months, he'd been in jail without bond, and during that time he'd found his faith in the legal system shaken. It had begun with the law enforcement officials and prosecutors, who should have been focused on chasing down every lead and finding the killer but instead seemed determined to frame him. Donna Parrish had spun wild tales. Roger Dale Chapman had lied to save his skin. Even

Bill's pot-smoking, drug-dealing friends, who were afraid of the cops, had testified that on the day of the murder he had been seen wearing the yellow Surf-It T-shirt despite the fact that he had never owned, worn, or even touched such a shirt.

Bill desperately found himself in the crosshairs of two men, aptly named Hunt and Slaughter—not to mention a dog named Harrass. Their names alone evoked a low-budget picture show in the theater of the absurd. To top it off, the man at the heart of the investigation—the lust-struck Detective Charles Slaughter—had conveniently never even taken the stand since his appearance would have tainted the prosecutorial process beyond recognition. As it was, the trial had felt at times like a farce and at other times like a surreal nightmare, a vast conspiracy too outlandish to believe.

But as frustrating as it had been to listen to all the conflicting testimony and misdirection, Bill still felt confident that once the jury heard his version of events, the truth would win out. He still believed in his heart that a jury of reasonable people couldn't convict him. There was no evidence to put him at the scene of the crime or link him to the murder. Hyper, brash, strong-willed—Bill took the stand ready to tell the truth.

Frank Clark began his direct examination of Bill by focusing on the young man's appearance. Bill, after telling the jury that he was six feet, four inches tall, testified that he couldn't grow a mustache. He had tried in the past, he said, but he couldn't grow much more than peach fuzz above his lip. Frank then showed Bill the infamous yellow Surf-It T-shirt and asked him whether he'd ever worn one even remotely similar. Bill said no, although he did confirm owning a yellow Pelican T-shirt.

"Okay," Frank said, "now I must ask you some questions of a rather personal nature, Mr. Dillon, but they're important. Are you—is your penis circumcised?"

"Yes, it is," Bill answered.

"Was that from birth?"

"Yes, sir."

"Now there's been some testimony from a John Douglas Parker that the man he picked up on the early hours of August 17, 1981, had a penis which he described as narrow and pointed. Is your penis in any sense of the word narrow and pointed at the end?"

"No," Bill answered, "it's exactly the opposite."

After asking a few questions about jailhouse snitch Roger Dale Chapman, whose testimony Bill flatly refuted, Frank returned to Bill's appearance on the night of the murder. "How would you compare the length and styling of your hair now, with the way it was on the night of August 16, 1981?"

"I'd say it was just a little bit longer than it is now," Bill said.

Bill then explained why he hadn't been sure about his whereabouts on the night of the murder when first questioned by the police. He hadn't been able to remember Charles and Roseanna's last name, he said, but he *had* been able to recall the Plumlees.

"Now," Frank said, "there's been some testimony that you jokingly said, 'I killed a guy down in the beach,' or whatever. Did you ever make that statement, jokingly or otherwise, to anyone?"

"No, sir," Bill answered soberly. "I killed nobody. I said nothing to that effect."

Bill recounted the events of August 16: his sister's plan to feed him pork chops for dinner, Donna's arrival in the Plumlees' red Mustang, the unbecoming drinking and bickering between the Plumlees at the motel in Cocoa Beach, Bill's retreat to the beach, and dinner with Charles and Roseanna Rogers. After giving a play-by-play of the evening's activities, he described going to bed around two o'clock in the morning and testified that he never left the Rogerses' apartment until the next morning.

"Now there's been testimony from a John Douglas Parker concerning a male he picked up, had oral sex with, and then dropped off at the A Frame," Frank said, "the man being described as being in cutoff pants six inches above the knee and shirtless and bloody. You saw that man testify. Have you ever seen him before in your life?"

"No, sir, I haven't."

"Were you at any time in the evening hours of the sixteenth of August 1981 in Canova Beach?"

"No, sir, I wasn't."

"How many miles is Canova Beach from Cocoa Beach?"

"I'd say about fifteen."

"Did you have any transportation of your own on Sunday, August 16, 1981?"

"No, sir, I didn't."

Framed

Eventually Bill's confused and sometimes conflicting interviews with the police came up. Frank, while discussing Bill's statement that he'd spent the night at the Bocci brothers' apartment on August 16, asked Bill whether he had been mistaken.

"Yes, I was," Bill answered.

"What was your emotional attitude when you were being questioned by authorities once you realized you were suspected of first-degree murder?"

"Once I was suspected of it or knew—they told me I was suspected of it—I was very nervous, and I knew I was not guilty of it. But I was still very scared at the time of being interrogated back and forth by police officers."

When Frank came to the subject of Donna's testimony, he asked Bill whether he had made any admissions or incriminating statements to her. "Was anything she said about your involvement in this murder true?"

"No, sir, it's not."

"Did you on Sunday evening, August, 16, 1981, buy any drinks at the Pelican?"

"No, sir, I was not at the Pelican."

"Okay. Were you ever at the Pelican that day or that evening?"

"No, sir, I wasn't."

"Did you ever visit the death scene in Canova Beach South, three hundred and thirty-five feet south of the Eau Gallie Causeway? Did you ever visit the death scene on that early morning hours of the seventeenth of August or at any other time?"

"No, sir."

"So, therefore, if you didn't visit it, you never saw Donna there?"

"No."

"Was there a night, Mr. Dillon, within a span of two or three days either side of the night of the sixteenth that you did, in fact, stay at Matt Bocci's apartment?"

"Yes, sir. Monday night."

"Was that Monday night, August 17, 1981?"

"Yes, sir, it was."

"Was Donna Parrish—did Donna Parrish spend the night with you?"

"Yes, sir, she did."

"And where did you sleep that night?"

"On the floor."

Bill explained that he had gone to sleep at about one o'clock in the morning and had woken up around seven or seven thirty the next morning. He described the weather as rainy and told the jury that people came back to the apartment that day because they couldn't work in the rain.

"On the day of the seventeenth," Frank said, "the full daytime hours of the seventeenth of August, did you have any injuries or wounds of any nature whatsoever on either of your hands or your body?"

"No, sir, I was checked."

"Okay, did you have a rash on your hands?"

"I have a skin problem. Dermatitis." Bill added that he had chapped hands, and because he was a mechanic, he had scars on his knuckles that didn't tan.

Frank finally homed in on the question on everyone's mind. "Did you have anything to do with the beating or the death of James Dvorak, the deceased in this case?"

"No, sir, I did not."

"Did you have anything to do with any attempt to rob him or anyone else the night of or the early morning hours of August 17, 1981?"

"No, sir."

Frank turned to Judge Wolfman. "No further questions."

Karen Thompson came out firing for the prosecution. "Mr. Dillon," she began, "are you telling us that you have the only penis in the world that doesn't have a point at the end?"

"Am I telling you that?" Bill asked.

"Yes, you said that your penis was not narrowed and pointed at the end," Thompson clarified. "It's just the opposite."

"Yes, ma'am, it is."

"Not pointed at the end like everybody else's."

"Oh, is everybody else's pointed?"

"I'm not gonna testify as to *my* experience," a cocky Thompson shot back.

Thompson then hammered Bill on the details around the case—the timeline, how his testimony conflicted with Donna's, and his lack of money.

"What's the last time—you said you were a mechanic, Mr. Dillon. When is the last time you worked as a mechanic?"

"In the service," Bill answered.

"And that was back in '79."

"Yes, ma'am."

"When did you last work at all?"

"July."

"And this was August," Thompson said, "so you didn't have any money in August."

"Well, I did some odd jobs in August," Bill said, "some carpentry, some trim, somewhat. It's off and on. It's sort of weekend work. It's when they need you."

"Do you recall a statement to Brian Kersey that you frequently went down to Canova Beach and rolled fags to get money?" Thompson asked, attempting to profile Bill as a gay basher.

"No, ma'am, I don't."

"Never said that to Brian Kersey."

"No, ma'am."

Thompson then went after Bill's conflicting statements to the police. After attempting to knock him off balance, she tried to dispense of the possibility that the police had failed to follow up on an important lead.

"And you did tell them that J.D. Novak knew something about someone who had done it, didn't you?"

"He did tell me that," Bill said.

"Suppose he was talking about you, Mr. Dillon?"

"No, ma'am, he was not," Bill said adamantly. "Why would he be talking about me, telling me about it?"

Unfazed, Thompson continued to pepper Bill with questions about his testimony, the timeline, and the diary Donna said she had kept to document her relationship with Bill.

"Donna was keeping a daily log of it from the second of August," Bill said of her diary.

"And if Donna says she wrote it all on the same day and she changed it, the dates, at your request, she's just lying?" Thompson asked.

Bill didn't blink. "Donna Parrish is a liar, yes."

"And I guess Matt, Tracey, Glen Zeller, Joe Bocci, Maggie, Genevieve, Mark Muirhead, John Preston, and Deputy McGee are all lying, too?"

"Ma'am, I wouldn't say that they were lying. They just seen me sometime between the week or so, but they do have their dates mixed up, yes, ma'am."

Thompson asserted that Deputy McGee had called into the dispatcher on the seventeenth after following Bill and the Pelican bouncer, Mark Muirhead, to Donna's house.

"Did he?" Bill asked.

"Didn't you hear him so testify?"

"I heard something mentioned about it," Bill said, "but I didn't hear him testify to that."

"And you heard Thom Fair testify that he had verified it had been called into dispatch on that date?"

"Thom Fair testified that he called it in?"

Frank intervened and moved to strike Thompson's question because it had previously been argued that the call-in log itself was the best evidence, and the log had not been produced by the prosecution nor entered into evidence.

Thompson withdrew the question, but only after the damage had been done. Despite the fact that the prosecution had produced no evidence of Deputy McGee's traffic stop, the jury was likely accepting it as a fact and associating it with the early morning hours of August 17.

The prosecuting attorney returned to Bill's conflicting interviews with the police, this time focusing on Bill's interview with Al Albright. She then moved on to his on-again, off-again relationship with Donna. Each question was asked with one clear intention in mind: to make Bill's testimony look self-serving, inconsistent, and ultimately unbelievable. When she returned to the subject of Donna's diary, she asked about the poem Donna had written about Bill.

"The poem consisted of 'Why, Billy, Why?'" Bill explained. "But it didn't consist of any type of death or anything, unless it's been changed or anything like that. It's sort of a love breakup that she suffered."

Thompson, though, was far from through. She focused next on the crossed-out dates in Donna's diary, forcing Bill to read aloud from it. It was a moment laden with theatrics—and one Judge Wolfman allowed in order to refresh Bill's memory, never mind the fact that the spurious document had never been entered into evidence, the prosecution had never established that Bill had even seen the diary after August 16, and there were multiple entries written over each other—who knows when?

Bill's naivety was quickly disappearing, replaced by the troubling realization that those in authority could easily tamper with the truth. Nothing was off limits.

Once finished with the topic of Donna's diary, Thompson grilled Bill on various comments attributed to him that painted him as abusive and homophobic, on his ability to grow facial hair, on his knowledge of karate and a pair of nunchucks he owned, on his alleged conversation with Roger Dale Chapman, on the yellow Surf-It T-shirt, on his encounter with Harass II at the courthouse, and so on. She even mentioned a man by the name of Larry Bunting, someone who had supposedly loaned Bill the yellow Surf-It T-shirt. Bill had never heard of him before, and tellingly, he never appeared in court.

Though the line of questioning continually changed, Thompson's main theme—that Bill was asserting everyone else was lying—stayed the same. "Are you telling us that Donna, Joe, and Matt and Tracey and all those other people are in a conspiracy to convict you of a crime that you didn't commit?" she asked in a condescending tone.

"Not the other people," Bill answered. "Donna Parrish? Yes, ma'am."

"And all those other people who have testified as to where they were that night and how they know it was that night and Deputy McGee, who phoned it in or called it in to the dispatcher—all those people are wrong and you're right."

"No, not all those people. Donna Parrish is lying, yes, ma'am. Very much so."

"Can you look each juror in the eye and tell them you didn't do it?"

"Yes, ma'am, I sure can," Bill said defiantly. "Every one of them."

"And all of these people who came in here and said that they had seen you in the area on Monday, the seventeenth of August, in the early morning hours, are coming into this courtroom and perjuring themselves in order to put you in jail."

Finally even Judge Wolfman grew tired of the endless grilling. "Ms. Thompson," he said, "the question's been asked and answered several times. Do not ask it again."

During his redirect, Frank returned to the topic of John Preston and his tracking of Bill at the courthouse. "Did Mr. Slaughter—there was a phone in the room where you and Mr. Slaughter were, isn't that right?"

"Yes, sir, there was."

"And did Mr. Slaughter before the dog came in use it more than once or twice, or how many times did he use it?"

"He used—when we first got in there, he was on the phone. I don't know particularly about that conversation. Then he got off. Then I told him that I had to go to the bathroom, and he called up and he said, 'We are going to the bathroom.'"

"Do you know if in that first call he gave the location to anyone of the room you were in?"

"I don't—"

Thompson interrupted to object, but Judge Wolfman overruled her.

"You don't recall whether he gave directions to someone or information," Frank said, continuing on.

"No, sir, I don't."

"What size T-shirt do you wear, Mr. Dillon?"

"I wear a large and sometimes an extra-large."

"All right. Have you ever worn a medium since you've grown up?"

"No, sir, they don't fit quite well."

"Handing you exhibit fourteen, what does this sticker on the back of the shirt say the size is? What letter designation is that?"

"It's a medium."

"All right."

Karen Thompson asked to approach the bench. "The state would like Mr. Dillon to try on the T-shirt," she said out of the hearing of the jury.

"It's not necessary," Frank said. "I don't think he has to be forced in to any exhibits."

"You asked him if he ever tried it on," Judge Wolfman said. "He's asking him what the size is, and that's it."

"Okay," Thompson said, relenting.

It was a minor, though fortuitous break for the defense. Had Bill tried on the shirt, it might have looked impossibly small on him—small enough to convince the jury he'd never worn it. Then again, had he tried to squeeze into it, he would have left his DNA on a key piece of evidence in the process. In 1981, DNA profiling—or for that matter, any use of DNA in forensics or the courtroom—was unheard of. But times would soon change.

CHAPTER 20
CLOSING ARGUMENTS

After Frank Clark finished his redirect, Bill was excused from the witness stand. Judge Wolfman then instructed the jury to break for lunch.

Bill had acquitted himself well, withstanding several minutes of tough, unrelenting questions from Karen Thompson. But he left the stand feeling hollowed out, as though whatever faith he'd had left in the judicial system had been drained from him. Much to his dismay, Thompson had been allowed to toss out an unsubstantiated assertion—that someone named Larry Bunting had loaned him the yellow Surf-It T-shirt—without a protest from Frank Clark or admonishment from the bench. Did such a character even exist, or had Thompson made him up? Her introduction of the man so late in the process was consistent with the prosecution's overall approach, which had been to throw as much mud as possible against the wall to see what would stick.

In a different courtroom, before a different judge, and against a different defense attorney, such a strategy might have failed. But the week-long trial to determine Bill's guilt or innocence had descended at times into farce. Bunting's name had been invoked without anyone batting an eye. McGee and the police had been allowed to assert a traffic stop without providing a log of said stop. Tracey Herman had claimed to have flown home on the night of August 16 but had never been required to provide proof of her flight. The burden of proof throughout the trial had been on the defense, not the prosecution, turning the basic premise of the American legal system—that one is innocent until proven guilty—on its head.

Thompson had openly mocked Bill's defense that multiple people were either lying or remembering dates incorrectly, suggesting he was conjuring up some kind of wild conspiracy theory. But from where Bill was sitting, it didn't seem so far-fetched. John Preston had pushed his debatable dog-tracking techniques as gospel. Roger Dale Chapman had fabricated a conversation that had never taken place. Donna Parrish had told an epic tale as dramatic as it was erratic. And the Bocci brothers had lined up behind her, perhaps responding to police intimidation, given their drug-dealing habits. Overall, the campaign to put Bill in prison had cut numerous corners and felt to Bill like an underhanded orchestration, and the man behind it all—Detective Charles Slaughter—was nowhere to be seen, his reputation and career having been sacrificed in a moment of lust with the star witness.

More hurtful than being accused of a crime he hadn't committed was having his reputation dragged through the mud. The prosecution hadn't just called Bill a killer and a liar. They had falsely profiled him as some kind of homophobe who routinely robbed gay people. But Bill had never had any negative feelings toward homosexuals. In fact, the subject of homosexuality was not important to him and had rarely, if ever, crossed his mind. The prosecution didn't have a shred of evidence to substantiate the smear. But then again, Bill had never been implicated in any muggings or other crimes on the beach either. It was enough to tar him with innuendo—innuendo that perfectly fit the narrative the prosecution had created.

The attorneys' closing statements were almost anticlimactic, coming as they did after so much combustible testimony. Karen Thompson began her final argument by explaining the contours of the case. The state was trying to prove three things, she said: that James Dvorak was dead, that Bill's attempt to rob him had caused his death, and that Bill had killed him. The first issue no one contested. As for the second two, Bill's innocence depended on whether or not his alibi was believable. But the state had multiple witnesses who contradicted it.

"In order to believe the defendant's alibi defense," Thompson told the jury, "you must believe that all of these people are either mistaken or lying and that the physical evidence is wrong. Mr. and Mrs. Rogers, the swinging motel managers, seem like basically honest people. They don't seem to be deliberately lying or trying to tell you a falsehood, but they're obviously confused in their dates. Both days were weekend days. Both of them had routine existences. Mr. Rogers said he went to work just about every day, and on weekends sometimes he went in in the mornings and then came home and had the afternoon free. And I submit to you that there is just too much conflicting testimony for their memories to be correct.

"I don't challenge their veracity or their belief that they're telling you the truth. They seemed like nice people. And I don't believe that they would—strike that. And they did not seem the sort of person who would come in here and lie to you. But there are just too many other people, including the deputy who called in the report of seeing Mr. Dillon with Mark Muirhead on the date of the seventeenth, and it's been verified by Mr. Fair.

"Donna's telling the truth. We know she is because all of the evidence backs her up."

Frank Clark began his closing argument in personal fashion. "Members of the jury," he said, "I would like to let you know that I have always thought ever since I became of age that the highest calling to which a lawyer could aspire would be to defend a person for his life on a charge of first-degree murder, and I'm honored and proud to be a member of that profession. Somewhere out there in this county or elsewhere walks a murderer. He is not in this courtroom and has never been, to my knowledge.

"This evidence that was put on by the state is neither the quantity of the evidence or the quality of the evidence that would justify a conviction of William Michael Dillon beyond a reasonable doubt on a charge of jaywalking, let alone first-degree murder."

Frank went on to explain the crux of Bill's defense. Bill's alibi, he insisted, was being ignored. As Charles and Roseanna Rogers had testified, Bill had not even been at Canova Beach on the night of the murder. Moreover, there was one piece of evidence that could settle the matter.

"With all the resources of the state of Florida and all the money that they have to develop evidence," Frank said, "they brought people from out of state, and this case has cost them a lot of money, there's no doubt about that. They could, by the simple expedient of subpoenaing Eastern Airlines flight records, of which they keep for many, many months and years, and brought a witness in here to say, 'Yes, here is the ticket that we sold Tracey Herman. It shows that she left Houston at six-thirty p.m., she arrived in Atlanta at eight, and there was an hour layover and she took flight 571 out of Atlanta and came into Melbourne.' Where is that evidence before you? It doesn't exist. It was available."

Frank went on to point out the many weaknesses of the prosecution's case: Donna's ever-changing testimony and admission that she had lied under oath, the lack of physical evidence tying Bill to the murder, the marked difference between Bill's appearance and the sketch of the hitchhiker John Parker had picked up on the night of the murder, and so forth.

Since Bill had elected to take the stand in his own defense, the prosecution got the last word. Thompson, in response to Frank's closing argument, ratcheted up her attacks on Charles and Roseanna Rogers. They were no longer a nice, though "swinging," couple. Now Roseanna was a submissive wife testifying in obeisance to her domineering husband's wishes. Bit by bit, Thompson addressed every argument Frank made, including his contention that the state should have provided records of Tracey Herman's flight in order to prove her arrival date.

"Now, Mr. Clark told you that the state of Florida could have subpoenaed the Eastern Airline records," she said. "Mr. Clark didn't tell you whether or not they erase their computer records after one week."

"I think that's an unfair comment on something that's not in evidence, your Honor," Frank said, interrupting Thompson.

"I think it was brought up by you, and she can comment on it," Judge Wolfman replied matter-of-factly.

It was a clever ploy by Thompson, who, after having successfully implied that the enormous airline didn't maintain any passenger manifests beyond one week, moved on to another subject without actually stating whether or not the records had been available—or whether the state had even looked into the matter. Not a single juror did so much as blink. From the beginning of the trial to its closing, Thompson and Hunt had managed to assert facts without proving them. And Frank Clark, to his everlasting discredit, had let them get away with it.

At 4:20 p.m., after Thompson finished, Judge Wolfman excused the alternate jury members, now no longer needed, and the rest of the jury began a long, drawn-out discussion on whether or not to break for dinner.

Bill, anchored to his place at the defense table by a sandbag tied to his leg, could only watch in amazement. His future, it seemed, was less important than the jury members' dinner plans.

After nearly an hour of debate, the jury made a decision: they would retire to the deliberation room to sort through the reams of evidence. There were mountains of material—easily a week's worth. How they would tackle it on empty stomachs was anyone's guess.

Despite the jury's petty behavior, a wave of relief went through Bill as the bailiff escorted him through the time tunnel back to his cell. It was almost over. He knew the prosecution hadn't proven anything, but he couldn't be sure how the jury would react to all the conflicting testimony, much of it based on deception and outright lies. Frank had assured him that the jury would either acquit immediately, based on the implausibility of the evidence, or be out for days poring over all the exhibits, statements, and testimony in an attempt to make heads or tails of the timeline and other particulars.

The bailiff locked the heavy steel door behind him, and Bill, alone once again in his cell, sank to his bunk, exhausted but not yet defeated. He clung to his faith that God would never let him be convicted. If anyone knew he was innocent, it was God. His God was a fair God.

He prepared himself for a long wait.

CHAPTER 21
A UNANIMOUS DECISION

Bill was shocked when the bailiff returned to his cell just two and a half hours later. The long walk back to the courtroom, where he felt contorted by anxiety, became a surreal march. His temples throbbed. His shallow breaths came rapidly, one after another.

Back in the courtroom, he took a seat next to Frank Clark at the defense table.

"A swift decision means it's good news," Frank assured him.

Bill nodded anxiously. Whatever the verdict was, he'd be hearing it without the support of his parents, who had attended every day of the trial but the last. His mother had been forced to stay home due to severe headaches, and his stepfather had gone home to check on her. The stress of the ordeal, it seemed, had been more than they could bear. Mr. Dillon, convinced the evidence against his stepson was flimsy and inconsistent, had confidently prepared a statement to read to the press in which he would thank the jury for acquitting his son.

At 6:55 p.m., Judge Wolfman called the court to order.

"Let the record reflect the jury has returned," the judge said. "State and defendant are both present." He turned to the jury members. "Has the jury reached a verdict?"

"Yes," Patrick Markey, the jury foreman, said, "we have."

"Will you please hand your verdict to the clerk?" Judge Wolfman said. "Will the defendant please stand?"

Bill stood to hear his fate, his shackles digging into his ankles. No one made eye contact with him. Not the bailiff, not the jury, and not the judge. He was frozen with fear.

The clerk read from the piece of paper handed to her. "We the jury find as follows as to the defendant in this case: the defendant is guilty of first-degree murder, so say we all, Patrick J. Markey, foreman."

Debbie Dillon, seated in the back of the courtroom, cried out in disbelief.

"Does counsel wish the jury polled?" the judge asked.

"Yes, sir," Frank said, clearly in shock.

"Will you please poll the jury?"

The clerk complied, and as each jury member repeated the verdict, Bill's sister, now hysterical in her grief, had to be escorted from the courtroom.

The clerk, after naming each jury member, asked, "Is that your verdict?"

And each jury member, in turn, gave the same answer: "Yes."

Bill's mind raced as Judge Wolfman spoke.

"Having been tried and found guilty of first-degree felony murder, the court will not impose sentence at this time but will defer imposition of sentence pending a completion of a pre-sentence investigation report, which the court at this time does hereby order. The defendant is remanded to the custody of the sheriff to await sentencing."

In that instant, Frank's attention lurched toward the prosecution table, and a moment later he whispered to Bill, "They just told me they never thought they would get a conviction. They threw a bunch of theories at the jury, hoping they'd pick one."

Even in the fog of disbelief, Bill had heard it too. It was a remarkable admission. One that implied the prosecution didn't believe in their own case. Jolted by the words, Bill wanted to explode, to vent his anger at the monumental injustice that had just been visited upon him. His world had just stopped. He couldn't move. Couldn't talk. Couldn't think—but those words would remain seared into his memory for decades to come.

The bailiff had to drag him by the arm, and as he was hauled from the courtroom, it seemed to Bill that the reading of the verdict had wrought a palpable change. He could feel the disdain of those in the courtroom as they stared at him with fear and suspicion. He was a vicious murderer now. It was official. And his life—the life he'd hardly begun to live, the life he would have done anything to reclaim—was being taken from him.

CHAPTER 22
DENIED

Bill was sitting alone in his cell a week later, awaiting sentencing, when a guard opened the steel door.

"Phone call," the guard said.

Bill followed him to the officers' desk, where he was handed a phone.

"You have an emergency phone call," the officer behind the desk said. "It's your sister on the phone."

Bill's mind raced. Was it his mother? She'd suffered terribly during the trial. Was she in the hospital?

"Hello?" he said worriedly.

"Billy, it's me."

It took him a moment to recognize the voice on the other end of the line, but when he did, he was furious. It was Donna.

"Haven't you done enough?" he said through gritted teeth.

"I'm going to recant," she replied in a shaky voice. "Everything's going to be okay. We'll be back together before too long."

Bill shook his head in disgust. After everything she had put him through, after all the drama and theatrics, she was still toying with his life.

"Yeah, sure," he said and hung up.

Was she drunk? High? All he knew was that she couldn't be trusted. The likelihood that she would make good on her promise was next to nil. If Donna had proven anything since Bill's arrest, it was that she was about as predictable as the weather during hurricane season.

Bill was shocked, therefore, when Frank called him on Thursday, December 17, just thirteen days after the jury had found him guilty, to tell him that Donna had recanted.

"I met her last night in my office," Frank explained. "She's full of regrets, Bill. But she's afraid of the state. She said they pressured her from the beginning. She admitted never seeing you near the body at the beach. She's recanted her testimony—all of it. And I got it on tape. I'm going to file a motion for a retrial."

Bill had gone so long without good news that he resisted the urge to smile, but his heart was pounding in his ears.

"They badgered her from the beginning," Frank continued. "They questioned her many times, put her in front of a grand jury. Every time they took her in for interrogation, her statements got more incriminating."

Frank relayed more from his conversation with Donna. The police, she said, had warned her she would "rot in jail" and be imprisoned for twenty-five years as an accessory to murder if she didn't cooperate. As for the body on the beach, it was a figment of her imagination—Donna claimed it was all an hallucination she'd suffered while taking drugs shortly after Bill's arrest. Many of the elements unique to the crime scene, such as the position of Dvorak's body or his wounds, she was aware of only because she'd overheard investigators talking and as a result had learned bits and pieces of the case.

Bill sighed deeply. Throughout the trial, he'd watched helplessly as prosecutors, officials, and various witnesses had chipped away at his faith in the legal system. But now, for the first time in weeks, he was beginning once again to believe in the possibility of a just outcome. Donna had come to grips with the damage her lies had caused. Now it would be up to Judge Wolfman to overturn Bill's conviction. The mere fact that Donna had been threatened with jail time would surely make the judge reconsider the way the entire case had been handled.

Bill spent Christmas alone in his cell. On that holiest of days, he felt abandoned. Abandoned by everything that was right and good in the world. Bill sat on the edge of his bunk and stared at the dusty spiderwebs on the ceiling. Not one for formal prayer, he began to speak out loud, "Why God, why? What have I ever done to deserve *this*?" "Why are they allowed to do this to me?" He sat in silence but no answers came. No sounds other than steel doors slamming and the clomp, clomp, clomp of the night shift patrolling the concrete hallway.

On the following Tuesday, December 29, he returned to the county courthouse in Titusville for a hearing to determine whether or not he would be given a new trial. Michael Hunt appeared for the prosecution once again. Judge Wolfman presided. The hearing, which took less than a day, was a near replay of the trial—minus the jury.

Frank Clark began by playing the eighteen-minute-long tape of Donna recanting her testimony. During the recording, Donna spoke about being threatened with jail time by both Detective Slaughter and Thom Fair if she didn't testify for the prosecution. She was told, in effect, that she had no choice but to back the prosecution's version of events. In truth, she told Frank, she had never seen the body. She had spent the night of the murder with Bill at the Rogerses' apartment. Likewise, she and Bill had been at the Bocci brothers' apartment the night *after* the murder, just as Bill had claimed on the stand. She had tried to convince the police of both of those facts, but the police, along with the prosecution, had browbeaten her until she had relented.

On the tape, Donna acknowledged the fact that she might go to jail for perjury. She then tried to defend her actions by explaining that, along with the police and the prosecution, her family had pushed her to testify against Bill. At the time, it had seemed easier to simply give in to all the pressure than actually tell the truth.

After playing the tape, Frank invited Donna to the stand, where she reiterated everything she'd just said. Just like she had at the trial, she then began spinning tall tales. She claimed Joanne Stinchcomb had told her that Bill had asked about Donna's ring size. She also said she had spoken with Bill for over an hour on Christmas Day, and he had been audibly upset, vacillating between tears and anger. Both claims were pure fabrication. The latter, especially, would have sounded ludicrous to anyone who knew the climate at the county jail, where no prisoner was allowed to monopolize the phone, especially on the biggest holiday of the year.

In fact, Bill hadn't spoken to Donna on the phone since she had tricked him and the guards into thinking his sister was calling. And that conversation, during which she'd promised to recant, had been brief. But it was clear Donna was worried about being charged with perjury. If she could convince the judge that she was acting out of love and that she was overwrought with emotion, there was a chance she might not be held accountable.

Michael Hunt cross-examined Donna and then called Thom Fair to the stand to further discredit Donna's testimony. Far from giving any credence to Donna's latest claims, Fair stuck with the police's story that Donna had voluntarily given statements implicating Bill in the crime and had led the police to the scene of the crime. Hunt, working in tandem with Fair, framed his questions in order to make it appear like Donna had known details that only someone who had seen the body could know, never mind the fact that Donna had already claimed she'd learned those details directly from the police.

During cross-examination, Frank asked Fair whether Slaughter had shown Donna photos of the crime scene. Fair could answer only that he had no idea. Slaughter, once again, was not called to testify. Frank also fought back against the notion, put forth by Hunt, that Donna had only recanted the part of her testimony about seeing Bill standing over a dead body. She had, in fact, recanted *all* of her testimony, Frank countered, and had done so on tape and just now in the courtroom.

Hunt was reduced to arguing case law. After citing numerous cases from the past, he argued that Donna's recantation did not mean a new trial was warranted.

Frank closed by trying to put Donna's latest testimony into perspective. "I don't think there is any doubt," he said, "if you took Donna Parrish's testimony of today and presented it to a jury and left the state with the testimony of John Douglas Parker, who put the mustache on the man he was with, and the cold trail dog tracking—that's all they've got. Because the Boccis and the young lady—they don't help put him at the murder scene; they put him five miles away. They don't put him anywhere near Canova Beach. None of them do. Their testimony merely is in conflict with the testimony of Charles and Rosanna Rogers. And another thing: suppose Donna Parrish goes to a new trial and testifies, 'Yes, we spent Sunday night at the home or the apartment of Charles and Rosanna Rogers.' Then I don't think it is not only probable—I don't think there is any doubt as to what the jury's verdict that would be brought in. I think this is a complete turnaround of the most material witness I have ever seen in a criminal case in thirty years. I have never seen a person whose testimony was condemning and more damning to William Michael Dillon than that of Donna Parrish. It is recanted now. The state can do nothing about it now, and I think the interest of justice requires that he is entitled to a new trial."

"The court will review the cases that have been cited by the state," Judge Wolfman said blandly. "As stated by the Supreme Court, recantation does not automatically grant a new trial. All of the circumstances must be considered, and the court wishes to review those cases which have been cited and the review of the recantation set forth today and the testimony of the witness at the trial, and I'll give the ruling after doing so."

As Bill was led back to his cell, he felt confident he would get a new trial. Donna had been the only person to put him at the scene of the crime. Without her testimony, the state didn't have a case and couldn't possibly continue with its charade. Judge Wolfman would have to cede there was reasonable doubt since Donna had just thrown suspicion on her entire testimony.

Just a few days after the first of the year, Bill got the paperwork from the request for a retrial. **DENIED** was stamped in bold letters across the top page. Bill sank to his bunk. Judge Wolfman, despite Donna's recantation and after nearly a week of reviewing the case, still felt there had been sufficient evidence to connect Bill to the murder of James Dvorak. It was a galling, mystifying decision, but Bill, trapped in his tiny cell, could do nothing to fight it.

Frank never called. Nor did he come to the county jail to check on Bill. Two and a half months crawled by, with each day more depressing than the last, before Bill, defeated and frightened, saw Frank at his sentencing at the Brevard County courthouse in Titusville on Friday, March 12, 1982.

Once again Judge Stanley Wolfman, a specter in his black robe, sat atop the square podium at the front of the courtroom.

Frank looked older than Bill remembered—a spent lawyer with his cards on the table and no ace up his sleeve. Diane Baccus Horsley, an assistant state attorney, sat at the prosecution's table.

"You're here for sentencing in regard to the guilty verdict in your case," Judge Wolfman said, addressing Bill and his attorney. "What legal cause do you have why the court should not impose sentence at this time?"

Frank bowed his head. "None, your Honor."

"Any matters in mitigation that you wish to present?"

"No, your Honor," Frank answered. "Simply I wish to state to the court that this is the first time—I know that the court has no discretion whatsoever based on the verdict. This is the first time in history that I can recall that I was unable to make a plea for the sentencing. I believe he's innocent. Nothing more."

The judge turned to Bill. "Mr. Dillon, I've known Mr. Clark a long time, and I think he presented a very fine case for you, and, perhaps, on an appeal you might be back before a court for another trial. But this court has an obligation of sentencing you at this time. The court does adjudicate you guilty of the offense for which the jury found you guilty, sentence you to life imprisonment with a minimum maximum time required by law. The court does advise you that you have the right to appeal the judgment of the court. If you wish to do so, it must be done within thirty days of this date. You have the right to be represented by counsel, and in the event that you cannot afford counsel of your own choice, then the court will appoint an attorney for you."

With that, the judge nodded to the two attorneys. "Thank you very much."

"Thank you, your Honor," Frank said, wiping a tear from his eye.

Bill watched numbly as Frank Clark fled the courtroom sobbing audibly. It was the last time he would ever see him.

PART II

CHAPTER 23
WHAT NIGHTMARES ARE MADE OF

Bill had been locked up for seven months, and during that time the days had dragged on inexorably, each one separating him further from his freedom, from his life as it had been before. But if time had marched slowly since his incarceration in the county jail, everything changed with his sentencing in March of 1982. Within an hour of his arrival at Florida State Prison,[3] the harshest prison in the state, he was brutally beaten, stabbed, and gang raped. And as he cried in vain for help, the absolute indifference from the guards and other prisoners told him everything he needed to know about his new home: he was on his own. If his thoughts had been on justice and freedom before, on his wrongful conviction and unfair trial, now he could think only of survival. As a captive of the State of Florida, he had a number—082629—and a cell. Beyond that, he mattered not.

After his attackers disappeared, Bill, battered and bleeding, began tearing his cell apart, piece by piece. The porcelain sink hit the floor first, followed by the toilet. Seven months' worth of anger and frustration, combined with the adrenaline rushing through his veins, filled him with superhuman strength, and he used that strength to destroy everything within reach. He could hear his grunts—guttural and animal-like—echo down the cement corridor as he attempted to rip the metal bed from the bolts

---

[3] Florida State Prison (FSP), also known as "Starke" prison by the inmates, housed the only death chamber in the state. "Old Sparky," the electric chair, was used from 1924 to 1999. The wooden chair was built by prisoners at FSP. After several botched executions, lethal injection became the standard method of execution.

fastening it to the wall. Other prisoners howled along with him, their voices merging with his.

"Pop it!" a prison guard roared outside his cell.

A second later, the steel door swung open noisily, and through it burst several guards in face masks. Bill turned in time to see a large, clear electric shock shield speeding toward him. Before he could respond, he was being mercilessly restrained by several guards. Overflowing with rabid energy a second earlier, now he could only collapse in exhaustion and defeat.

"Who attacked you?" one of the guards asked.

Bill, unable to hide his injuries, nevertheless knew he would be a dead man if he talked. He refused to answer.

He was therefore physically extracted from his cell and dragged to solitary confinement, otherwise known as "the Hole," where he was brusquely tossed onto the cement floor and charged with destroying state property.

The double door slammed shut.

This would be his home for the next thirty days: a cramped, broiling cell with no bed, only a coarse gray blanket. Bill, spent and dazed, stared in confusion at his new surroundings. There was no chair, no furniture, no sink—just a hole in the floor for a toilet. For the next month, he would have no human contact, aside from his twice-weekly showers, for which he would be escorted to and from the showers by armed guard. Meals would come through a slit in the double door.

Having just earned his first DR, or disciplinary report, Bill sank into an uneasy sleep, with only the shrieks of mentally deranged inmates to keep him company.

After his stint in solitary confinement, Bill was returned to the general population. The next morning, he was jolted awake at five thirty when his heavy, electronically operated cell door popped open in unison with the rest on the block. Moments later, screams from the young and vulnerable began to echo through the corridor.

Bill leapt to his feet and hurried to his door, but he was too late. Once again he was overpowered by a group of fellow prisoners, and once again he fought back in vain. As the second youngest inmate in the prison, he would have to learn to sleep with one eye open. For now all he could do was try to fight off the rapists who routinely terrorized the pod. He knew by now that no one would come to his aid. His only hope was to survive with minimal injuries. This dehumanizing experience would, like the popping of the doors and the tasteless breakfast still to come, become part of his bleak daily routine.

Cells had to be clean by six o'clock each morning, but the predators in the prison used the tiny window of time between wake-up and breakfast to target weak and inexperienced prisoners. Soon everyone was lining up to be searched before entering the chow hall. Each cell block took turns eating breakfast, and when his group's turn came, Bill fought off the pain to grimly follow the others into the chow hall. This morning's nourishment: a scoop of watery grits, plus a biscuit.

Still wincing from the attack, Bill felt his stomach turn as he stared at the unappetizing meal.

"Eat it," a grizzled inmate sitting across from him said. "You'll need your strength."

As sick as he felt, Bill did as he was advised.

Later, back in his cell, he vowed to be vigilant, to lock his door each morning when it was popped. But no amount of sleep deprivation could compensate for the hostile environment that had become his new home. He was a "lifer," a prisoner doomed to live out the rest of his natural life in one of America's most notorious and dangerous prisons. He would have to remain stoic, to show no signs of fear or weakness. He would have to fit in with the others and with the prison culture, to make alliances, to do whatever it took to survive. The fact that he was innocent, that he didn't belong here, no longer mattered. He would whine to no one. Broadcasting to others that he had been framed for a crime he hadn't committed would only target him for further violence.

Bill began to adapt to his daily existence. He grew accustomed to fear, torture, and violence. He hardened himself to hunger, surviving on paltry rations of mystery meat, tasteless powdered eggs, white rice, and the seldom served piece of chicken. And he learned to cope with the endless hours of boredom—maddening and unbearable boredom.

As a lifer in the 1980s, Bill was not allowed to get an education or take classes. The State of Florida, unlike other states, was unwilling to invest a single dime in the education, much less the rehabilitation, of its prisoners with life sentences. The most it would do was warehouse people like Bill, whose chance of release was remote at best. But Bill understood his only hope of survival lay in bettering himself—or at the very least *busying* himself. Thus he began reading whatever he could get his hands on.

He also tried to get assigned a job. Many lifers, he was learning, didn't want to work. They didn't want to be a slave to the system. Indeed, most jobs in prison didn't pay anything. Those lucky enough to get a paying job earned a paltry fifteen cents an hour, which was deposited directly into a prisoner's account. They were then free to spend up to twenty-five dollars a week at the canteen, where prices were exorbitant and only prison-issued coupons were accepted. Many prisoners believed someone somewhere was making an enormous profit off the captive customer base. Nevertheless, Bill knew the alternatives were bleak at best. Without a job, he would have to depend on others to fund his account, which at the moment was empty. But if he could find work, he could save up for some peanut butter or tuna at the canteen.[4] Better still, he wouldn't be stuck in his cell all day with nothing to do. As a young man with boundless energy, he knew he had to do *something*.

Although not in need of any more incentive to go to work, Bill got exactly that when his skin broke out in a severe rash in reaction to the prison-issued soap. Lye-based and caustic, the soap was part of the basic supplies—all of them of the lowest quality—issued twice a month to the prisoners. Bill had been applying the soap liberally and regularly, despite the dangers associated with using the showers. Many of his fellow inmates refused to bathe for weeks at a time for fear of what might happen to them in the showers, where guards, often just as fearful, offered no protection. But as much as he feared the possibility of being raped or even killed while taking a shower, Bill was also well aware of the possibility of getting a staph infection or, worse, necrotizing fasciitis, the deadly flesh-eating bacteria. The prison was a lethal breeding ground for all kinds of viruses and bacteria.

Covered head to toe in a painful rash, Bill was assigned a job in the notoriously dangerous kitchen, where he thought he might earn enough money to buy better soap, among other luxury items. But he was never sent there. The guards, aware that he would likely be mercilessly attacked in the kitchen, diverted him to the laundry. Perhaps they had grown tired of watching—and listening to—the repeated assaults against him. In any case, Bill was put into AC, or administrative custody, which was mandatory confinement meant to protect a select prisoner from his fellow inmates.

---

4   Peanut butter was sold in squeezers, not jars, since jars could be broken and fashioned into weapons. Likewise, tuna was sold in foil packets, not cans.

He'd had a chance to go into PC, protective custody, upon entering but had passed. Now he wasn't being given a choice.

On his first day on the job, Bill was led down a hallway and past two gates to the discharge clothing room, which was stocked with brand-new clothes and shoes.

Guthrie, a civilian officer, unlocked the room for Bill. "You're not allowed to go here by yourself," Guthrie explained. "And only I can let you in."

In other words, Bill could only go to work if Guthrie was working.

Once Bill was situated, Guthrie turned and left.

Part of Bill's job was to issue new uniforms to incoming prisoners. Soon enough, he met a new prisoner who was clearly frightened.

"Don't look too vulnerable," Bill advised him. He knew well the fate that awaited anyone who appeared weak.

In the days to come, Bill would learn how to use a sewing machine, repair clothing, and even make custom-fitted clothes. One of his customers, an inmate who went by the name of Ragu, weighed more than five hundred pounds and had needed a special bed constructed for him. Bill sewed together two pairs of fifty-inch-waist pants to make one pair that could contain all of Ragu's girth.

While working in the laundry room, Bill met several inmates on death row, including Robert Sullivan. Bill was sent to Sullivan's cell to measure him for a suit. Technically, it wasn't a full suit, just a cheap jacket and matching pair of pants, which he would be forced to wear during his execution. A huge guy in his own right at 350 pounds, Sullivan had been convicted of murder. The jury had recommended a life sentence, but the judge had imposed the death penalty. He had been on death row for a decade and was about to go on "death watch," which meant he was scheduled to be executed in seven days. For the next week, he would have no contact with anyone. Not the prison guards, who would slip food through a slot in his door, and not his fellow inmates, from whom he would be isolated. In effect, Bill was the last person Sullivan would talk to before the state strapped him into the electric chair.

Sullivan had dark hair, a big square face, and a genial disposition. "I didn't commit the crime they have me here for," he said as Bill measured his inseam.

Bill, sick to his stomach, said nothing in response. He was still new here—and still reeling from the trauma he'd already endured.

The prison administration zealously publicized Sullivan's looming execution for seven days straight, and by execution day, everyone was buzzing with anticipation. But when the moment finally came—and everyone knew because the lights blinked on and off for several seconds—the corridors fell silent. It was a blatant show of might, a message to the prisoners to remind them who was in charge and just how lucky they were to be breathing still. Bill, alone in his cell, shuddered as the lights finally stopped flickering. Like him, Sullivan had insisted on his innocence. But unlike Bill, Sullivan had gone to the chair. It was a strange thing, Bill thought, to feel heartbroken *and* fortunate. As hellish as his new home was, at least he had a future, however grim.

CHAPTER 24

THE LORDS OF JUSTICE

The system had been designed to make people like Bill Dillon disappear. Convicted killers, after all, deserved neither rehabilitation nor redemption. They had only to rot in prison—or better yet from some people's perspective, die a violent death at the hands of their fellow murderers. But what the system failed to take into account was that some of those languishing in the Florida state prison system were innocent. Bill began writing letters to Frank Clark, who upon Bill's conviction had immediately filed an appeal, submitting additional grounds in support of a new trial and detailing Donna's recantation.

Predictably, Judge Stanley Wolfman issued an order denying the motion for a new trial, stating that, "after examination of the entire case, it is the opinion of this court that there is substantial, competent evidence to support a guilty verdict and that said motion for a new trial should be denied."

The appeal came back stamped DENIED, and Frank Clark, for months now the only person in Bill's corner, simply disappeared.

Bill, refusing to give up, redirected his letter-writing campaign to any attorney whose name and address he could get his hands on. But in his darker moments, he was beginning to feel completely alone. Without a single ally to defend him, and with no one to turn to, he became acutely aware of how cut off from the world he was. As a maximum security prisoner at Florida State Prison, he was not allowed to use the phones. And even his incoming and outgoing mail, his only means of communicating with anyone beyond the prison walls, was opened and read by the guards.

As for visitors, he had none. His friends had long abandoned him, and his parents, after one fearful visit, were so intimidated by the maximum security prison and its menacing reputation that they became afraid to enter the gates. But that was the point, Bill realized in short order. The barbaric institution didn't want to deal with family members. That would only complicate things. Now that Bill was locked away, his former supporters had, for all intents and purposes, thrown away the key.

No one had been more deeply wounded by the public humiliation than Bill's mother, who since the trial had hidden herself way from friends and acquaintances. The whole family appeared to believe what the police were telling them. They were a military family, after all, and military families were trained to believe what the authorities told them. Bill's parents no doubt thought it foolish to mortgage their home to pay for the defense of someone who the state had determined was guilty. Why end up penniless and on the streets for such a lost and dubious cause?

Then there were Bill's siblings. Joe, clearly devastated by the jury's decision, had left town as fast as he could to join the navy, the first branch of the military that would take him. Debbie, feeling conflicted about how to deal with the pain of her brother's conviction, distracted herself with her teaching career. She would soon be married, a mother, and busy with her own family. Finally, David, Bill's youngest brother, was likely suffering the most. Too young to understand everything that was going on, he was no doubt being teased at school by his schoolmates. To be the brother of a convicted killer was to carry a social stigma with him wherever he went.

Bill had repeatedly told his parents that he was innocent, and he couldn't understand why they had never hired an attorney on his behalf. Tortured by the thought that his family doubted his innocence, Bill could do nothing but hope to one day vindicate himself, both for his sake and theirs.

For the moment, however, his primary focus was on surviving the daily perils of Florida State Prison. Violence could happen anywhere or anytime, such as on the indoor basketball court, where rival gangs vied for power and often enacted deadly revenge in a never-ending spiral of retaliation. Any prisoner thinking he'd been disrespected felt duty-bound to respond with violence.

Bill was in the recreational facility one night watching a film, Charles Bronson's *The Mechanic*, when he suddenly felt what he thought was warm water spraying him in the face. It was blood. Someone had snuck up on the prisoner sitting beside Bill and slit his throat. A second later, the room erupted in violence, with chairs flying and prisoners tussling in the dark. The guards eventually intervened, and Bill, covered in someone else's blood, was rounded up along with the guilty parties. Although just as confused and surprised by the incident as everyone else, he spent the next thirty days in solitary confinement while authorities conducted an official investigation.

It wasn't the last time Bill would see a man injured or killed, often over the most trivial of offenses. His fellow inmates, he was learning, could fashion a weapon out of almost anything. When the administration distributed new footlockers to the inmates, it unwittingly introduced four thousand knives into the prison. Each locker had two metal handles, one on each end, which could be filed into sharp daggers by rubbing them against a hard surface. Within hours, every single handle, having been broken off its respective locker, had disappeared into the population.

Bill could only watch in disbelief as inmates intentionally flooded their cells, started fires, and threw excrement and other foul substances at the guards. They broke windows and burned mattresses, destroying anything they could get their hands on. The savagery was unremitting.

On Thanksgiving Day, Bill was standing in line in the chow hall, waiting for his Thanksgiving dinner, when an inmate working in the kitchen passed a butcher knife to a prisoner named Moore, who was standing in line. Moore leapt the waist-high guardrail, which ran the length of the room all the way up to the tray rack at the food counter, and everyone scattered. A second later, Moore was repeatedly burying the butcher knife into another prisoner's back and neck, just feet away from where Bill stood. The wounded prisoner crashed into a table, his face colliding with his tray, and then rolled to the floor, already slick with his blood.

"Lockdown!" several guards screamed in unison.

Doors in every direction slammed shut.

Moore, having completed what had clearly been a well-orchestrated hit, turned with his hands in the air to the guards and calmly allowed them to apprehend him. He was carted away, and the doors relocked, after which time a medical team came to tend to the victim.

The rest of the prisoners were given an option: stay and eat or go back to their cells.

Bill chose the latter. He'd lost his appetite.

Back in his cell, Bill felt keenly aware of his own vulnerability. Young and defenseless, he was a prime target for the very kind of violence he'd just witnessed. Soon, he fretted, someone like Moore, someone he had unwittingly offended or merely rubbed the wrong way, would kill him. For now, it was all he could do to fend off the gang of rapists who repeatedly assaulted and beat him. As the attacks continued unabated, he slowly began to lose his identity. Overcome with grief and self-doubt, he couldn't understand how fate could be so cruel.

His second Christmas behind bars arrived, and with it came the sense that he would never again celebrate with his family. The stark reality of living out the rest of his life in prison, including cherished holidays, was too much to bear. Somewhere beyond those bars, life was going on without him, but here, locked away, he was dead to the world. Holidays came to be dreaded, not rejoiced, for they stood as torturous reminders of all that had been lost—and all that was unattainable.

Adjusting to prison life meant learning to absorb disappointment. Some disappointments were relatively trivial, such as when the prison administration removed athletic equipment from the gym and vitamins and nutritional supplements from the canteen in order to prevent inmates from getting too big and strong.

Others were harder on the psyche. After several months of working in the laundry room and on death row, Bill realized that only the prisoners he measured for suits were executed. The others on death watch never went to the electric chair. In other words, the last-minute appeals and the flurry of activity that preceded a prisoner's execution or stay were all just theater. The powers that be knew ahead of time who was going to die and who would be spared. If a prisoner was doomed, Bill was sent to his cell to fit him for a suit a week in advance of his execution. If not, Bill never went in to take the prisoner's measurements.

The New Year came and went. Bill had been in prison for a little over a year when Cynthia Karl-Stamm, his new public defender, sent him a letter informing him that she was going to file an Anders brief on his behalf. This was the first time Bill had ever heard from Karl-Stamm. It was also the first time he'd ever heard of an Anders brief. When he spoke of it to a fellow inmate, the inmate's reaction surprised him.

"Don't let her Anders brief you," the inmate said angrily. "That means she's giving up on your case."

"I thought it was some kind of freedom thing," Bill said in alarm.

"Nope. It means she'd be admitting there are no grounds for an appeal—that even *she* thinks an appeal would be frivolous."[5]

Bill shook his head indignantly. Ever since being assigned his first public defender, he'd been designated a "pauper" by the state. After his arrest, he had been required to file papers detailing the extent of his wealth. Nothing had changed in the interim. At that moment, he was worth about sixty cents, all of which was in his prison account. Being a pauper meant accepting whatever appeals attorney the court assigned him. Cynthia Karl-Stamm, as far as he could tell, was no more competent or helpful than the very first attorney he'd been assigned, the man who'd stayed on his case for less than twenty-four hours before vanishing.

Furious that his latest attorney had already given up on him, Bill sat down in his cell and wrote to Karl-Stamm to demand that she not Anders brief him.

A few weeks later, a second letter arrived from the attorney. In it she asked what she should put in the appeal.

Bill replied at length by outlining the merits of his case and the basis of an appeal. It would be his job to educate his attorney. The appeal, he wrote, could be reduced to three basic elements: the prosecution's failure to prove prima facie robbery-murder, the impossibility of confronting the witness against him—the dog, Harrass II—and Donna's recantation.

Karl-Stamm eventually resubmitted the facts as Bill explained them, this time as a writ of certiorari, which would go all the way to the US Supreme Court. It came back to Bill on his twenty-fourth birthday, August 31, 1983, and was stamped with three words, the first in all caps: DENIED, without comment.

How? Why? Bill couldn't understand why everyone, including his own attorney, was arrayed against him.

Bill was eventually assigned to another laundry facility, this one on the prison's second floor. Not long afterward, during one of his work shifts, he met the infamous Ted Bundy.

---

5   *Anders v. California*, 386 U.S. 738 (1967), was a United States Supreme Court case in which a court-appointed attorney filed a motion to withdraw from the appeal of a criminal case because of his belief that any grounds for appeal were frivolous.

"What's going on out in the population?" Bundy asked one day while Bill was delivering his laundry.

Smart, handsome, charming—Bundy kept his cell obsessively neat. Like the rest of the death row inmates, he was kept in constant lockdown, which meant never mingling with the general population. But he did enjoy one luxury not afforded to regular prisoners: a television in his cell. It was on whenever Bill stopped by with Bundy's laundry.

"They stabbed two officers this week," Bill answered, "and the papers say they're getting ready to sign some more death warrants."

It was unnerving, Bill thought, to be making conversation with one of the most notorious killers in the world. Bill was innocent. Bundy was not. But they were both prisoners here at Florida State Prison.

Bundy opened his mouth to reply but then paused, suddenly transfixed, when a woman appeared on the television in his cell. This wasn't the first time he had drifted off, mid-conversation, at the sight of a woman on the screen.

Unable to break the spell, Bill moved on to the next cell.

Two years into his incarceration, Bill met with his classification officer, a heavyset African American man named Desue.

Bill had met Desue months earlier, during his classification "callout," when the two men had discussed Bill's behavior, his job, his health, and how he was getting along with the other prisoners. After that, Bill had seen Desue in passing several times. But this was his first official classification meeting, and it had come sooner than expected.

They met in a nondescript office, and Desue, who had to tip the scales at close to 350 pounds, cut straight to the chase.

"What are you doing here?" he asked.

"They sent me here," Bill answered with a shrug.

"Why?"

Another shrug. "I was convicted of murder."

"That doesn't mean you should be *here*," Desue replied. "I'm going to get you transferred out of here. It won't be easy, but I'm going to do my best. You don't belong here."

For more than a year now, Bill had suspected that he'd been sent to the barbarous prison by special request. His mind retraced the words of the nurse who questioned him on his first day at Florida State Prison:

"How did you get yourself into FSP at such a young age?" she asked. Bill replied that he got a life sentence. "But why did they send you *here*?" she probed.

Putting the pieces together, Bill was convinced someone high up had wanted him to disappear, and there was no better place to make a man disappear than Florida State Prison. Now Desue was confirming his suspicions that the state knew it had facilitated the conviction of an innocent man. It had sent him to Florida State Prison to literally bury the evidence. After all, most men who ended up here were either murdered or went insane.

The latter were easy to pick out. They inhabited the psych ward, where they could be seen doing the "two-step" all day long. Two steps forward. Two steps back. Hopped up on psychotropic drugs that had been prescribed for them, they inhabited their cells like mindless zombies, babbling to themselves, drooling, totally vacant. The men who ended up in the "experimental wing," as the prisoners called it, rarely came back. If they did, they came back as hollowed-out versions of their former selves. They were human guinea pigs. The prison administration liberally handed out drugs in an attempt to control behavior, and it was widely known that the doctors experimented on the prisoners, strapping them to beds and giving them Thorazine and other drugs. In the psych ward, the walls, floors, and doors were all solid. Prisoners couldn't see up the tiers like they could in other wings.

Such woeful medical treatment wasn't reserved just for the mentally ill patients. Inmates had no say in what medications they were given, and most illnesses were simply left untreated. Cancer patients, rather than being given the standard treatments of the day, were sent off to what was euphemistically called "the little house on the prairie," another prison where they lived out their final days in agony. As opposed to being kept comfortable in a hospice, they were sent away to a place where no one could hear them moan in pain. When death finally took them, their broken, unclaimed bodies were then buried in the prison's sprawling graveyard.

Most prisoners at Florida State Prison, abandoned by their families and forgotten by their communities, were destined to never leave. In his darker moments, Bill assumed his body would one day rest in the prison cemetery. But as bleak as his future looked, he never seriously considered hastening his death. He was too much of a coward, he told himself, to take his own life. There were, though, times when he wished someone would do it for him. If he made a run at the fence, he thought, the guards might shoot him. Of course, with his luck, he would end up paralyzed and have to endure prison life as a cripple, a fate worse than the one he currently suffered.

In fact, men were committing suicide all around him. Some slit their own throats. Others hung themselves with their bedsheets. But as despondent as Bill was, he was also harboring a deep anger, a nearly bottomless hatred for the people who had put him in prison, and it was that anger that kept him alive. He wanted to survive this hell hole, to live long enough to prove his innocence. More than once, he woke up from a dream in which the authorities had admitted their mistake or found the real killer. In one recurring dream, the real killer came forward and Bill was exonerated. Every time he awoke, he was jerked painfully back to reality. But the dreams gave him hope, a small burning ember that fed his soul. If he died, the powers that be would win, for dead men didn't talk. But if he went on living, if he could somehow continue to survive, there was a chance he would find vindication.

One day, alone in his cell, inspiration hit. He reached for a piece of paper but then thought better of it. He was only allotted two pieces of paper and two envelopes every two weeks, which meant he had to reserve the good stuff for his letter-writing campaign. Instead, he would have to use toilet paper. His story, unvarnished and raw, came to him in verse, one after another. The bitterness. The heartache. The injustice. For each new verse, he uncoiled another length of the gritty prison-issue toilet paper. Before he knew it, he had scribbled out nine verses and was staring at his first completed poem, "The Lords of Justice."

It often felt to Bill like no one was listening, like no one cared. But in taking his first step toward becoming a poet and later, a songwriter, he was preserving the truth by telling his story, even if, for the moment, he had no audience. He folded up the toilet paper and placed it in the small box that held all of his earthly possessions. For now, it was enough that he was writing.

CHAPTER 25

THE LAST STOP

The most violent prisoners at Florida State Prison never left their cells except to pace small pens beneath the hot sun. They lived their lives in perpetual lockdown. But most in the general population could earn a little recreational time in exchange for good behavior. Bill spent the bulk of his playing on the softball team. For each game, Bill and his teammates, weighed down by leg shackles and handcuffs, were loaded into a van and driven through the prison gate to Union Correctional Institution, also known as "the Rock," which stood directly across from Florida State Prison and was surrounded by endless rolls of razor wire.

Coach Hopp, a civilian who ran the recreation department, was an older black man with broad shoulders and a barrel chest. He wasn't much taller than five feet, but he had an outsized, jolly personality. As the only person who treated the inmates like human beings, he earned Bill's and the others' gratitude and respect. Hopp included his players in strategizing sessions before each game. His best idea, "murderer's row," included Bill, who was among three convicted murderers—all home run sluggers—that Hopp placed one after the other in the batting order. If an opposing team purposely walked the first among them, they still had to face the next two. If they walked all three, they loaded the bases.

Bill's team reached the prison state championship in 1984, and Bill hit two home runs to help his team take the title. For a brief, bittersweet moment, as Bill celebrated the victory with his teammates, he felt a sense of camaraderie, even freedom. Memories of his first home run as an eight-year-old kid came flooding back to him. It was a high fly ball that sailed over the rickety schoolyard fence and rolled away. But it was contested. Did it go over the fence or did it go under the fence, the umpire questioned. Bill was abruptly stopped on second base unable to advance as an intense conference ensued on the mound. Bill's heart pounded. Were they going to steal his first victory? No! "It was a fair ball!" the crowd roared. The umpire finally signaled, and young Billy rounded home plate with a smile as wide as his home state of California beaming across his face. That foreboding moment was the beginning of a love of the sport that never left his soul, but it also foreshadowed that others had the power to sabotage his destiny with one swift decision.

Bill's continued appeals for another hearing, meanwhile, were summarily denied in Florida's Eighteenth Court of Appeals as well as its Fifth District Court of Appeals. When he submitted a writ of habeas corpus in 1985, Louie Wainwright of the Department of Corrections and Attorney General Jim Smith ruled it had no merit and dismissed it. Shortly thereafter, on August 26, exactly four years to the day after Bill's arrest, former state prosecutor John Dean Moxley, now a powerful judge, reaffirmed Bill's conviction and signed an amended life sentence. Bill couldn't believe his appeal had gone back to the very people who had participated in his wrongful conviction. How would he ever get a fair hearing? Why was this allowed? There was no one to answer his questions and his anger surged. He was furious with a system that seemed to be conspiring against him, and at least for the moment, he was furious with God. His faith in a fair and loving God was waning to an all-time low. It was a very lonely place.

When one of his teeth began giving him grief, Bill went to see one of the prison's dentists.

"I think I have a cavity," he told the dentist. "Can you fill it?"

The dentist, a young, skinny, talkative man who wore eyeglasses, chuckled. "We don't do fillings. I can give you an aspirin to put on it, but you'll be back when it's painful enough to sign the paper to have it pulled."

Bill left with the offending tooth still in his mouth. But the dentist was right. He would eventually come back to have it pulled. Most prisoners in the 1980s lost some if not most of their teeth to the abysmal Florida Department of Corrections dental program.

Back in his cell, meanwhile, Bill caught a whiff of cigarette smoke, which meant some prisoner nearby was smoking a cigarette in his cell. Cigarettes could be bought at the canteen. They were called "rips" and had to be rolled. Lighters, too, could be bought. But no matches. The sulfur from matches could be used to make zip guns, improvised firearms capable of firing .22 caliber bullets. As for cigarettes, they weren't allowed in the cells, but that didn't stop prisoners from smoking them in their cells. Typically a prisoner would light up while standing in front of his cell's window, blowing the smoke through the bars. A guard might smell it but would be unable to trace the odor to the offending prisoner.

In any case, the guards made a habit of looking the other way so that all kinds of nefarious activities—from smoking to gang-rape—could go on uninterrupted in the prison cells. Many of the guards, in fact, were running their own schemes at Florida State Prison. Some dealt drugs, turning prisoners into crack addicts in order to make a few bucks, usually off prisoners' friends and family members on the outside. Others smuggled in contraband, including green money, which the prisoners in turn would use as an underground currency, since only prison coupons were legal tender. Some guards even extorted money from concerned family members, who were told they needed to pay guards to protect their loved ones on the inside. But such practices worked both ways. Prisoners often paid guards to look the other way when a hit was planned on another prisoner.

When officials came to inspect the prison, everyone played dumb. No one dared mention how easy it was to buy marijuana or how often the guards stood idly by while an inmate was raped or even murdered. Furthermore, there was no whistleblowing on the sadistic guards who used the showers as their own personal torture chambers. Punishment came in all forms. Inmates tied to chairs were ordered to soap up with caustic lye-based soap. The guards who controlled the water temperature and flow from behind the wall would then turn off the water and wait until the soap burned and blistered the prisoner's skin. Only after they didn't want to hear the screaming anymore, did they allow the prisoner to rinse off. Alternatively, they would turn up the temperature high enough to scald a prisoner and wouldn't stop until he pleaded for his life. No guards were singled out or exposed for their part in the corruption and abuse. A code of silence was maintained on all fronts. To breach it was to dig your own grave.

Even the female guards took part in the corruption, albeit at their own peril. Some openly flirted with or teased the inmates. Others had consensual sex with the prisoners and even became pregnant. But some were raped or assaulted by convicted rapists and murderers who, knowing they would never see freedom again, were willing to take any risk to be near a woman. Some female guards were appreciated for their compassion and femininity. Some were even revered for their beauty. But those among them who forgot they were among hardened criminals often paid a hefty price.

"The Last Stop." That was what many prisoners called Florida State Prison. Indeed, it was the end of the line for many. The five-year rule, a rule that ensured the transfer of prisoners to another prison every five years, prevented prisoners from learning the ropes of any particular institution or causing too many problems. But Florida State Prison was different. The five-year rule didn't apply here, and as a result, it was nearly impossible to get a transfer. Florida State Prison was where prisoners went to die.

Nevertheless, Desue, Bill's classification officer, eventually made good on his promise to get Bill out of Florida State Prison.

One evening, shortly before his transfer, Bill was walking back to his cell from his job at the laundry when several guards appeared in front of him pushing a gurney.

Bill jumped back to get out of the way, and as he did, he saw the man's face. On the gurney was the dead body, bloody and beaten, of Nasty T, the ringleader of the gang that had repeatedly assaulted and brutally raped Bill. From the looks of it, one of his victims had finally evened the score.

Bill gasped as he stared at the lifeless corpse. Karma could be a vicious thing to those who abused it. God, Bill was certain, had kept him at Florida State Prison just long enough to witness the fate of his cruelest tormentor. Maybe, just maybe, he wasn't alone on his journey after all.

CHAPTER 26

LIFELINE

In late 1985, just before fall gave way to winter, Bill was transferred to Avon Park Correctional Institution in Polk County, where he was relieved to find the prisoners older, wealthier, and less violent. Many were white-collar criminals, as opposed to the hardened thugs at Florida State Prison. The environment allowed Bill's parents to begin visiting, which was a blessing not only to Bill but to Amy and Joe Dillon as well. Determined to stay out of trouble and mind his own business, Bill avoided conflict whenever he could, all the while leveraging his reputation as a good softball player. Like Florida State Prison, Avon Park boasted a softball field, and everyone, it seemed, wanted him to be on their team. There, on the field, he felt connected to his past, to the athlete he could have become. The prison walls seemed to fade into the horizon as he focused on the game. For a few short hours, he could become a young boy again and dream of life in the big leagues.

Unfortunately, his fellow inmates' respect for him didn't extend beyond the field. There were still plenty of dangerous men at Avon Park, which, like Florida State Prison, was a maximum security facility, and when they got wind of Bill's reputation as someone who (a) could be assaulted and (b) wouldn't name any names, they tried to take advantage of him.

Bill, still recovering from the deep physical and emotional scarring he had suffered at Florida State Prison, was thankful for the fresh start and began to slowly change his stature among the population. Had he been forced to stay at Florida State Prison much longer, there was no telling how—or *if*—he would have survived. After landing a job as a butcher in the kitchen, he met a friendly civilian in the recreation department.

Older, white-haired, the man had been working for years at Avon Park and, like Coach Hopp, seemed to genuinely care about the prisoners.

Bill asked him for a job in the recreation department, and when Bill got the job, he made an even bigger request. "Could you talk to the higher-ups about resurrecting the band program?" Bill asked the older gentleman.

"I don't know. The last time we had it, the prisoners abused the instruments and equipment."

"I'll take responsibility for the band room," Bill said. "I'll make sure everything is handled properly."

Bill kept working on him.

Finally one day the man presented Bill with a pile of catalogs. "Okay," he said cautiously but optimistically, "you have a six-thousand-dollar budget. Order what you need to outfit a band program."

Elated, Bill rounded up the other prisoners who were musicians and pored over the catalogs with them. Six thousand dollars was more money than Bill had ever seen, but he still had a lot of instruments and equipment to order. Eventually, he and the others came up with a list that included microphones, keyboards, drums, mixers, and about ten Palmer guitars at sixty dollars each. They soon had everything they needed to offer a full lesson program and outfit several bands for performances. Better still, Bill was enjoying himself immensely in his new job. He had found his calling, in fact. He encouraged every prisoner who wanted to learn music to get involved.

Although an inmate couldn't take a guitar back to his cell, he could check it out for an hour and use it in the yard. If the guitar was returned in good condition, the inmate could use it again in a few days. If not, the inmate lost his privileges. Soon inmates were teaching and taking lessons, and bands were playing for the population on weekends.

The inmates who participated in the program visibly changed. So, too, did Bill, who, along with overseeing the program, began taking guitar lessons from other prisoners and practicing every chance he got. Music gave him something positive to think about, which was far better than focusing on the many injustices that had been visited upon him. It offered him an outlet for his energy and emotions and a chance to spread a little good will. He would sit for hours in his cell writing songs about life in prison—as well as the life he couldn't have. And when others learned he could sing, he became the lead singer in two of the bands, which earned him respect among his fellow inmates.

"Sing, Bill!" an inmate would shout down the corridor at night. "Sing!"

More than willing to oblige, Bill would croon one of his original tunes, and the corridor, noisy just seconds before, would fall eerily silent as the inmates listened.

"Someday my songs will be on the radio," Bill told several prisoners.

It was a gutsy boast, given his life sentence, but Bill had a hunch that somehow, someway, the day would come when the world would hear his songs. He was keenly aware of music's healing powers, as well as its transformative ones. If it could heal the savage beasts around him, if it could change his own heart, then surely it could change those on the outside. Imbued with optimism and a sense of possibility, Bill set out to write the world's prettiest love song.

Along with working in the band room, Bill landed a job assembling furniture for Prison Rehabilitative Industries and Diversified Enterprises, or PRIDE, a program that put prisoners to work for private companies. At first, he worked for free, other than the occasional cheeseburger he was given for his efforts. But eventually he began making fifteen cents an hour—still a steal for a company selling low-quality furniture to government agencies at exorbitant prices. After some creative wheeling and dealing, Bill was able to save up enough money to buy a small transistor radio on the black market for five dollars.

Bill searched the dial for something—anything—to listen to, but with Avon Park located in the backwoods of Polk County, radio reception was poor. He finally found a few local music stations and some talk radio shows, and soon he was keeping up with some of his favorite bands. The tiny radio, a cheap assemblage of transistors and wires, was his connection to the music of his youth, not to mention the outside world. In short, it was nothing less than a lifeline. The fact that it wasn't on his property list weighed heavily on his mind. He could only hope the guards wouldn't take it from him.

Bill had been at Avon Park for three years when, in 1988, Frank Clark contacted him out of the blue, offering to help him with his appeals. All Bill had to do was send Frank all of his legal work. Encouraged to hear from his former attorney, Bill sent Frank nearly everything he had—and never heard from him again.[6] Worse still, Frank never returned any of the documents, many of which would be needed to file future appeals.

Bill would have no choice but to make do. During his five-plus years at Avon Park, he tried to focus on the music program. But he was still in prison, still living a substandard life in substandard conditions. Dental problems continued to plague him, and when he developed a painful abscess in one of his teeth, he had no choice but to see the dentist. Sure enough, the dentist pulled the tooth rather than fill it.

On August 5, 1991, Bill was transferred to Holmes Correctional Institution in Bonifay, a tiny town in northwestern Florida. There he became a literary vocational assistant and taught other prisoners how to read. The work was fulfilling, and Bill found himself a natural teacher. It was his third prison in a decade, however, and Bill was dealing with a degree of depression. Each time he hit bottom, Bill agonized over the odds of an escape attempt being successful.

The endless hours of idle time allowed him to create painstakingly detailed plans. They were intricate and complex and would constantly change according to the layout, activities, and schedules at each prison. Opportunity and timing would be the success-limiting factors.

While at Holmes Correctional, Joe Dillon Jr., Bill's stepfather, became gravely ill. His doctors felt his only chance at a normal life would be to undergo a risky bypass surgery. Bill, having long ago repented for his brash attitude toward his stepfather, had since developed a deep and special love for him. The thought of not being able to see him before the surgery that could very well end his life caused Bill intolerable anguish. He knew it was time to execute.

"God," he prayed as he fell to his knees. "You know I'm an innocent man. I wouldn't do this for myself, but I need to do this for my dad. Please, if you don't want me to do this, please give me a sign." He prayed as he plotted out the route he would take. Bill had watched for weeks as the very pregnant officer assigned to the guard tower made her trek up the long flight of stairs to the lookout station high above the prison. As each week of her pregnancy passed, it took her longer and longer to get from the ground to the top of the tower. It was in that small gap of time that Bill would have to make his run for it. Each night, Bill watched the clock until he knew exactly how long it would take her to reach the apex. He knew he had twenty-three seconds to reach "station one," a shaded spot under an overhang at the back of his housing pod. He would then have an additional

---

6   Frank Clark passed away two years later, in 1990.

forty-two seconds to reach "station two," a tree where he could be spotted if anyone was up in the tower. From there he would have to duck under the searchlight and sprint to the fence in less than twelve seconds in order to scale the metal barrier by the time she reached her chair.

Bill had spent the past weeks amassing the items he would need to launch. Magazines that would wrap around his legs to protect him from the razor wire, green money he got by trading his few possessions he would leave behind, and pepper from the chow hall to throw the dogs off his scent if he was lucky enough to vault the fence before he was shot. Where he would go from there, he knew not. The swamps around Holmes Correctional were teeming with alligators and poisonous snakes. He would have to make it to a road before count time if he hoped to survive. He would need civilian clothes and a way to get to his father before they took him to the hospital. After that he would play it by ear.

When night fell Bill stayed behind at his job, pretending to work late. Once his boss called in the count and count was clear, at just the right moment he slipped out to station one, his heart pounding in his throat and adrenaline gushing. His eyes focused on station two, and as he crouched like a cheetah ready to pounce, an officer sauntered out of the back gate and knelt down to talk to someone sitting on the ground under the very tree he needed to reach or his plan would be foiled. Bill could see that the man on the ground was a prisoner, a well-known snitch in fact, likely cutting a deal.

No! he fumed to himself. *No one was supposed to be out there after dark!* He knew it was over. Bill would be missed if he didn't make it back to his dorm on the double. Once inside he tore off the magazines and sat on his bunk. God had, in fact, sent a sign, and Joe Jr. would go to surgery without his stepson there to wish him well.

After his stint at Holmes, Bill was moved to Union Correctional Institution, a.k.a. "the Rock." Just a few years earlier, he'd been at Florida State Prison staring across at the Rock. Now he was at the Rock staring back at Florida State Prison. Each time he was transferred to a different prison, he had to learn the ins and outs of surviving that particular institution. New friendships had to be made. New hierarchies had to be learned. It was always dicey, but as he got older and more experienced, it became easier to figure out who he could trust and who he should avoid.

Not long after arriving at the Rock, Bill made friends with Nate Johnson. Nate, a former drug dealer, had been selling weed when two men had tied him up and tried to rob him. When it had become apparent they were going to kill him, Nate had reacted with rage and had ended up killing both of his captors. After being convicted of murder and put on death row, he'd had his sentence commuted to two life sentences. By now, Nate was back in the population and had served twenty years in prison, as opposed to Bill, who'd totaled a dozen. Nate, along with being astute when it came to legal issues, radiated religious wisdom. When he spoke, he spoke with utter sincerity.

"You'll be free someday," he repeatedly told Bill. "Just keep your faith."

"Nate, sometimes I wonder if God is really fair. Maybe he doesn't have to be fair. I mean, he's God after all."

"Billy, it's the world that's not fair. It *will* happen," Nate reassured. "All in God's time."

Bill shook off his despair enough to join a softball team at the Rock. During his very first game, an African American prisoner, older and balding, hit an inside-the-park home run. But as he reached home plate, the man collapsed. He was having a heart attack.

Bill worriedly glanced around at the other players and coaches.

Nobody moved.

Not willing to watch the man die, Bill rushed to him and began performing CPR, which he had learned in the military. Just as he was getting a faint pulse, the guards stepped in, "Get off him, you dick," they said as they pulled Bill off the man gasping for breath.

The guards then took their sweet time tossing the man onto a cart and then wheeling him to medical. Not surprisingly, by the time the man arrived at medical, it was too late. He died.

Bill could only fume in disgust. Had he been allowed to continue CPR on the man while someone fetched a medic, the man might have survived. Instead, the guards, lacking compassion and common sense, had dragged the man away and let him die en route.

The incident soon faded from view, and Bill, once again working for PRIDE, busied himself assembling metal furniture. His starting pay, despite the fact that he'd already logged a few years with PRIDE, was a measly twenty-five cents an hour.

Still saddled with dental problems, Bill went one day to visit the Rock's dental ward, where jars full of teeth were proudly put on display. Several of Bill's teeth would soon be in those jars. All told while in prison, he lost all of his bottom molars on one side of his jaw and most of the upper molars on the opposite side. He was left with no chewing surface and had no choice but to chew all of his food with his front teeth. Not only were the prison authorities bent on taking his freedom; they seemed determined to take his health as well.

As had been the case at Holmes, Bill's stay at the Rock was a relatively short one and amounted to only a few years, but those years passed by slowly and were full of danger. The place was so old and "war torn" by turmoil, it would be condemned as unfit for human habitation a few years later. He was soon transferred to Polk Correctional Institution in Central Florida, where he would be incarcerated for roughly a dozen years.

At Polk, Bill worked once again for PRIDE, this time in customer service. Handling complaints regarding damaged or faulty products took more people skills than assembling the furniture, and again Bill earned a starting pay of twenty-five cents an hour. Later, he would head up the laundry operation, during which time he would use the sewing skills he had learned at Florida State Prison to repair and tailor prison uniforms, all while receiving no pay.

In such an economy, prisoners regularly bartered with anything they could get their hands on: sugar packets from the chow hall, matches, cigarettes, and of course, homemade knives or other weapons, which went for the most money. Pets, too, fetched a high price. When Bill caught a lizard in the yard, he knew he could have sold it for twenty-five or thirty dollars. But, fearing that the reptile might be mistreated, he kept it on a string in his cell and fed it insects. The two bonded, with "Godzilla" sleeping above Bill's bunk. Bill was therefore devastated one morning when he found the lizard dead in his bed. Sometime during the night, it had fallen onto the mattress and Bill had rolled over and crushed it. In prison, where friends were few and true companionship was rarer still, losing a beloved pet, even a small lizard, was an emotional blow.

CHAPTER 27

EPIPHANY

As the years wore on and Bill was transferred from one prison to the next, one thing remained constant: his letter-writing campaign. He wrote letters to lawyers, to law professors, to congressmen, to the Innocence Project, to total strangers, to anyone and everyone who might take an interest in his case. With each letter, he included return postage—no small expenditure, considering his meager prison wages.

Despite sending out hundreds of letters, he never received a single response. The silence was deafening. Demoralizing. But he pressed on with still more letters, as well as appeal after appeal. In the appeals, he outlined Donna's recantation, never heard by a jury; her affair with Detective Slaughter, also never heard by a jury; the fact that he'd been questioned for hours before being read his rights; and the impossibility of challenging Harass II's identification of him as a suspect. Over the years, each appeal was denied, but Bill continued filing them, knowing that if he did so, the state would not be allowed to destroy his case files or any of the physical evidence from his case.

In 1996, a few years into his stay at Polk, a short, stout prisoner with brown hair approached him.

"Are you William Dillon?" the inmate asked.

Bill looked down at the five-foot, six-inch man guardedly. "Yeah, I'm William Dillon. Why?"

"I'm Dencil Chapman," the man said. "You know Roger Dale Chapman?"

"Yeah, I know the slimy liar," Bill answered in a testy tone. "Why? Are you his brother or something?"

Dencil nodded. "He lied on the stand during your trial."

"Are you for real?" Bill asked.[7]

"Yes. He set me up too. Roger and Mr. Hunt always work hand in hand. Roger will lie and set someone up, and Mr. Hunt will then drop whatever charges there are against Roger."

Bill felt his heart pounding in his chest. Finally he had proof that he had been framed. "Would you be willing to repeat what you just said to my cellmate?"

Dencil agreed, and Bill's cellmate, a certified Department of Corrections law clerk—that is, a jailhouse attorney—wrote up an affidavit for Dencil to sign. The affidavit read as follows:

> I, Dencil Chapman, do hereby swear that the following statement is true and correct and made from my own free will, from my own personal knowledge:
>
> Roger Chapman was a witness in William Dillon's murder case. Roger made blatant statements to me that Dillon really never told him that he did it, but had to say that Dillon did it, because that's the only way that Mr. Hunt would drop Roger's sexual battery charge. Roger has made numerous statements that he and Mr. Hunt had made deals before to get him out of trouble. From what Roger told me, William Dillon should never have been charged for the murder. When I asked Roger, "You mean there is really a murderer out there?" he replied, "I don't care. My charge got dropped."

Bill filed the appeal shortly thereafter, and the appeal was summarily denied by Judge Tanya Wainwright, who, curiously enough, shared the same last name as Bill's official jailer, Louie Wainwright, who in turn had been party to denying Bill's habeas corpus petition a decade earlier. Judge Wainwright based her conclusion on the belief that Dencil's statement only impeached Roger Dale Chapman and by itself wasn't enough to ensure that a jury would have come to a different verdict. The judge neglected to mention Donna's recantation. Moreover, she didn't take into account the fact that, without Roger Dale Chapman's testimony, there was also no jailhouse confession from Bill, contrary to what the prosecution had insisted.

Astounded that Judge Wainwright had been unable—or unwilling—to connect the dots in his case, Bill filed for a rehearing. And to his continued

---

7 Was Dencil indeed Roger's brother, as he claimed? Melissa Montel of the Innocence Project of Florida has voiced skepticism. As of this date, we don't have evidence to confirm or deny his assertion.

chagrin and astonishment, his request went to the same judge a second time and was flatly denied. No amount of evidence, it seemed, was sufficient to cast doubt on his conviction. Without Donna's testimony, without Chapman's, all the state had was a half-blind eyewitness and the dubious results of a swaggering dog tracker.

Slowly, inexorably, the anger welling inside Bill began to poison his soul. The state had taken everything from him—his freedom, his youth, his future, his reputation, even his *teeth*—and no matter how hard he worked to regain all that had been stolen from him, he found himself repeatedly steamrolled by a monolithic system intent on his destruction. He was in essence a political prisoner, and his captors were shining their badges and promoting their careers on the back of an innocent man. His faith in the justice system, long gone, had been replaced by bitterness, despair, and a rage so potent it was incapacitating. The darkness threatened to swallow him whole. He got into fights and paraded his foul attitude. Embraced the bile billowing up from deep within. And when he wasn't striking out in anger, he was repeatedly asking the age-old question every victim of injustice asks: *Why me?* In short, institutionalization was changing him—and he didn't care.

Then one day Bill was sweeping the floor in the rec room, a square room with rows of wooden benches and a fifteen-inch television mounted high in the far corner, when a program on the TV caught his attention. It told the story of several country music stars, including Tim McGraw, visiting children in the cancer ward at St. Jude's Hospital in Memphis, Tennessee. The children were young, between the ages of two and ten years old, and had bandannas on their heads and tubes in their arms. Many only had a short time to live. Yet they were smiling and singing and clearly happy to meet the musicians.

As he watched the terminally ill children face adversity with such courage, Bill felt something powerful sweep over him. He fell into a rickety chair and dissolved into tears. He knew it was time to change his life. For years he'd considered himself the most unfortunate person in the world, but suddenly he realized there were people, just kids, who had it worse than him. They would never even have a chance to grow up. He, on the other hand, had his health, more or less, and many years still ahead of him, even if he would never see freedom again. Moreover, he had managed to hold on to his sanity, despite the physical and emotional torture visited upon him in prison.

It was time to make something out of his life, he realized, even if his life wasn't the one he had chosen. God, he thought, had placed him in the rec room at that precise moment to open his eyes to the possibilities before him. It wouldn't happen all at once. It would take hard work. But he nevertheless made a commitment, right then and there, to change the way he thought about the world. He would become less angry. He would think positively. He would accept his circumstances with as much equanimity as he could muster. He would spread love, rather than hate, and most of all, he would heal his relationship with God and reinforce his faith. He began a new and diligent letter-writing campaign, but this time the letters didn't begin "Dear Professor" or "Dear attorney," they began "Dear God" and always ended with the same salutation: "Your son Bill."

After his epiphany in the TV room, Bill began counseling other prisoners about changing *their* outlooks. He'd seen countless inmates over the years get released from prison only to return for a second, third, fourth, or even fifth time. They were stuck—unable to change their habits. It was true that he would never be free, Bill thought, but that didn't mean he couldn't help others find their way to a happier, more productive future. Indeed, if he could make a difference in even one prisoner's life, then he could rest easy in the knowledge that he'd served a worthy purpose and that his life hadn't been for naught. Hatred and bitterness, he now realized, were self-destructive emotions that ate a man alive and kept him in his own spiritual prison. He came to terms with suffering, cruelty, and humiliation. He began the process of letting go.

Bill was experiencing nothing short of a rebirth of his soul, and with that rebirth came countless transformations in and around him. Other prisoners began treating him differently. The guards respected him. An inner freedom, even behind bars, became possible once again. And his sense of resolve, cultivated daily, grew exponentially. He'd made a conscious decision to dispense of his anger and establish a purposeful life. In a place of unending misery, he began to spread happiness.

In 1996, nearly fifteen years into his sentence, Bill received an unexpected visit from his brother Joe and Joe's eight-year-old son Zach, whom Bill had never met before. It had been years since Bill had last seen his brother, who had served in the navy for several years before returning to civilian life. At that time, he was working as a detective for the Palm Bay Police Department in Florida.

"Joe," Bill said in a determined tone, "I'm an innocent man and have been here all these years. There must be something somebody can do about it."

Joe managed to get copies of Bill's case files and approached the Innocence Project of Florida and others to see whether they could offer any help. But he soon hit multiple roadblocks and was unable to do anything further to help his brother get the needed attention paid to his claims of innocence. Joe was up against the same machine that was determined to keep Bill shut away forever.

Visits from the rest of Bill's family, meanwhile, became less frequent. They had their own lives to lead, and Bill could sense that it was difficult for them to visit him, for it brought back all of the pain they had endured during the arrest and the trial. Moreover, although prison officials claimed otherwise, the prison system made it difficult for families to visit. Every prison Bill had called home so far was situated in the state's farthest reaches. Thus his parents and siblings were forced to travel long distances to see him, and they often had no choice but to take a day off from work and stay overnight in a hotel. When family members arrived, they were frisked for contraband and monitored by the guards, who hovered nearby during the visit. No displays of physical affection were permitted beyond a brief hug at the beginning and end of the visit. Although Bill had been the one to go to prison, his whole family suffered with him.

So, when Bill did get a visit, it stayed with him for days. It was a veritable lifeline to know he hadn't been forgotten. Most of the letters he received were from his stepfather who even began depositing small amounts of money into Bill's prison account so Bill could afford a few things at the canteen.

Was peace possible for a man who was serving a life sentence for a crime he hadn't committed? For the first time since his incarceration, Bill was learning to accept the unacceptable, to tolerate the intolerable. He'd been dealt a lousy hand, certainly, but it was possible, even here behind bars, to find a certain measure of composure. Maybe his life hadn't turned out the way he'd envisioned it would. But it was still *his*, and he was determined to make the most of it.

CHAPTER 28
CHOKEHOLD

In 2002, Bill was transferred to his sixth prison in twenty years, Okeechobee Correctional Institution in south-central Florida. Before arriving at Okeechobee, he stayed for a week at Lake Butler, where he got his first glimpse of "the little house on the prairie," the hospital ward next to Lake Butler where prisoners were sent to die. The ward, painted red, reportedly housed mostly terminally ill prisoners. Whether dying of cancer or AIDS, they rarely were seen or heard from again. After their deaths, their bodies were buried in one of the prison graveyards.

At Okeechobee, meanwhile, Bill landed a job with the recreation department digging up dirt and reseeding the softball field. Along with working, he made a conscious effort every day to keep his mind sharp. Okeechobee, just like the other prisons that had housed Bill, had its own set of unwritten rules and unofficial alliances. To survive, he would have to learn them as quickly and painlessly as possible.

Shortly after arriving there, Bill met "Rat," a young man whose cell was located on the second floor, near the TV. After the two became friends, Bill often sat with Rat in his cell, which had a decent view of the TV. Rat had gone to prison at age fifteen for shooting his parents. His mother, the only one to survive, had testified at his trial that his father had repeatedly abused him, physically and sexually. Nevertheless, he had been tried as an adult and was serving a life sentence without the possibility of parole. A scrawny boy among men, Rat was vulnerable to the violence and abuse regularly dished out at Okeechobee. He was also the most talented artist Bill had ever met and spent most of his free time painting. Tattoos were illegal in prison, but Rat had perfected an underground method of tattooing called "pick and poke" and could turn almost anything—a guitar string, a sewing needle attached to the end of a toothbrush—into a tattoo needle. By burning newspaper or any paper with ink on it and using the ashes as tattoo ink, Rat could create gray-blue tattoos that looked as good as any tattoo available on the outside.

Bill had for years sported an ugly tattoo of an eagle on his left arm. He hated it. It looked like a chicken. After scraping together fifteen dollars, he paid Rat to cover it with a new tattoo, and for the next three days, the two men hid from the guards, using doors and bunks as cover, as Rat worked on his masterpiece. The young artist began by drawing a beautiful wolf freehand on Bill's arm, and by the time he had finished, Bill was the proud owner of a gorgeous tattoo. Years later, it would still look brand new, although Bill would shudder at how lucky he'd been to walk away from the experience without contracting hepatitis, or worse, AIDS.

It was tragic, Bill thought, that a brilliant young artist like Rat was destined to never share his art with the world. But other men fared far worse. More than a few were classified as Psych 3s, 4s, or 5s, which meant they were suicidal. Some, known as cutters, would cut themselves with razor blades. Others overdosed on medication or contraband drugs.

Then there was Jason, whom Bill met on the softball team. When Jason's wife wrote to tell him she had decided to move on with her life, Jason blocked his tiny cell window with a piece of paper, which he fastened with toothpaste. He then locked his cell and, after tying his bed sheet around his neck, leapt from the top bunk. When count time came, his cellmate couldn't get into their cell, so he called the guards, who popped the cell open and found Jason's dead body hanging from the side of the bunk.

At Okeechobee, Bill was thrilled to receive his first-ever visit from Dave, his youngest brother, who was now a full-grown adult. Dave came accompanied by his girlfriend, Jane, a pretty woman with sparkling blue eyes, a big smile, and a friendly disposition. In the weeks that followed, Jane and Bill became pen pals, and months later, after she broke up with Dave, she continued to visit Bill at the prison. Jane spent much of her visits talking to Bill about holding on to his faith. The visits from Jane, whose compassion Bill felt was literally a godsend, became more frequent. It had been years since anyone had been so kind to him. When he felt hopeless, she brought him hope. When he felt cut off from the outside world, she helped him feel connected.

In early 2005, as Bill approached his twenty-fifth anniversary in prison, Jane helped him prepare for his first parole hearing. As his advocate, she would be the one representing Bill at the hearing since prisoners weren't allowed to attend their own parole hearings in the state of Florida. Bill was serving "life with a mandatory quarter," which meant he was finally eligible for parole. But, he learned, he was trapped in a Catch-22. He would have to show remorse for the crime he had been convicted of committing—a key requirement of the parole commission—in order to be granted parole.

As sad as he was that James Dvorak had lost his life in such a pointless and brutal murder, he refused to apologize for a crime he hadn't committed and continued to proclaim his innocence.

On the day of the hearing, fearing the worst, Bill waited until that evening to call Jane and ask her how things had gone.

Jane, clearly upset, could barely choke out the words. "It was a disaster," she said through tears. "The board ruled against parole. They said your next possible parole date is 2041."

Bill would be eighty-two years old.

Crushed by the news, Bill hung up the phone. He had already spent a quarter of a century in prison, watching helplessly as the prime years of his young adulthood had receded day by day, never to be regained. Now approaching middle age, he wasn't sure he had the energy to face the grim news that freedom, always a faint hope at best, would never again belong to him. He would die here. He would be buried along with the other lifers. He was tired: tired of being a prisoner, tired of continually forging ahead, tired of living without hope.

Later that year, as the weather cooled, Bill entertained his first Thanksgiving Day visitors in twenty-five years. Jane, along with Bill's Aunt Aggie, dropped by, and the three dined on ham and cheese hoagies, chips, and soda in the visitors' room, surrounded by guards. Holidays were usually depressing times, emotional gauntlets the prisoners did their best to get through without too much inner turmoil. But for once Bill was able to bask in the moment, to relish each second spent with loved ones.

After saying goodbye to Jane and his aunt, he returned to his cell, only to find it ransacked. Everything he possessed, including all of his personal letters and photos and his entire collection of handwritten songs, was gone. Bill's mind raced. Who was the bastard that had riffled through his belongings? Although he lived in a two-man cell, he was currently sharing it with no one. But Okeechobee, perhaps more so than any of the prisons he had thus far called home, was a chaotic place. Along with the fights and riots and suicides and racial tensions, there were the lackadaisical guards who often popped doors when they heard prisoners yell out the cell door number, never bothering to check whether the prisoner indeed belonged in that cell. In this case, Bill had a pretty good idea of who had broken into his cell. Weeks earlier, a fellow inmate had given Bill a lock for his footlocker. Now that lock was *gone*, not broken. Someone, most likely the original owner, had known the combination and stolen everything inside the footlocker before walking off with the lock itself. He'd been set up.

Bill sank to the cement floor and sat, motionless, surrounded by the mess the thief or thieves had left behind.

A few hours later, the guards tried to get him to move, but he refused. He wouldn't eat. He wouldn't get up onto his bunk for the daily head count. He just wanted to go to sleep and never wake up. The flame that had burned inside him for twenty-five years was quickly fading. Hopelessness, the deadliest emotion a prisoner could feel, had him in a chokehold.

CHAPTER 29
AN ANGEL

Bill was moved to the psych ward and put on suicide watch. Stripped of his clothes, which he could in theory use to hang himself, he was allowed only a "suicide blanket." As far as he could tell, the psych ward wasn't much different from the hole. But it didn't matter. *Nothing* mattered. He refused to eat. Spit out his meds. Declined to talk to the guards or the doctors. He wanted only to die.

After a few weeks, though, something inexplicable began to change. Slowly, steadily, he began to regain his strength, and by the time he was released back into the general prison population, he felt ready to face his future with a renewed spirit. A voice inside him, growing louder by the day, was as resolute as it was relentless: *Don't let them win*. He was determined to someday tell his story, and the only way to do that was to survive, to keep moving forward at all costs.

Back in his cell, he meditated about his life and the many injustices he had weathered. Although the elaborate escape plans he had drawn up in his mind over the years were all but abandoned, he replaced those dreams with positive thoughts about gaining his freedom. He fanned himself with a lightweight piece of cardboard, heavy enough to move the air around him but not so heavy that it required exertion to keep it in continual motion. The sweat on his skin lingered just long enough to cool him before it evaporated in the fanned air. Half art, half science—proper self-fanning required a Zen-like concentration. It was a skill Bill had mastered out of necessity, for none of the maximum security prisons he had called home over the years had ever offered air-conditioning in the cells. At Okeechobee, huge fans at each end of the corridor sucked in hot air from the outside and blew it around aimlessly, carrying with it the stench of urine, sweat, and feces. Even after he had drifted off, his right hand continued to move automatically, cooling the air and providing a steady hum to drown out the noise all around him.

Though still in his forties, Bill had gained the wisdom of a much older man. In his spare time, he visited the library, where he read almost anything he could get his hands on. Ironically, the library was air-conditioned. The books, though outdated, were treated better than the inmates reading them. Determined to make sense of his life and what it all meant, Bill devoured novels, old classics, self-help books—whatever was on the shelves. *Knowledge and faith*, he thought, would hold the answers he was seeking.

He was in the library several months later, in the spring of 2006, when an older inmate appeared in front of him. Slender, barely five feet tall, the man had jet-black eyes, graying hair, and sideburns that suggested he was in his late fifties or early sixties. Bill had seen him on occasion in the law library next door, where the man worked as a law clerk, dispensing legal advice to his fellow inmates. But now he was marching straight toward Bill as if he'd been sent specifically to see him.

"Bill," he said in a friendly voice, "have you ever had a DNA test?"

Bill was surprised the man knew his name. "No, I haven't."

"I know you've been in prison a long time," the man said, clearly knowing more about Bill than Bill knew about him. "You should file a motion to get one."

Bill had heard of DNA testing but had never understood how it might apply to his situation. After listening to the man briefly explain the science behind it, he said, "I've been in prison for twenty-six years now. I don't know if there's any evidence left from my case to test. The state has done everything possible to shut me out. They won't listen."

"This is science, Bill. They *have* to listen," the mysterious man replied with a deliberate tone.

With that, the man gave him a form, about seven or eight pages long, along with a set of instructions on how to fill it out.

"You know what they say about a man who represents himself?" Bill retorted humorously.

"Just file it," he urged. "You've got nothing to lose."

To date, Bill had relied on public defenders or jailhouse attorneys, none of whom had been able to help him. He was doubtful that he would fare any better representing himself, but he had no money to pay for legal services and thus would have to bring himself up to speed on all the requirements.

As he studied the form, he saw that he would have to state where the evidence from his case was being stored.

"How do I answer this?" he asked the man. "All these years I made sure I filed all of my appeals on time, so I know the state isn't allowed to throw out my evidence. It has to be *somewhere*, but I have no idea where it might be."

"Where were you tried?" the man asked.

"Brevard County."

"Then just write down that it's in the sheriff's office in Brevard County."

"All right," Bill said, still somewhat hesitant. The whole thing sounded like a long shot, but he knew that if they could possibly locate the Surf-It T-shirt, his DNA would not be on it.

"You'll have to get on it, man," the clerk said, "a new statute is being passed and they're going to shut down all *post-conviction* DNA testing in Florida a week from now. You only have a short window of time. After that, no more requests will be accepted for review."

Bill was alarmed to learn that the window would be closing on June 6. *Was there an expiration date on innocence?* he thought incredulously. It was May 30. He had a scant seven days to fill out all the paperwork and submit it. *It would take a miracle*, he thought.

He rushed back to his cell and spent the next week diligently learning how to become his own attorney. Bill researched two cases that were eerily similar to his. In each case, a man tried in Brevard County had been convicted based on the expertise of none other than John Preston, the arrogant dog handler, and his so-called magic dog who had helped send Bill to prison. Moreover, each case had involved a jailhouse snitch testifying that the suspect had confessed in jail. The hair on the back of Bill's neck stood at attention when he read that many of the same people from the sheriff's department and the state attorney's office, including John Dean Moxley, had been involved in each case. Bill suddenly realized he wasn't alone. Nor was his case an isolated one. The state, in conjunction with the police in Brevard County, had employed the same MO against all three men.

Promisingly enough, both men had eventually been released. One of the men, Juan Ramos, had escaped execution after being on death row for five years. In Ramos's case, the Florida Supreme Court weighed in and ruled that the dog tracking was an untested and unproven method. Ramos was acquitted at retrial and released in 1987.[8] The other, Wilton Dedge, had actually been convicted *twice* of rape—he was granted a second trial, and the state used the testimony of a serial jailhouse snitch to convict him a second time. In exchange for his bogus testimony, Clarence Zacke, a dangerous murderer, had been granted a reduced sentence. In other words, the state had stolen the freedom of an innocent man while *reducing* the jail time of a convicted killer. Dedge had only later earned his freedom after DNA testing proved he could not have been the perpetrator.

Dedge's case struck particularly close to home, for Bill had actually met Wilton while playing softball at Avon Park. Bill and his second baseman had never discussed their cases, so it was a shock to learn how much they had in common.

Up against the clock, Bill did his best to cobble together a coherent handwritten motion. In it, he explained to the judge why he should be granted DNA testing, summarizing once again the contours of his case. Bill managed to file it, just under the wire, on June 6. Before sending it off in the mail, he offered a silent prayer, hopeful that this time, finally, his efforts would prove fruitful.

Two months later, in August, Bill was transferred to his seventh prison, Hardee Correctional Institution in Bowling Green. Starting at the bottom once again, the only job available was a grueling one: picking up garbage under the hot Florida sun. As taxing as the work was, he was more than willing to endure it, for his new boss was also in charge of the band room, and Bill was positioning himself to get a job where he could continue to hone his musical skills.

Bill was working in the yard one day in early October when he got a callout for legal mail. He was then escorted to the mail room, where a female officer opened his mail to make sure it contained no contraband. She handed the letter to Bill, and he hurried back outside to read it in the yard.

---

8   Juan Ramos's death penalty conviction was overturned in 1987, just five years after Bill's conviction, due to doubts about John Preston and Harass II's abilities. Yet, no one looked into Bill's conviction or any other convictions the dog handler participated in. Bill questioned John Preston's dubious abilities in all his appeals, including the inability to cross-examine a dog. All were denied.

According to the letter, a Brevard County judge by the name of W. David Dugan had received Bill's motion and was requiring the state to show "just cause" why Bill shouldn't be allowed DNA testing.

"What's this mean?" Bill said, handing the letter to his old friend Nate Johnson, whom he had first met years earlier at the Rock.

Nate studied the letter a moment and then smiled. "This is good, Bill. The judge is making the state say why you *shouldn't* get the DNA test." Nate waved the letter in the air, his voice filled with joy. "You're knocking at their door, Bill. You are knocking at their door!"

It took the state attorneys roughly a month, but by November 6, they had submitted a confusing counterargument that led Bill to believe they had either forgotten about him or were hoping merely to fudge the truth and make the case go away. Bill quickly put together a rebuttal and sent it to Judge Dugan, once again fashioning an exhaustive narrative that covered all the details of his case.

Bill was astonished a week and a half later when the judge granted him a hearing. He reread the letter from Judge Dugan, his hands trembling with excitement. The tide was turning. He could feel it. There was a chance, a legitimate chance, that his prayers had been answered and that soon the world would know the truth.

He set the letter down on his bunk and remembered the diminutive older prisoner from the law library at Okeechobee who had helped him, in the nick of time, back in May. Bill never had the opportunity to thank him. He disappeared as mysteriously as he had appeared, and Bill never laid eyes on him again. Was this sheer happenstance? Luck? A coincidence? Or, Bill wondered, was he an angel?

For the first time in two and a half decades, Bill hadn't relied on a stranger to do his legal work. He had put his own hand to the task, and it was blessed. Maybe, just maybe, this was the first time Bill didn't have a fool for an attorney. He could taste freedom.

CHAPTER 30
EVIDENCE LOST... AND FOUND

After being transferred to the new Brevard County Jail in Sharpes, Florida, Bill found himself sharing a two-man felony cell with two other men. He slept on the floor. Such crowded conditions were common at the jail, which was brimming with men awaiting trial or sentencing for murder, rape, and other violent crimes. Each felony cell helped make up the felony pod, a cluster of cells packed to the gills with mostly hardened men awaiting their day in court. The place was cleaner than the old "bullpen" back in Titusville, whose county jail and courthouse had been torn down, but just as poorly run.

Having been granted his motion for DNA testing, Bill was now entitled to a public defender for the first time in decades. Michael Pirolo and Bill met for the first time in the attorney conference room.

Michael, dressed in a suit, entered the room after Bill. Young, handsome, and clearly fit, he had dark hair and looked to be in his thirties.

A glass window separated them.

Speaking through five small holes arranged in a circle in the center of the glass, Bill told the young attorney everything he knew about his case.

Michael listened intently. It was obvious by the questions he asked, each one delivered with just a hint of a New York accent, that he had done his homework. "You know something?" he said after Bill had finished. "I believe you. I'm going to do everything I can to help you."

As worried as he was about Michael's youth and inexperience, Bill couldn't deny that the kid was earnest. He clearly meant what he said. Only one question remained in Bill's mind: how good of a lawyer was Michael?

Unbeknownst to Bill, Michael Pirolo had recently left a high-paying law firm in the Big Apple to accept a far lower-paying gig at the Brevard County Public Defender's Office. The antithesis of the stereotypical public "pretender," Michael oozed fire and passion for his work. He had moved to Brevard County to help the less fortunate obtain legal representation against the good ol' boys that ran the county. That meant going up against the powerful machine. It also meant reforming the justice system one difficult case at a time. More than willing to be a big fish in a small pond, Michael wanted to make a difference. In the months to come, he would be an outspoken critic of the state attorney's office, regularly shining a spotlight on its frequent corrupt practices. After their meeting, which took less than an hour, Bill returned to his cell feeling guardedly optimistic. He knew DNA testing could prove his innocence, assuming there was any evidence remaining from his case, but he was afraid to get his hopes up. Prison had taught Bill to keep a lid on his expectations at all times. The alternative was to be continually disappointed when things went south, as they so often did.

In January of 2007, one of the guards approached the two-man felony cell Bill was sharing with two other inmates and handed Bill a piece of paper.

After reading the note, which stated that Dan Billow, a news anchor at Channel 2, wanted to interview him, Bill put a check next to the box marked *yes* and then signed it. Although wary of the press, he felt he was given the opportunity for a reason.

To his dismay, members of Bill's family expressed disappointment that he had agreed to the interview, fearing that Bill would hurt his chances of earning parole in the future if he publicized his wishes to have his DNA tested. Bill was confident he knew better. He was innocent and he knew that the only way DNA evidence could work against him would be if the state tampered with it. As risky as it was, DNA testing was the *only* method still at Bill's disposal that might prove his innocence.

Dan began the interview with a simple question. "You've been in prison twenty-six years," he said. "Why are you here in the county jail?"

"I'm here for DNA testing," Bill answered. "I want to be granted a new trial and to have the DNA test results admitted."

The interview took several minutes, and afterward, while the cameraman was breaking down his equipment, Dan turned to Bill and said, "You know I'm the reporter who interviewed Wilton Dedge before his DNA tests came back and exonerated him."

Bill believed it was a heavenly omen. He knew that one by one, the missing pieces of the puzzle were being put in place by an invisible hand.

In fact, just a few days later, Bill was sitting in his cell in the felony pod, at the moment crammed with more than seventy men, when he was told he had a legal call and was escorted to the phone. Bill assumed the person on the other end of the line was Michael Pirolo, his new public defender, but instead he was greeted by Seth Miller, Jenny Greenberg, and Richard Junnier in a conference call from the Innocence Project of Florida, or IPF, in Tallahassee. Miller and the others explained that they had seen Bill's interview with Dan Billow on Channel 2 and were eager to represent him.

Bill knew that the Innocence Project used DNA testing to help exonerate wrongfully convicted prisoners. Beyond that, he knew very little about the organization. As he would learn later, the Innocence Project of Florida consisted of several passionate, underpaid attorneys, many of whom believed so strongly in justice that they had given up potentially lucrative careers in order to fight for penniless prisoners. When circumstances warranted it, they resurrected old cases that had been tried before the advent of DNA testing. Other key contributors among the dynamic, talented group in Tallahassee included attorneys David Menschel and Melissa Montel, the newest member of the team.

"Would you like us to represent you?" a friendly voice asked.

"Yes! Please!" Bill replied, as he reflected on his nearly three-decades-long letter-writing campaign. In all that time, and after sending out hundreds of letters, not a single lawyer had stepped forward to help Bill prove his innocence.

A few days later, Melissa Montel, dressed from head to toe in a white tailored pantsuit entered the visitors area to greet Bill. Her flowing white-blond hair and icy blue eyes sparkled as she stretched out her hand. To Bill, she looked like an angelic vision of hope. By her side was investigative reporter for *Florida Today*, John Torres. John, a handsome ambitious young writer was passionately delving into cases of injustice in Brevard County. He and Melissa were determined to discover the truth behind Bill's conviction. John would begin a journalistic campaign to tell Bill's story and follow his new journey through the swampy waters of Brevard County's justice system. Bill brought them up to date on all the particulars and explained that Mike Pirolo was already representing him through the public defender's office. To their mutual credit, Pirolo and the Innocence Project of Florida would eventually coordinate their efforts and work together on Bill's behalf.

After amassing all of the files related to Bill's case, the Innocence Project of Florida turned its attention toward rewriting the post-conviction relief motion that Bill had handwritten on notebook paper. The original motion would have allowed the state attorney's office to conduct the DNA testing at the Florida Department of Law Enforcement (FDLE) laboratory. But the new motion insisted that the DNA testing be conducted at an independent, accredited lab with no interest in the outcome. The lab would also have access to more advanced types of DNA testing than those used at the state lab.

After the Innocence Project of Florida and Pirolo refiled the motion, Judge Dugan read it and scheduled a hearing for July, several months away. In the meantime, several "status hearings" were held to determine whether or not any evidence from the case still existed.

Predictably, the state attorney's office, whose team included attorney John Parker (no relation to John Douglas Parker—the half-blind eyewitness who picked up the bloody hitchhiker near the crime scene), attorney Wayne Holmes, and original prosecuting attorney Michael Hunt, objected to the process itself, insisting that the results would be irrelevant as to innocence. Pirolo, on the other hand, was requesting that the state locate not just the yellow Surf-It T-shirt but a total of twelve items of evidence, all of which he wanted DNA tested. During each status hearing, the attorneys for the state emphatically represented that they couldn't find any of the evidence. The Brevard County Sheriff's Office also represented that it had in its possession *no* evidence from the case. This served to infuriate Pirolo, who rightly pointed out that Bill had filed all of his appeals and motions in a timely manner and that the state, as a result, had had no right to discard or destroy any of the evidence.

Bill's hopes were eroding, and he began to fear the state would go to any length to make sure he remained in prison forever. Hunt and the others had used every delay tactic in the book to slither away from testing the very evidence they had used to convict Bill two and a half decades earlier. With no evidence to test, this would be the end of the line for Bill; his only chance for exoneration sabotaged.

Suddenly, in a surreal moment, the clerk of the court stood, took a few steps forward, and matter-of-factly said she had possession of the yellow T-shirt in her evidence room! Bill and Pirolo smiled ear to ear as the prosecution's jaws hit the floor.

Pirolo immediately insisted on a search of the clerk of the court's evidence room. He was determined to locate all of the remaining physical evidence. It was a long shot, considering twenty-six years had passed since Bill's trial and, more importantly, current procedure dictated that the clerk of the court return evidence held by the clerk to the state's main evidence room after each trial. But Pirolo was determined to leave no stone unturned, and if the T-shirt was there, he surmised, other evidence would be there as well.

Thus Pirolo, state attorney John Parker, and Monica Levsen, the clerk of the court, met in a courtroom on May 22, several weeks before the final hearing granting DNA testing of the evidence. With no judge present, Levsen carried into the courtroom several boxes from the case. Though she hadn't been the clerk of the court during Bill's trial in 1981, Levsen had held her current position for many years. To Pirolo's consternation, none of the fingernail clippings, cigarettes, blood samples, or swabs from the victim or contents vacuumed from John Douglas Parker's truck remained. But to his relief, the most critical piece of evidence—the yellow Surf-It T-shirt—had been preserved! Also present were several other items of clothing that had been found at the crime scene, plus four loose hairs. All told, seven of Pirolo's twelve requested items were still in the evidence boxes. Where were the other five pieces? Where had they gone? If they had been destroyed, who had given the orders? Pirolo wanted to know.

With no job to do and no guitar to play, the days in the county jail crawled by. Bill was sitting at a table in the felony pod one day when the notorious James Phillip Barnes approached him. Already serving a life sentence for killing his wife in 1997, Barnes had just been charged with a second gruesome murder and was awaiting trial. Although a confessed killer, the burly convict appeared genuinely concerned about Bill and his case.

"Hey," he said as he sat down beside Bill. "I've been hearing about your case. I noticed we had the same prosecutor, Michael Hunt. Do you know Hunt requested I be sent directly to Florida State Prison, even though I wasn't sent to death row?"

Bill was startled by the statement. "You know something? I always figured someone requested *I* go to Florida State Prison, since everyone always said I didn't belong there. They said, 'They send you there to die.'"

Barnes nodded grimly. "Yeah, rightly so. You need to know what you're up against here in Brevard."

"Do you have proof of that?" Bill asked.

"You bet."

Barnes, who was representing himself, had a sharp legal mind, not to mention direct access to all his legal files and documents. He disappeared briefly to his cell and then returned a few minutes later with a folder stuffed with hundreds of pages. After peeling back half the stack, he showed Bill a document bearing the letterhead of the Brevard County State Attorney's Office. There, in black and white, was a recommendation from Michael Hunt to the Department of Corrections. It appeared Hunt had formally requested that Barnes be sent to Florida State Prison, adding that he considered Barnes extremely dangerous.

Suddenly Bill understood that his assignment to the notorious state prison hadn't been an oversight. He been sent there by design. But by whom? And for what reason? He couldn't say. All he knew for sure was that *someone* within the Brevard County legal system had likely known he was innocent—and had done everything they could do to make him disappear.

While the two sides argued over the evidence and what was left of it, Bill had nothing to do but wait. He therefore requested a transfer back to Hardee, where he had happily landed a job in the band room prior to being sent to the county jail. At Hardee, he would be able to continue working in the band room, practicing guitar, and sharpening his songwriting chops, all of which was preferable to sitting in the county jail and staring at the wall all day. If anything could bring him peace while he waited for the slow gears of justice to churn, it was music.

After several long months, Bill was transferred back to the county jail for the July 3 hearing, presided over by Judge Dugan.

Judge W. David Dugan, dressed in a black robe and sitting atop the podium, appeared to be in his early to mid-fifties. The bespectacled judge still had a full head of hair, which was graying and parted on the side. He had a thick neck, broad shoulders, and an intense gaze. In contrast to Judge

Stanley Wolfman, who decades earlier had hurried witnesses on and off the stand in his quest to finish Bill's trial before the weekend, Judge Dugan appeared to be intently listening to each attorney. He actually seemed to care about the case.

Bill glanced from the judge to Michael Hunt, who had aged noticeably since the 1981 trial. He was a more or less familiar sight in an otherwise new-to-Bill courtroom. The old courthouse in Titusville had been demolished, along with the old jail, and replaced by this modern facility in Viera. Instead of walking the old "time tunnel" from the county jail to the courthouse, Bill had been driven in a van from Sharpes to Viera.

As part of his request for DNA testing, Pirolo was asking that a private lab do the testing. To begin with, the FDLE lab wasn't equipped to conduct the sophisticated testing required due to the age and condition of the evidence. Secondly, there was only a limited amount of material available for testing. It was possible the FDLE lab would use up all of the evidence while attempting to obtain results using inadequate test systems that might produce no, or inconclusive, results. A private lab with superior expertise could conduct all of the necessary tests with the available evidence. Additionally, Pirolo argued, the FDLE lab was backlogged with piles of cases, which meant the results would likely be a long time coming back. And finally, on top of all of the technical reasons, was the conflict of interest inherent in the FDLE lab's involvement. The state, after all, had been fighting Bill's claims of innocence for more than two and a half decades and now was fighting the DNA testing.

Pirolo was laser-focused on finding out what happened to the remaining missing items of evidence. When state attorney Wayne Holmes claimed the state didn't know where the missing items were, Pirolo, his temper flaring, told the judge he wanted to conduct a full investigation. Judge Dugan responded by saying it was the state's burden to prove that the lost items didn't exist.

Pirolo smelled a cover-up. The state seemed pleased those items were missing. "What does the state have to lose to test these items?" Pirolo asked the judge. "We either have an innocent man who's been saying he's innocent for the past twenty-five-plus years come out that he's truly innocent, or they're just gonna prove that they have their guy. What is there to lose in the end? We certainly don't want another Wilton Dedge here. The same things that happened to Wilton Dedge happened here. The same officers were involved, the same facts—not necessarily the same facts, but very close to the same—the same Preston, and so forth, Judge. It would be sad to know that in Brevard County, Wilton Dedge was not the only one, that Mr. Dillon was sitting in DOC for twenty-five years of his life for something he never did."

The evidence custodian for the Brevard County Sheriff's Office's evidence unit, took the stand and stated that she had searched the files from the Dvorak case but had come up empty. There was no evidence that a court order had been issued to destroy the missing items. In fact, the paperwork didn't indicate that anything had been destroyed. That said, her records indicated that nothing remained in the sheriff's evidence room.

"Where would they have gone?" Pirolo asked.

"Nothing is indicating where these items are," she answered carefully.

"Is it possible it was destroyed? Doesn't each item have to be accounted for? If they are missing, then they were destroyed—or they magically disappeared?" Pirolo turned to the judge. "As a records custodian, she should know the procedure. Isn't it fair to assume the sheriff's office destroyed it?"

The custodian was visibly upset. "I can't find the paperwork that says it was disposed of."

"If there is no form that gave authority," Pirolo said hotly, "then isn't it fair to assume it was destroyed without authorization? So are you going to stick with the fact that it magically disappeared?"

Not willing to let anyone off the hook, Pirolo asked how she had conducted the search, step by step.

The custodian replied that she had pulled the folder under the proper case number and had found it empty. "If I could find the paperwork," she said through tears, "I could find what happened to it."

Pirolo then put Michael Hunt on the stand and began grilling him about the missing evidence.

Hunt claimed that the state attorney's office hadn't gotten anything back from the clerk after the trial and as a result had no property receipts to show the evidence had been returned. "I can almost say with absolute certainty that we didn't get it back," he testified.

"How do you know that you don't have it?" Pirolo asked. "What have you done to make sure you don't have those items?"

"We don't have an evidence room," Hunt answered.

It was a curious statement. If the state attorney's office didn't have an evidence room, where did they keep the evidence?

Hunt went on to explain that they had limited space for guns and other items. "I presume a search was made of that limited area. We've moved about four times since 1981." An offsite file storage area existed, he said, but it hadn't been searched because any evidence would be at the clerk of the court's office or at the sheriff's office. "The clerk's office has also been moved several times," he added.

"Isn't it possible that these items were destroyed without a court order?" Pirolo asked.

"It would be speculative," Hunt answered nonchalantly, "but anything's possible." Along with being unapologetic for the state's role in losing the evidence, he seemed both unconcerned and unfazed by Pirolo's steady stream of questions.

Pirolo put Monica Levsen on the stand next, and Levsen explained everything she *had* found in her evidence room back in May, including the yellow Surf-It T-shirt. She told the court that she always held on to everything. Had she been the one to transfer the evidence, she said, she would have retained a property receipt, but she couldn't speak for anyone else's procedures. "Other people, clerks, if evidence was only marked for identification, it was returned to the state attorney's office," she said. "It was not a written rule, but it was a common practice in 1981." There was no written standard operating procedure, per se, she said, so clerks were free to transfer evidence as they saw fit. "In the old days, I remember that anything not marked into evidence sometimes we did return the items to the state attorney's office."

State attorney Parker was quick to speak up. "And then they would be handed over to the law enforcement agency," he said in an obvious attempt to deflect blame and redirect it at the sheriff's office.

Pirolo was clearly running out of patience. "Items don't just disappear," he said in an exasperated tone. "Where are the items?" He called for another hearing, one that would bring back *everyone* involved in the 1981 trial, including attorney Karen Thompson, the clerk of the court at that time, and anyone who'd had access to the evidence. "I just find it extremely concerning, Judge, and very suspect that those items just disappear, and no one's got a clue of where they're at. No one. Everyone's pointing the finger."

As angry as Pirolo was, Bill began to sense that this hearing was nevertheless going in his favor. The Surf-It T-shirt, the state's prized piece of evidence—the one they'd used so successfully against him in the trial—was still intact—and available for DNA testing.

Not surprisingly, Holmes began to argue against the T-shirt's inclusion in the testing, suggesting that it be used only for "the limited purpose of obtaining a profile for future testing or comparison to other results." He added, "I think the focus should be on the shorts and the underwear."

Serological evidence from the 1981 trial had shown that Bill's blood was not on the shirt, but Karen Thompson had successfully muddied the understanding of the blood test results just enough to confuse the jury. Now, though, DNA testing could help unravel the state's entire case, which had hinged on Bill's wearing of the yellow T-shirt. No doubt fully aware of this, Holmes was now in the dubious position of arguing that, since the serologist had excluded both Bill and the victim from wearing the shirt back in 1981, there was no need to test the T-shirt for DNA. But Pirolo shrewdly countered that if another person's DNA were to be found on the T-shirt, such a finding would surely constitute reasonable doubt—enough for a jury to think twice about convicting Bill.

Holmes, not willing to concede the point, put Harry Hopkins, his FDLE crime lab supervisor, on the stand. Could the evidence have been contaminated in 1981? Hopkins responded that he couldn't vouch for the lab techs that had handled the evidence. In fact, he couldn't even say whether or not they had worn gloves and masks. Once again, the state was impugning its own evidence. Chain of custody, transfer of evidence, contamination of evidence—when it came to the proper handling of evidence, the state had, since Bill's trial, continually tried to tarnish the soundness of the evidence by discrediting their own people's procedures and expertise.

DNA testing, being only as good as the integrity of the specimen, can be more damaging than helpful if the specimen itself is compromised or the testing isn't handled competently. But that didn't stop Holmes from arguing that his own people—the very people who the state claimed had botched the handling of evidence at every turn—should perform the testing, so long as the testing fell within the FDLE's range of capabilities. If, after the FDLE finished the testing, it was determined the FDLE couldn't perform a specific test requested by the defense, then and only then would an independent lab need to participate in the testing.

Pirolo countered that the evidence should not be split between labs for the obvious reason that such a convoluted process could compromise the results. Rather than risk losing the evidence in transport between labs or worse, using up all the evidence at an FDLE lab before it could be tested elsewhere, Pirolo argued that the tests should be conducted by one highly competent, *independent* lab.

The hearing continued for several grueling hours, and Judge Dugan, after listening to arguments from both sides, finally granted the DNA testing of six of the seven pieces of evidence remaining. Pirolo withdrew his request for the seventh piece, the crumpled-up piece of paper that had been used in the so-called scent lineup, but he didn't waive his right to test any of the evidence that was currently missing from Bill's files, should any of it be found in the future. More importantly still, Judge Dugan granted Pirolo's request that the DNA testing be conducted at an independent laboratory within thirty days. The evidence was to be forwarded to Orchid Cellmark Laboratory in Farmers Branch, Texas, a state-of-the-art lab deemed credible, professional, and above all, neutral by the Innocence Project of Florida.

Pirolo turned to Bill, and the snarl he'd been wearing all day disappeared. They had won this round.

It had to be an epiphanic plan, Bill thought, that he'd won this crucial victory on July 3, just a few short hours before Independence Day.

But the state, still dragging its heels, tried to stall progress wherever and however it could. It began by claiming it had not properly preserved the blood evidence from the victim. Had the move been anything other than a delay tactic, the state would have then requested an exhumation of James Dvorak's body in order to obtain viable DNA samples for comparison analysis. But the state was just getting started. Thirty days soon became sixty and then ninety, and before long more than a year had gone by without the state turning over all of the evidence to be sent to the lab.

Finally, Judge Dugan ordered another hearing, which he used to chastise the state attorneys for their failure to comply.

Bill watched in amusement as the judge essentially told the stammering state attorneys to shit or get off the pot. If they didn't fully comply with his orders to turn over all evidence for DNA testing, Judge Dugan warned them, he would order Bill's release.

With no choice but to comply, the state finally made good on its obligations, and a few weeks later, in late July of 2008, Bill received a phone call at Hardee. The whole Innocence Project of Florida's office was on speakerphone.

"Bill," Melissa Montel said after informing him that she had some good news to share, "the DNA is back, and they have proven that your

DNA is *not* on the Surf-It T-shirt. They found the DNA of two males on the shirt, and neither is yours."

Bill felt twenty-seven years' worth of waiting drain from his shoulders. "I already knew that!" he said excitedly. "I'm the only one who knew that."

In fact, his DNA had not been found on any of the evidence tested. The results did, however, prove that it was James Dvorak's blood on the shirt, which meant that the serology results presented at trial that had excluded both Bill and Dvorak from the blood stains on the shirt had been half wrong. It also meant that Bill's supposition, that the T-shirt used by the prosecution to convict him hadn't belonged to the crime, was also wrong. Bill had posited in his motion for DNA testing that the T-shirt should be tested because neither his nor Dvorak's blood had been found on it. The serologist's original findings, that there were certain blood enzymes on the shirt in common with Bill and the victim but no blood type match, had been used as a smokescreen to convince the jury that the results had been inconclusive. But this hadn't stopped Hunt from waving the shirt in front of the jury during his closing statements and insisting that it *was* Bill's shirt. Now there was definitive proof that Bill had not worn the yellow Surf-It T-shirt—and that Dvorak's blood *had* been on it, after all.

Pirolo called for Bill's immediate release.

The state responded by dragging things out for another four months, even backpedaling on the importance of the yellow Surf-It T-shirt. Just because Bill's DNA hadn't been found on it, they argued, didn't mean Bill hadn't committed the crime. It was a galling statement, considering Michael Hunt and Karen Thompson had mentioned the shirt sixty-two times during the trial, including eight times in their opening arguments and four times in their closing arguments. They had considered it damning evidence, which John Preston and his dog Harass II had supposedly linked to Bill. Now the state wanted to disown it.

Refusing to concede defeat, the prosecution grasped at straws trying to find a way to connect Bill to its prized shirt even if the DNA didn't. Suddenly, out of thin air, Sandra Weeks, a former professional surfer, mysteriously came forward to claim that she had dropped Bill off at the Pelican on the night of the murder. The prosecution, trying to pull a rabbit out of a hat, proposed that Bill may have gotten the Surf-It T-shirt from her, and leaked their newly proposed theory to the press. Never mind the fact that she had never appeared at the trial—or that her narrative was at odds with the one Michael Hunt and Karen Thompson had so carefully created decades earlier. Even without Donna's testimony, without Roger

Dale Chapman's testimony, without Bill's DNA on the Surf-It T-shirt, and with the sensational John Preston being exposed as a fraud, the state, in a desperate move, was still trying to build a case against Bill all the while still using the shirt!

Perhaps had Frank Clark still been acting as Bill's attorney, the state might have succeeded in its latest ploy. But Mike Pirolo, furious that the state was playing dirty, had his staff do a little digging, and what his team unearthed was nothing short of infuriating. Weeks, a former convict, had violated her probation and was awaiting re-sentencing. The circumstances surrounding this previously unknown witness were suspicious to say the least and evoked shades of jailhouse snitch Roger Dale Chapman. Perhaps she was offered a favor and the state was once again more than willing to deal.

Bill, though still locked up, was ecstatic. Yes, it was discouraging to see the state was still plotting against him, but at least he wasn't alone. His brave new team of attorneys was going toe to toe with the machine that had put him behind bars for twenty-seven years. Rather than standing idly by while the state trotted out Sandra Weeks, Pirolo and Co. had done their homework and discredited Weeks before her story could gain any traction. Not surprisingly, the prosecution abandoned its latest gambit and never again mentioned Weeks.

On November 14, Judge Dugan vacated Bill's sentence. The judge scheduled an immediate hearing for later that same day, and in that moment, Bill knew he had won.

Two guards hurriedly escorted Bill to the loading dock, and there he was callously stuffed into a dog cage for the trip to the county jail. His back ached—the cage was too small for his rangy frame. And his hands, tied between his legs to a metal loop on the floor of the cage, would be unavailable to him should the van transporting him get into an accident. The cage was a death trap, but he had no choice but to endure this one last indignity. Neither guard seemed to care. Bill was still a maximum security prisoner, still unworthy of humane treatment.

At the courthouse, Bill stood before Judge Dugan. Twenty-seven and a half years earlier—a lifetime ago—he had been sentenced to life in prison. In that time, he had lost his youth, his dreams, his brash naivete. He had been hardened by brutality and indifference, enduring one mortification after another. He had been dehumanized and nearly destroyed. All for a crime he hadn't committed.

"Your sentence has been vacated," Judge Dugan informed him. "You will be remanded to the county jail for a new trial."

An overpowering wave of tension and fury that had been building for twenty-seven years began to break. Finally, people were beginning to believe in his innocence.

Four days later, on November 18, 2008, Bill returned to the courtroom for his bond hearing, and Judge Dugan, after setting a low bond, released Bill into the custody of his brother Joe, pending a new trial. Bill would have to wear an ankle bracelet with a GPS monitor attached to it, but he would be free.

He was driven back to the county jail in Sharpes, where he changed into civilian clothes for the first time in twenty-seven and a half years: new slacks, a new black T-shirt provided by the Innocence Project that read NOT GUILTY and a brown blazer. He then waited in a small, nondescript room for his release. On the other side of the door was an outer lobby, beyond which lay the jailhouse exit and a long ramp to the outside world.

A guard entered the room and addressed Bill. "There's been a holdup. You're going to have to hold on."

Bill tried to shake off a wave of anxiety. Was the state still fighting his release? They'd likely break any law, he worried, to make sure he didn't go free.

Finally the guard nodded and opened the door for him.

Bill, relieved, walked quickly through the door and did a double take as soon as he saw the crowd of people assembled in the lobby. Waiting for him were his family and friends, Mike Pirolo, everyone from the Innocence Project of Florida, and news reporters.

His family rushed to his side, and Bill, overwhelmed at the sight of so many well-wishers, embraced his parents and siblings in a giant bear hug. For years he'd felt like a terminal cancer patient burdened by his inescapable fate, fearfully awaiting his final breath. Now he knew he had something much more potent on his side than any corrupt power broker could dish out. He had the unbeatable combination of breathtaking cutting-edge science and the truth.

It has been said that DNA is God's signature—that every nucleus in our body contains the language of God. At that moment, Bill knew God had authenticated his innocence and had signed off on his freedom.

CHAPTER 31

FREEDOM

Just eight months shy of his fiftieth birthday, Bill was a free man trading hugs and handshakes with his supporters in the county jail lobby.

"It's a feeling I know I will never feel again," he told the press, referring to the exhilaration that nearly overwhelmed him. "It's like a man wandering in the desert who finally finds water."

But even that comparison fell far short of the euphoria now buoying him.

Before he could catch his breath, he turned to see none other than Wilton Dedge, a brother in pain and endurance, a man who had spent twenty-two years in prison for a crime he hadn't committed before DNA evidence had exonerated him. The two men greeted one another warmly. They had given a combined total of nearly fifty years to the State of Florida, each man spending the prime of his life in prison due to false evidence. Now they were both free.

As someone who had suffered an even longer incarceration, Bill now owned the dubious distinction of having served the longest sentence to date of any DNA exoneree[9] in America.

Bill, still overwhelmed by all the fanfare, proceeded down the ramp that connected the jail to the free world, his family and supporters in tow, and as he walked toward the sunlight, he felt like angels were carrying him down the concrete ramp. He paused briefly to answer questions from the press; his brother Joe and his mother joining the tearful Q&A session.

---

9   Exoneree—A person who was convicted of a crime and later officially declared innocent of that crime. Today there are exonerees who have served longer sentences.

"When I first went behind the bars," Bill said, choking on tears, "I couldn't believe it happened. And then . . ." He paused to gather himself. "I never thought it would be corrected."

While Bill's family consoled him, Joe finally requested that the group be allowed to go home. It was time to celebrate and begin to heal.

Seth Miller and David Menschel of the Innocence Project of Florida spoke to the media next. Miller, the executive director, was dressed in a dark suit and bow tie. His dark hair, meticulously groomed beard, and calm delivery belied his relative youth.

"The fact that they're even entertaining a retrial is somewhat preposterous," he said. "It's high time the state drops the charges in this case and ends this charade."

David Menschel, the legal director, spoke next. Trim, handsome, with sandy brown hair and a clean-shaven face, he was in his prime, just like Miller, and had a sharp legal mind to match his passion. Though he was dressed casually, with the collar of his dress shirt peeking above his sweater, his fiery delivery was anything but casual.

"This is a case not just about a corrupt dog handler," he said after pointing out that the state's best witness, Donna Parrish, had already admitted to committing perjury on the stand. "This is a case about a corrupt sheriff's office and about a corrupt state attorney's office. Governor Crist needs to come in and figure out exactly who was doing that, investigate, and *arrest* the people who were doing that."

Miller and Menschel, far from appearing satisfied by Bill's release, had just reminded the media that justice was still in the balance. Bill still had a case pending against him, and the people who had wrongfully convicted him had yet to face any consequences.

At Joe's house, meanwhile, Bill ate lasagna and salad, did an interview with the local TV news, and tried to get used to the idea of living without bars for walls. Before the night was over, he played his nephew Zach's guitar and sang one of his favorite songs, "Lucky Man," made famous by the country music duo Montgomery Gentry.

Later, after all of his well-wishers had departed, Bill retired to the guest room and lowered himself to the bed. In prison, he'd grown accustomed to sleeping with lights on in the corridors and guards shining flashlights in his face to make sure he was in his bunk. As a result, he'd lost his night vision, not to mention his ability to orient himself in the dark. He'd also developed a powerful fear of the dark. But tonight he was just happy to be a free man.

He had rehearsed this moment a million times in his head, and now it had finally arrived. With the light on and the TV flickering in front of him, he gradually drifted off to sleep.

There was only one thing Bill had wanted as much as his freedom: a fair trial. Now he hoped to get one with the help of his feisty public defender. Michael Pirolo told Bill he was determined to get all of Bill's charges dropped, but since Bill had been released pending a new trial, Pirolo wisely filed a "swift and speedy trial" request, with the deadline set for February 14, 2009, just three months away. This would force the prosecution to make its case posthaste—or quit it altogether.

Bill, meanwhile, tried to adjust to the twenty-first century. Computers, cell phones, flat-screen TVs, debit cards, robotics—all were new to him. So was Barrack Obama, who was only weeks away from being sworn in as the first African American president of the United States, and the International Space Station, which had just received a payload from the space shuttle *Endeavour*. Bill felt like he'd just emerged from a time capsule.

Bill had assumed that, upon his release, there would be a government program of some kind to help him adjust to life outside of prison. But there was no local, state, or federal program in place to help ex-cons who had been *wrongly* convicted of a crime. In fact, had he been guilty and paroled, he would have received one hundred dollars and been entered into an assistance program. But he was innocent, which meant no vocational, educational, or financial support would be forthcoming from the state. Nationwide, precious few men or women were ever exonerated, and those lucky enough to win their freedom found themselves in no-man's-land.

The Innocence Project of Florida would, in the days and weeks to come, help Bill meet some of his critical medical expenses, but most of its resources were earmarked for legal defense and DNA testing. Thus most of Bill's support came from his family, particularly his brother Joe and sister-in-law Traci, who had offered Bill their home as a temporary place to stay until he was back on his feet. But even Bill's family, though willing to offer support, was unprepared to help him rebuild his life. Bill was essentially a stranger to them. He had been through harrowing trials and tribulations that they could hardly fathom.

For his part, Bill didn't know how to live like a free man. He turned his brother and sister-in-law's guest room into a kind of cell, rarely venturing out and even eating his meals there. When he did leave his room and the house, he invariably got lost, which only reinforced his desire to stay put. His long-lost sense of direction, still dormant, coupled with his rusty driving skills, kept him anchored in place.

Bill caught a lucky break a few days after his release when a kindhearted man at the local NAPA, auto parts, store in Melbourne heard his story and offered him a job. Bill, knowing full well that he wasn't qualified to do anything other than perform manual labor and that his résumé included a twenty-seven-year stint in prison, gladly accepted.

After about a week on the job, Bill purchased a 1996 Dodge pickup truck for $1,200—a loan from his parents. Each day, he drove to NAPA at seven thirty in the morning, GPS ankle bracelet still attached, ready to go to work. Although grateful for the opportunity, he was leery of being out in public with charges still pending against him. How would people feel about him? Would they assume he was guilty? He spent most of his first day performing small chores, some of which he found hard to remember. It had been a long time since he'd been entrusted to do anything beyond maintaining a band room or picking up litter. But soon enough, he was assigned to the stock room, where he learned to manage the inventory and spent endless hours lifting and moving heavy steel cylinder tractor trailer wheel hubs, brakes, and huge twelve-cell batteries from the loading dock. On most mornings, he was the first to arrive and would spend a few minutes in the cab of his pickup truck eating the same breakfast: two chocolate donuts from Dunkin' Donuts.

Occasionally Bill's supervisors would ask him to deliver parts around town, and inevitably Bill would get lost and have a hard time finding his way back to the store. Sometimes he'd get so confused he would forget where he was supposed to be going in the first place. He was easily distracted by the fast-paced activity going on all around him and often felt overwhelmed or frustrated as a result. The simplest tasks—such as figuring out what to buy on a small salary at a bustling grocery store bursting with countless products—felt daunting. To compensate, he kept things as simple as possible. Thus every day he ate a peanut butter sandwich for lunch—sometimes two.

Mike Pirolo, too, was keeping things simple in his defense of Bill. No longer willing to be pushed around by the state attorney's office, Pirolo had filed multiple subpoenas to depose several of the state's own attorneys, the detectives involved in Bill's case, and even a number of other witnesses for the prosecution. It was time to get to the bottom of what was really going on. The state was hiding something, and Pirolo was going to make everybody—the state attorneys, the cops, the state's witnesses—raise their right hands and give testimony under oath.

On December 10, twenty-two days after his release, Bill was standing in Joe and Traci's driveway when he got a call from Pirolo.

"We got a fax this morning from the state attorney's office," Pirolo said. "You're a free man."

Bill felt his stomach leap. "*What?*"

"It's called a nolle prosequi order," Pirolo explained. "All charges have been dropped!"

"Just like that?"

"Just like that. They didn't even bother to call or send us a letter or give us any kind of heads up. They just sent the news in a fax. You can get that monitor taken off anytime."

Bill couldn't believe his ears. The state, facing the daunting prospect of having its *own* people called to the stand, had declined to retry him for the murder of James Dvorak. Moreover, if the prosecution failed to file new charges before February 14, which by now was only two months away, Bill could never again be tried for the same crime. Pirolo had done it: he had countered the state's slippery tactics with a hard-nosed, take-no-prisoners campaign and had won Bill's freedom as a result.

Bill had the GPS monitor removed from his ankle—and was charged two hundred dollars for its use. He had to fork over the money *before* the authorities would remove the monitor.

Afterward, Bill's brothers and nephew happily threw Bill, fully clothed, into his brother's pool. It was time to celebrate.

Bill spent Christmas and the New Year with his family, and in February he met with John Torres, the hip, charismatic journalist at *Florida Today* who had been assigned to Bill's case long before his release and had visited Bill at the county jail. Torres and his crew followed Bill around with a camera and chronicled the challenges inherent in transitioning from prison life to freedom on the outside. Although it would take several months to complete, the resulting documentary, entitled *A Lifetime Lost*, would eventually air by year's end on local television as well as *Florida Today*'s website.[10]

---

10   The critically acclaimed documentary would go on to win an award for excellence in broadcasting.

In the meantime, Bill was slowly realizing that it wasn't just vindication he sought. He wanted a future. Unfortunately, everyone around him seemed to have set their expectations for him awfully low. Perhaps others thought it was enough for him to work for minimum wage at a dead-end job or wait for the state to someday compensate him. But he felt compelled to do something with his newfound freedom, to take strides toward fulfilling his destiny, even if he was unsure how to move forward. It was possible he was overestimating what he was capable of achieving, but he didn't think so. He felt certain he could do more than manage the inventory at NAPA. He could help others—touch them on some deeper level.

Bill took a step closer to securing a more resonant future when February 14 came and went without the state refiling charges against him. He could never again be charged for the murder of James Dvorak. To his chagrin, the state wouldn't admit that he was innocent, only that it didn't have enough evidence to bring him to trial. But Bill, rather than focusing on the limits of his victory, instead chose to recognize the symbolic nature of the occasion. Back at Polk, more than a decade earlier, he had made a conscious decision to let go of the hate that was consuming him. Instead, he had chosen hope. He had chosen love. It was that choice, he now knew, that had led to his freedom, for he had purposefully allowed goodness to enter his life. From that moment on, angels had appeared in his life to help guide him: the mysterious law clerk at the library in Okeechobee; the indefatigable Michael Pirolo, who had willingly put his career on the line for Bill and gone toe to toe with corrupt officials; the good people at the Innocence Project of Florida, each of them passionately dedicated to justice; Judge Dugan, who believed in uncovering the truth; and of course, the soft-spoken clerk of the court, Monica Levsen, who had located the bloody Surf-It T-shirt in her evidence room and had brought it forth with no hesitation.

Without any one of those angels, Bill thought, he might very well be living behind bars still. But he had opened himself up to the possibility that his life might amount to more than one long, dark winter, that even as he approached the age of fifty, he still might drink in the promise of a new spring. Thus it was that his future was officially rescued on Valentine's Day, 2009. For such an auspicious moment to arrive on such an emblematic day, he knew could only mean that sunnier days lay ahead, that the love he had so obstinately clung to might someday be returned to him.

PART III

CHAPTER 32

STUCK

On March 20, 2009, William Dillon and I crossed paths for the first time at the Innocence Project Conference in Houston, Texas. I was networking. He was taking in the spectacle of 150 ex-cons, attorneys, and others congregating under one roof. While I was there in my capacity as the president and CEO of DNA Diagnostics Center, the event's sponsor, Bill was only four months removed from prison. He had come to the annual conference at the behest of the Innocence Project Network, which had invited recently exonerated men and women from across the country to attend.

For me, traveling to the event was nothing unusual. Every week, I commuted from my residence in Chapel Hill, North Carolina, to my job in Cincinnati, Ohio. In addition, my job often required travel. Bill, on the other hand, hadn't been on a plane in nearly thirty years. For him, the trip had been a startling revelation. The world was moving at a much faster pace, and nowhere was that frenetic energy more evident than at the nation's airports.

After shaking Bill's hand at Cabo, the lively "Mix-Mex" grill hosting our event, I pegged him for an attorney, what with his mellifluous speaking voice and his horn-rimmed glasses.

But he quickly disabused me of that notion.

"What's your story?" I asked, looking up at the handsome, blue-jean-clad man.

"I spent twenty-seven and a half years in prison for a murder I didn't commit," he answered casually.

Not only was I taken off guard I felt punched in the gut. Regardless of the occasion, I didn't expect that response. Frankly, he didn't fit the "profile" that we are all trained not to acknowledge but instinctively can't seem to ignore.

Bill had been talking to Cassie Johnson, a forensic scientist at the Texas lab that had tested Bill's DNA against the evidence reluctantly supplied by the Brevard County Sheriff's Department. Cassie explained to me who Bill was and how her lab had aided in his exoneration.

Then Bill smiled and shyly offered to buy me a drink.

"I'm on duty," I replied, "but I'd love a Diet Coke."

He bought me that Coke and then, with the restaurant buzzing around us, told me his story.

Captivated by his words, I saw a man who had been stripped of everything—liberty, dignity, opportunity—yet had somehow managed to hold on to his humanity as well as his sense of self. His broad smile radiated warmth, even if his blue eyes hinted at the hardships he had endured. By some miracle, prison hadn't stolen his intellect. Nor had it hardened his soul. He possessed a rare combination of open-hearted naivete and gentle wisdom. From the first moment he began speaking in his baritone voice, I trusted him. After hearing his story, I never doubted his innocence.

My head spun. How could such an injustice be visited upon an innocent man? The details of his case shook me to my core, and I found myself asking him several personal questions. They were none of my business, but I couldn't help myself.

"How are you doing?" I asked. "Have you seen any doctors? Are you getting any psychological help? Do you have a place to stay? What are you doing for money?"

Bill answered each question calmly and matter-of-factly. But after telling me he was working at NAPA and staying with his brother, he became emotional. "I feel stuck," he said. "I'm free now, but I feel stuck. I don't really know what to do."

I could feel his vulnerability. "I understand," I replied. "I've felt stuck at times in my life also, but the amazing thing is that each time I've felt stuck, something or someone came along that got me unstuck. It will happen to you too," I tried to reassure. Little did I know at the time how much soothsaying there was in my words.

I was eventually pulled away and into another conversation, but as the night wore on and I worked my way through the restaurant, I noticed Bill shadowing me. When I walked out onto the patio, he followed. And when I went downstairs, so did he. I could feel his eyes on me, but I wasn't in the least bit frightened or put off by his behavior. He had a sincere expression on his face.

If Bill and I didn't make a more lasting connection that night, it wasn't for his lack of trying. Unfortunately for him, I was in business-mode and was too busy meeting and greeting other people to think too much about the attention he was paying me, although the instant rapport between us made a strong impression on me.

Finally, Bill approached me and said somewhat bashfully, "I really like you. I'm never like this, but I really want to talk to you."

I handed him my business card.

He glanced at the title next to my name. "So you're a big cheese, huh?" he said.

I laughed off the compliment.

A few minutes later, I spotted him on the opposite side of the second-floor buffet room looking in my direction while he spoke on the phone. I didn't know it at the time, but he was leaving me a message on my cell phone.

Eventually it was time for me to leave. I had booked an early flight the next morning and needed to get back to the hotel for some much-needed sleep.

Bill chivalrously walked me outside. "The next time you're in Florida," he said, "I want to take you out to dinner."

I noticed his phone message the next day and realized he was interested in pursuing a friendship.

"Hi Ellen," his message began, "This is Bill. I'm not a stalker. I just really enjoyed talking to you and was hoping we could talk again."

Bill? I thought for moment. *Who was Bill? Oh, the friendly stalker!*, I remembered, laughing to myself. But unfortunately, he hadn't left his phone number, and for some reason my old BlackBerry hadn't registered it. Knowing how fragile his confidence was, given everything he'd been through, I couldn't help but conclude that it had likely taken some courage for him to call me. I didn't want him to think I was avoiding him because he was an ex-convict, albeit an innocent one. So I asked for help from two of my employees who had been at the conference, and eventually their sleuthing led us to the Innocence Project of Florida, which put me in touch with Bill. Soon enough, a friendship was struck.

"I can tell you're all business and everything," Bill said after we spoke on the phone a second time, "but is there a woman in there also?"

"I hope so," I replied with a laugh.

That was when the proverbial light bulb went on above my head. He was clearly reaching out to me on a more personal level—and I didn't mind. In the days that followed, we spoke regularly on the phone. I asked him what he wanted to do with his life, and he seemed pleased that I was curious about his dreams and wasn't simply telling him how he should live his life.

"I want to work on my music," he said.

He had hundreds of songs that he had written in prison, he explained, and was eager to get to work polishing them.

I was excited for him, but also fearful. I felt he was indeed stuck in Florida, not really living his life. Worse, I worried that he wasn't safe there. The media had begun regularly covering his story. That, combined with his many public speaking appearances, made him a high-profile figure. The press loved Bill's story, and this time the cameras were focused on the nefarious tactics of the county and the state. The public outrage was palpable. Neither the Brevard County Sheriff's Department nor the state attorney's office had ceded that he was innocent. Would there be retribution? I couldn't help but wonder. After we had gotten to know each other better, Bill invited me to visit him in Florida. He still wanted to take me out to dinner. I readily agreed and asked him to meet me at my hotel near the airport in Orlando since I'd be flying there. Unbeknownst to me at the time, I was putting Bill in a difficult position. He had rarely ventured out of Brevard County since his release and, not surprisingly, got terribly lost. He drove in circles for hours before finally calling me on my cell phone.

"Where are you?" I asked.

"I don't know," he answered in a frustrated tone. The worry was palpable in his voice. By now he'd driven through numerous tolls—ubiquitous in Orlando—and was probably running out of money.

To my relief, the front desk agent at my hotel was able to guide him to the hotel, and Bill, after a grueling and confusing drive, eventually found me.

I was acutely aware of his living situation and knew he didn't have any money to speak of. Yes, he was saving some expenses by living with his brother and sister-in-law, but how much could he have possibly amassed after working at NAPA for a few months? I couldn't in good conscience let him buy me dinner.

"Will you let me treat?" I asked.

"No," he said adamantly. "I invited you here. Plus, I've wanted to buy you dinner ever since I met you in Houston."

We argued over who would pay until Bill finally came up with a compromise. We walked two blocks to the convenience store on the corner and bought a loaf of bread, a package of bologna, a package of pre-sliced American cheese, a tiny jar of Miracle Whip, and a bag of Lay's potato chips. Then we walked back to my hotel, took the elevator up to my suite, and there Bill made us sandwiches. It was our first date—and the most romantic thing any man had ever done for me. He had next to nothing, yet he wanted to share it with me. The gesture didn't just endear him to me; it offered me a deep glimpse into his soul, into the kind of man he was.

After dinner, we talked late into the evening, and I was amazed by the breadth of his wisdom.

"Do you know how smart you are?" I asked.

He responded with a smile. "Well, yeah . . . for a prisoner, that is."

"I'm sure you already know it," I said, unwilling to let him off the hook so easily, "but just in case you don't, you need to know that you're exceptional intellectually. Don't ever let anyone make you think otherwise."

"Well, I wasn't too smart back when I was convicted, was I?" Bill retorted. "I never for one minute thought I could get convicted without real evidence."

As wise as I thought Bill was, I also knew that he was terribly inexperienced in the outside world. He had been told he was nothing but a piece of garbage for his entire adult life. Did he have enough self-confidence to resist manipulation? Would he make an easy target for others? I wanted him to know that he should trust his own mind and not let anyone push him into doing something he didn't want to do.

Bill and I continued to talk on the phone and visit whenever we got the chance, and every time I spoke with him, I learned something new, not just about his case but about the resilience of the human spirit. Despite everything he'd been through, he radiated strength, grace, and forgiveness. He didn't wallow in self-pity. On the contrary, he maintained a self-deprecating sense of humor and often poked fun at himself.

In June, Bill was contacted by Guy Spearman, a well-respected lobbyist from Tallahassee who owned a home in Brevard County. Guy had helped Wilton Dedge receive compensation for twenty-two years of wrongful imprisonment. At the time, Spearman had been forced to file a special claims bill on Dedge's behalf in order to win compensation from the state, but not long afterward, the Florida legislature had passed the Victims of Wrongful Incarceration Compensation Act, which provided $50,000 per year of wrongful incarceration. Thanks to the bill, exonerees didn't need to hire expensive legal counsel in order to obtain financial relief. It was automatic—with one exception. A "clean hands" provision, cleverly embedded in the law, prohibited compensation to anyone with a prior felony, even a nonviolent one.

Bill, of course, had been pulled over by the police at the age of nineteen and caught with exactly one joint and one Quaalude in his pocket. At the time, he had been given the option to plead-out so the third-degree felony would never show on his criminal record, and for the past thirty years, that was where his youthful indiscretion had remained—off the record. Until now. When Bill, with the help of Spearman, began seeking compensation, the drug possession mysteriously reappeared on his record.[11] One Quaalude pill, a pill he had never intended to take and had merely accepted from a car full of college kids, had the potential to cost him $1,350,000, the amount of money he was owed from the state under the compensation statute.

Spearman, undeterred by Bill's criminal record, offered to help. Although he didn't know Bill personally, he believed in doing the right thing, which in this case meant marshaling his considerable influence and connections to help Bill on a pro bono basis file a special claims bill in the Florida legislature. Since Bill didn't qualify for automatic compensation, Spearman would need to secure an attorney *and* a sponsor for Bill. Spearman had only one person in mind for the job: Sandy D'Alemberte, past president of the Florida Bar, past president of Florida State University, and

---

11 Bill's pre-sentencing report, which is the report a judge reviews before handing down a sentence, shows that he was charged for possession of Methaqualone (the Quaalude pill) and that the possession was discharged as "Poss. Methaqualone, 3 yrs. Probation, Adj. W/H [Adjudication withheld]." To this day, it is unknown who changed Bill's record—or how it was changed.

a former Florida legislator. Although D'Alemberte was out of the country at that time, Spearman promised he would contact him as soon as possible.

In the meantime, my client list expanded to include the folks at the Innocence Project of Florida, and when I met one day with Seth Miller and Melissa Montel, they indicated a desire to see Bill leave Florida, at least for the time being. Like me, they were concerned the Brevard County Sheriff's Department might try to implicate him in something—all while trying to refurbish its own tarnished reputation. Given how suspiciously the police had conducted the investigation of James Dvorak's murder, it didn't seem like much of a stretch to imagine them doing something to deflect the scrutiny they were currently facing in the community. And the corruption didn't end there. The state attorney's office seemingly had done everything it could to destroy an innocent man.

For his part, Bill was showing more self-assurance every day. As we grew closer, he seemed more comfortable sharing his deepest fears with me, including his concerns about his situation. As much as he appreciated his family's support, he felt like they were still treating him like the twenty-one-year-old kid who went to prison. It was as if they couldn't relate to him as an adult. Not that he blamed them. Who could fully fathom what he had been through? He felt stuck in Florida, where the reality of daily living had not lived up to the dreams of freedom he had played over and over in his head while behind bars.

"I feel like I'm still in prison in a way," he said one day. "I can't imagine things ever getting better."

"Come to North Carolina," I said without hesitation. "You can stay at my house in Chapel Hill. There's plenty of room for you."

It was a rather bold move on my part, but I felt strongly that he needed to be somewhere where he could get unstuck, where he could settle his mind and start over, minus all the baggage that weighed him down in Florida.

Bill packed everything he owned into a few boxes and headed north. On the day he moved, July 31, 2009, CNN aired a special report on his case, with TV anchor Anderson Cooper narrating the story of John Preston and his fraudulent dog handling practice.

As we sat in the living room watching the program, Bill appeared energized and comforted by his surroundings. I was sure he was experiencing a bit of culture shock. He'd never had the luxury of space, and it was decades since he had any of the finer things in life. Now here he was, moving into a contemporary four-bedroom house that totaled nearly four thousand square feet.

Previously, I was a vice president of Laboratory Corporation of America, (Labcorp) directing the company's DNA Identification Testing Division. This was a position I held for twenty years, and Chapel Hill made for a great base of operations.

For the first time in nearly three decades, Bill said, he felt like he had a home. But it would only be his home on the weekends. When I gave him the option of spending each workweek alone in Chapel Hill or accompanying me to Cincinnati, where DNA Diagnostics Center was renting me a small house, he chose the latter. It was a ten-hour commute between the two homes, which meant we spent most of the weekend on the road. So we started coming home less and less. But each time we made the trek to Chapel Hill, Bill said he loved North Carolina.

When our first Monday morning in Cincinnati rolled around, after a quick shower and breakfast, I said goodbye to Bill and left for work. When I returned that evening, he was famished.

"Didn't you have lunch?" I asked.

"I haven't eaten since we had breakfast," he answered.

I looked at my watch. It was almost seven thirty. "Why didn't you have something?"

He shrugged. "I didn't know what to eat."

"But the cabinets are full of food," I replied, confused. "You just need to pick something when you're hungry."

"I know," he said, "but I couldn't decide what to eat, so I just waited for you."

We had the same conversation the next evening—and the next and the next.

Finally, I started making him a lunch before I left for work each morning, either a sandwich or something he could heat up in the microwave. For a while, the lunches went untouched. But eventually he started nibbling at them, and finally he was eating the whole meal. Simple choices, I was learning, overwhelmed Bill. While at NAPA, he had eaten the same meals—two chocolate donuts for breakfast and a peanut butter sandwich for lunch—every day, never deviating from the routine. If I took him to a restaurant, he struggled with the menu and all the choices—usually giving up and asking me to order for him. Fancy restaurants didn't interest him.

Words like *balsamic reduction* and *mesquite* sounded like a foreign language. He preferred fast-food restaurants, where ordering was less convoluted.

One day, determined to help him regain a measure of independence, I asked him to go to the grocery store and get some soap. He needed to take small steps, I reasoned, to rebuild his confidence, and since he'd just begun to drive again and run small errands by himself, this one seemed doable. But when he got to the grocery store, he was so overwhelmed by the number of options, he returned without any soap.

While I found his behavior baffling at first, it didn't take long to understand why choices were so difficult for him. For nearly three decades, he'd made hardly any decisions for himself, and now he was being bombarded with choices every day. The net effect was incapacitating.

Anthony Scott, a social worker with the Innocence Project of Florida, had arranged for Bill to see several counselors and doctors near our house in Cincinnati. But it was a doctor we located in Chapel Hill who made the diagnosis one day in September: Bill was suffering from post-traumatic stress disorder (PTSD). All the hallmark symptoms were there: crowds terrified him, he was always looking over his shoulder, he was easily startled, he suffered nightmares and flashbacks, and he feared that someday the state would fabricate a reason to put him back in prison. Being diagnosed only added to Bill's anxiety. How would he cope? Would things get worse? What did the future hold for him?

Bill began seeing a therapist several days a week. She taught him coping skills and employed strategies used by the military to help soldiers returning home from war. It would be a long road to recovery, but Bill was determined to conquer his challenges.

In a just world, he would have qualified for disability assistance, but the Social Security Administration didn't recognize him. Although he had worked for the State of Florida for nearly three decades, an innocent man trading away his labor for slave wages or no wages at all, he had been granted no points in the Social Security system. Nor had he qualified for retirement benefits. The state had taken everything from him, including his entitled security.

CHAPTER 33
ANOTHER RECANTATION

By the time fall rolled around, Bill had settled into a routine of working on his music all day while I was at the office. One night after coming home late from work, I was getting ready for bed when Bill called to me from the small office next to the bedroom.

"What is it?" I asked from the office doorway.

He was seated at the computer and had an astonished look on his face. "It's an email from Douglas Cheshire's son. The Florida Innocence Project forwarded it to me. He heard about my release and wanted to personally apologize to me for the actions of his father and his father's administration."

Bill was clearly touched and buoyed by the gesture. "That couldn't have been easy for him."

I knew enough to know that Douglas Cheshire had been the chief state attorney during Bill's arrest and trial—and that Cheshire's administration had been rife with corruption. But I was only vaguely aware of the details.

We sat down on the bed, and for the next hour Bill brought me up to speed on the powerful role Cheshire had played in Bill's case. State attorney Douglas Cheshire was widely believed to have been running a crooked organization. Many had known at the time how unscrupulous the office could be—from its reliance on shady jailhouse snitches to the grooming of the fraudulent John Preston and his dogs as a go-to witness for the state—but no one had ever been held responsible for the corruption. It was chilling to hear Bill trace the malfeasance at his trial back to Cheshire. Why hadn't anyone investigated the man or his administration in the years since?

Bill accidentally deleted the email before he could respond, and to this day hopes to someday thank Cheshire's son for the gesture. The email from Douglas Cheshire's son was all part of my education as I slowly learned the myriad details of Bill's case. I didn't want to push Bill, so I never sat down and interviewed him. Instead, I let the stories come out slowly, as he was ready to share them. The last thing I wanted to do was force him to relive any troubling experiences. He was in the midst of a healing transition. I didn't want to deter his progress by dredging up the painful past.

In fact, as the months went by, Bill began to sleep better, eat better, and exhibit more confidence. He was smiling more. Laughing more. He was regaining his health as well as the understanding that he belonged in the world. He wasn't an alien.

Later that fall, I helped Bill establish the William Dillon Freedom Foundation, which he created to raise awareness of the plight of exonerees and the lack of resources available to them. He worked hard on launching the website, and in the process learned a lot about graphic and web design. No longer a victim of circumstances, Bill had a clear mission: to spread the word about wrongful convictions. His website and his music would serve as dual platforms from which to communicate his message.

Lobbyist Guy Spearman, meanwhile, contacted us with some great news: he had succeeded in bringing aboard attorney Sandy D'Alemberte, the man with a legal and political résumé a mile long. Guy and Sandy had successfully represented Wilton Dedge in his efforts to obtain compensation from the state, tirelessly battling the Brevard County State Attorney's Office, which had done everything in its power to prevent Dedge from being fairly compensated. Now Sandy, a true Southern gentleman and a highly respected figure in Florida, had agreed to represent Bill on a pro bono basis, quipping that the payment for his efforts was to be exactly double what Guy was receiving.

Guy and Sandy worked diligently behind the scenes with the Brevard County delegation and Florida Senate President-Designate Mike Haridopolos, a Republican from Melbourne. Their efforts paid off when Senator Haridopolos agreed to sponsor SB 22, a claims bill to compensate Bill.

On Monday, November 2, 2009, Bill and I traveled to Tallahassee for a special hearing on the bill. At the entrance to the Administrative Law Building, a full-scale security check, much like those at airports, was in place. After walking through the full-body scanner and having our belongings checked, we proceeded to the hearing room, a starkly appointed, plain vanilla space. Judge Bram Canter, special master of the hearing, sat in the front and was flanked on his right by Tom Thomas, a staff attorney appointed by the House of Representatives. To the judge's left was an empty witness box. Those in the audience sat in long rows of upholstered wooden benches. I took a seat next to Taylor Nix, Guy Spearman's assistant, in the front row. Bill joined Sandy and Seth and Melissa from the Innocence Project of Florida at a long table right in front. A large contingent of local television and print reporters, including one from the Associated Press, was also on hand.

The hearing would function as a mini-trial of sorts, after which Judge Canter and Representative Thomas would make their recommendations to the Florida legislature as to the merits of compensating Bill. Not surprisingly, Norman Wolfinger, the chief of the state attorney's office at that time, had two months earlier issued a formal statement opposing SB 22. Wolfinger, refusing to call Bill innocent, had explained that the only reason the state wasn't retrying Bill was because nine of the original witnesses had since passed away and another was too sick to testify. Despite all of the other exculpatory evidence, Wolfinger had said that he didn't feel the absence of Bill's DNA on the Surf-It T-shirt had exonerated him.

In effect, Bill was being tried all over again. Only this time he was presumed guilty. He would *now* have to prove "actual innocence," the standard that had to be met in order for him to qualify for compensation from the state.

Twenty-nine years older and dressed in a suit and tie, Bill entered the witness box for the first time since his trial. And as Judge Canter and Representative Thomas grilled him on the events leading up to the 1981 murder, forcing him to revisit his painful past, Bill broke down in tears.

To Bill, the money was of secondary significance. He wanted something far more important: vindication. He wanted everyone, from the media to the authorities to the people in the audience, to know that he was innocent, that he had been dealt a huge injustice. There was an awful lot at stake, and Bill's tears proved it.

Judge Canter and Representative Thomas asked Bill about the events surrounding his supposed jailhouse confession to Roger Dale Chapman, and Bill reiterated what he had explained long ago: that he'd been in the bullpen, a large cell populated by more than twenty inmates, at the time when Chapman claimed the two had met, and that he hadn't known Chapman and didn't remember speaking to him in jail. He certainly never confessed to the stranger.

Bill was finally excused from the witness box, and Sandy D'Alemberte, dressed in a dashing gray suit and bow tie, stood. With his silvery-white hair and wire-rimmed glasses, the elder statesman exuded a remarkable combination of wisdom and calm.

In an astonishing move that electrified the courtroom, Sandy called a surprise witness. Roger Dale Chapman, aged and skinny, entered the witness box. He had just been released from prison and, surprisingly to us, had insisted on making an appearance at the hearing rather than submit a written statement. He had something to say to Bill—and wanted to deliver the message face-to-face.

I could only imagine what was going through Bill's head. It was the first time he had laid eyes on Chapman since the trial.

As the rest of us looked on, spellbound, Chapman recounted to Sandy the events leading up to his appearance at Bill's trial.

According to Chapman, he had been accused of rape and was in jail, awaiting trial, when he received a call from Detective Thom Fair, who was inquiring about the murder of James Dvorak. According to Chapman, Fair told him it was in his best interest to become an agent of the state, which would mean entering the bullpen where Bill was being held and quizzing Bill about the murder. Chapman did as he was told, but when the story of the murder came on the television and Chapman asked Bill about it, Bill vehemently denied any involvement. Shortly thereafter, Fair returned to meet with Chapman. According to Chapman, he held out his hand and said, "I have your life in the palm of my hand, and if you don't give me something on Dillon, I can make that rape charge come back."

"I said, 'Look, he said he didn't do it,'" Chapman told Sandy and the rest of us gathered at the hearing. "He said, 'You are going to say this or you're going to go back to prison.'"

Chapman went on to testify that Fair had called Bill their "fall guy." His recorded statement on August 27, 1981, had been orchestrated by Fair and Officer Wilmer. Chapman reported that he had been escorted to an interrogation room, and after the audio tape had started rolling, Fair had asked him questions while the other detective had held up cue cards telling him what to say.

To back up Chapman's shocking testimony, Sandy entered into evidence secret handwritten notes that had been found in Bill's case files, recently obtained from the clerk of the court's office. In addition to representing that seeking the death penalty for Bill had indeed been on the table, the notes, handwritten by now *Judge* John Dean Moxley, the chief assistant state attorney in 1981, indicated that Chapman had likely been made an agent of the state before Bill had even been assigned an attorney. The notes also showed that Chapman had already been given a bond reduction. Scrawled in Moxley's own handwriting, the notes included two telling admissions: "weak sexual battery charges" and, even more incriminating still, "maybe we should deal." The scandalous evidence was a smoking gun. They knew they didn't have a good case against Chapman, but they still held the charges over his head in order to get him to play the "snitch" and lie at Bill's trial. After Chapman had testified at Bill's trial, the rape charges against him had been dropped.

"Is there anything you want to say to Bill?" Sandy asked Chapman.

Chapman, with a tear in his voice, turned to Bill. "I'm very sorry for what happened." Reporters' cameras flashed as he stood up, left the witness stand, and extended his trembling hand toward Bill. "Can you forgive me?"

Bill hesitated only briefly. He took Chapman's hand and said, "I know you were used. I know they pressured you."

It was a powerful moment. Two men, both abused by the system, with one sacrificing the other's freedom in exchange for his own, were, for the moment at least, on the same side. As Bill would tell me afterward, he had for years fantasized about chasing down Chapman in the prison system, where certainly the odds favored them meeting again, and confronting him for the major role he had played in Bill's wrongful conviction. But now, facing the weak and frail Chapman, Bill could only feel sorrow for the man and relief that the truth was finally finding the light of day. Chapman was merely a pitiful product of a corrupt system. Although not innocent, he was a victim, and there were countless others like him who had been used by Brevard County and the State of Florida to unjustly put other innocent men behind bars.

Bill shook Chapman's hand and fled the courtroom to compose himself.

The hearing lasted just shy of four hours. There were other riveting moments, such as when Cassie Johnson, the expert responsible for testing the DNA on the yellow Surf-It T-shirt, testified by phone from Fort Worth, Texas. She told everyone assembled that her results concluded Bill's DNA was not found on the shirt and that two other unidentified individuals' DNA was found in a mixture on the garment. A new advanced technology was required to analyze the DNA. MiniFiler had the ability to obtain DNA results from difficult samples that previously would have yielded limited or no genetic data. The test was indeed more sophisticated than Florida Department of Law Enforcement's capabilities would have allowed. Her findings indicated that Brevard County Sheriff's Office's investigation completely missed tracking down the true perpetrator. Then there was a brilliant demonstration when attorney Sandy D'Alemberte asked Bill to try on a shirt that measured identically in size to the bloody Surf-It T-shirt. Bill admitted he'd gained a few pounds since his arrest but just the same couldn't get the tiny shirt over his head and shoulders. It was Sandy's "If the shirt doesn't fit . . ." moment and was one more perfect strike against the Brevard prosecutors' bogus theory.

Sandy, after doing everything he could to prove Bill's innocence, closed with a comparison between Bill's case and the case of the recently compensated Wilton Dedge. Both men had been sent to prison on the strength of testimony from a jailhouse snitch and the now thoroughly discredited dog handler John Preston, now deceased.

We left Tallahassee guarded but hopeful. Bill's compensation was now in the hands of the state Senate and House. Two bills, SB 22 in the Senate and HB 61 in the House, would go to committee hearings in each governing body, with Senator Haridopolos sponsoring the Senate bill and Representative Steve Crisafulli, also a Brevard County resident, sponsoring the House bill. Where they went from there was anyone's guess. But one thing was certain: Roger Dale Chapman's testimony had blown open the lid on the corruption in Brevard County and at the state attorney's office. Chapman testified he had been made an agent of the state, but the state had insisted during Bill's trial that no such deal had been made. Such misconduct, typical of a sheriff's office intent on arresting someone regardless of facts, is called "tunnel vision" by those in legal circles, but it was indicative of a broader problem in Brevard County during the 1980s when county and state officials had often employed a pattern and practice of using suspicious, coerced, or even fabricated evidence to make numerous prosecutions stick. Behind Bill's conviction lay this culture of corruption, and it was finally being exposed.

Chapman's testimony was the tip of the iceberg. As Seth Miller wrote on the Innocence Project of Florida's website shortly after the hearing, "I suspect it won't be the last we hear."

CHAPTER 34
NO TIME TO WASTE

When news of Chapman's recantation hit the streets, Brevard County sheriff Jack Parker, bowing to pressure from state legislators and the public, had no choice but to act swiftly. "In light of the sworn testimony provided at yesterday's legislative hearing," Parker told journalist John Torres of *Florida Today*, "we have decided to reopen the homicide investigation involving the murder of James Dvorak, which took place twenty-eight years ago. We need to do everything we can to determine the truth in this case, regardless of whether or not it can be successfully prosecuted."

Seth Miller, sharing his skepticism with Torres, wasn't confident the sheriff's office was capable of investigating itself. "They had the wrong guy in prison for twenty-seven years," Miller was quoted as saying. "I'm surprised it took them a year to do this. If their intentions are in good faith, then everyone should be supportive. Solving murders is their job."

Thom Fair, not surprisingly, called Chapman's new testimony "slanderous, libelous, and defamatory." As far as he was concerned, Bill was still guilty of murdering James Dvorak. He had retired from the sheriff's office in 2000, having served twenty-five years. But now Fair had other things to worry about. What would the sheriff's newly opened investigation reveal about Fair's conduct during Bill's arrest and trial?

For his part, Bill was excited at the prospect of the sheriff finally uncovering the truth. Was Sheriff Parker a good man? Would he try to find the real killer? Bill was hopeful on both fronts. The reinvestigation had the potential to fully exonerate him and finally put to rest any rumors about his involvement in James Dvorak's murder. If there was a downside to Sheriff Parker's decision to reopen the case, it was that Bill's case files would once again be sealed while the investigation was ongoing, but that seemed like a price worth paying if it led to Bill's exoneration as well as the discovery of Dvorak's real murderer.

A presentation to the DNA Diagnostics Center's investors took me to New York City the week of Bill's first anniversary of freedom. I invited Bill to come along for our own celebration in the Big Apple. He had never been to New York, and the city presented a magnificent yet intimidating experience of sights and sounds. While I attended my meeting, he stayed in the hotel room, hesitant to venture out alone. The next day, November 18, 2009, a year after his release, Bill and I paid tribute to his first anniversary as a free man by taking a Hudson River dinner cruise. The city's glowing skyline shone on New York Harbor as we floated beneath the Statue of Liberty, which, bathed in spotlights, stood defiantly against the night sky. While the onboard band played Irving Berlin's "God Bless America," we saluted those Americans who had struggled to come to the promised land in order to escape tyranny and oppression and to live their lives in freedom, unafraid of being persecuted for their beliefs or customs. Standing on the bow of the ship, tears in our eyes, we knew Bill's experiences were unique, that what had happened to him didn't define America any more than it defined him. In fighting to clear his name, we were fighting to protect others from injustice and wrongful convictions.

That fight, we knew, would be a long one. A month and a half later, on New Year's Eve, John Torres's documentary *A Lifetime Lost* aired for the first time. It was gratifying to see Bill's story told, but parts of the program were difficult to watch.

Karen Thompson, the lead prosecuting attorney at Bill's trial and one of several to be interviewed for the documentary, was still as smug as ever. "He came across cocky, immature, and guilty," she said of Bill. "The jury didn't have any trouble at all finding him guilty. They were only out about an hour and a half." Thompson felt that Frank Clark had also contributed to Bill's conviction, saying, "Mr. Dillon had his choice of private counsel. Had he made a different choice, there might have been a different outcome." In other words, she indicated, the best attorney had won, regardless of the truth.

Bill could only stare at the television in anger. Was a kid who had been unfairly arrested and tried for murder supposed to show contrition while fighting for his life? What had mattered more? His indignant attitude or the fraudulent evidence compiled against him? In her interview, Thompson failed to mention that Bill had been deprived of his public defender because the state attorney's office had made Chapman an agent of the state. Citing a conflict of interest, the court had then assigned Frank Clark to Bill as a substitute. Bill, penniless and without financial support, had been forced to accept Clark's counsel. No other choice had been available to him.

Judge Stanley Wolfman, also interviewed for the program, likewise blamed Frank Clark for Bill's conviction. "The part that troubles me," he told Torres, "I recall this, was the dog tracking, uh, evidence. You know it was kind of flimsy. They had this dog going across A1A, tracking across A1A with all the traffic that had gone by there. Uh, you know, I just kind of shook my head and, uh, internally on that evidence. I don't think Mr. Clark did a good enough job in regard to that. Had he pressed it, I certainly would have gone along with anything he might have suggested, because it was just poor evidence as far as I could see."

Another incendiary statement. Judge Wolfman had known that evidence was suspect—and Frank Clark had gone to great lengths to first suppress it and, when that had failed, to refute it. Now, nearly thirty years later, the judge told Torres and a televised audience that he would have gone along with any suggestions from Clark. In the trial transcripts, 125 pages were devoted strictly to the dog handler's supposed evidence, all of which Frank Clark vehemently protested and Judge Wolfman now admitted had been flimsy at best.

The corruption was about to hit the fan—this much seemed clear from Torres's documentary—and those public officials responsible for Bill's arrest and imprisonment were now jockeying for position, carefully absolving themselves of any responsibility.

That winter, Bill experienced his first snow and below-zero temperatures since his incarceration—a bracing contrast from the sweltering heat of the non-air-conditioned prison cells he had called home for nearly three decades. Not surprisingly, he spent most of his time indoors. While I worked at the office each day, he continued tinkering with his songs and recording them, which meant teaching himself how to use computers, the internet, and the latest software. He told me he had always envisioned himself as a songwriter whose songs would be performed and recorded by others, but I encouraged him to sing his songs himself. Soon enough, he was taking online guitar lessons and poring over thick software manuals in order to master the art of digital and analog recording.

Bill felt his ongoing education was owed to him. He had missed out on so much. Now, hungry for achievement and exploration, he knew there was no time to waste. He was living life at a hundred miles an hour, finding inspiration and information everywhere he looked. Suddenly, I noticed that along with writing songs about his wrongful conviction, Bill was prolifically writing songs that honored the military. Songs of freedom and patriotism flowed from his pen. I was awestruck to see that he still believed in his country after suffering so much oppression. His wisdom was clear; he didn't blame his country for the sins of a few. He cherished America and the freedoms the soldiers gave their lives for. He was paying homage, making good on the promise he made when he left the military so many years ago.

One night during a big snowstorm, Bill was sharing a few details about his story when I blurted out. "You know, you really need to write a book."

He threw me a reluctant look. "I'd rather write songs."

"I wish I had the time to do it," I replied. "I would love to do it for you. But it's impossible right now."

His story, we both knew, needed to be told. Not for revenge. Not even for vindication. But for the potential it had to educate and raise awareness. How many other wrongly convicted men and women were languishing in American prisons? How many others had lived the best years of their lives behind bars?

A few days later, Bill started narrating his story into a cheap handheld tape recorder we'd bought at the mall. His words, put to tape, would form the basis of a sprawling, epic tale, one that would take me a few years to organize. For now, though, it was enough that he was simply talking.

In January of 2010, I took a couple of days off, and Bill and I flew to New York City so he could give an interview to television journalist Paula Zahn for her Investigation Discovery Channel program, *On the Case with Paula Zahn*. The interview afforded Bill another opportunity to get his story heard, this time by a large national audience. If the right people saw it, they might demand an investigation into the conduct of the county and state officials responsible for Bill's and others' wrongful convictions.

Bill and I traveled to Atlanta a few months later for a weekend Innocence Project Conference. There we sat down with Barry Scheck, a famous attorney who, along with being one of the first attorneys to introduce DNA into the courtroom, was a cofounder of the Innocence Project. With his dark hair a bit disheveled and his attention clearly rooted on his work, Barry reminded me of a younger and more refined Peter Falk, a.k.a. Lieutenant Columbo, a man who could always put the pieces of a puzzle together and root out the truth. His dark eyes conveyed caring *and* fearlessness; a no-nonsense guy who liked to get right down to business.

In Bill's case, that meant talking about the possibility of bringing a civil suit against the state attorney's office and the Brevard County Sheriff's Office. No one had ever won such a suit in Florida, he explained, because Florida had strict sovereign immunity laws in place that protected it from civil suits to a greater degree than any other state in the country. That said, after listening to Bill describe his story, Barry said that Bill's case was worth exploring, but he would need to partner with a first-rate Florida-based legal firm with a strong track record in criminal defense, government investigations, and civil rights.

Six months earlier, Bill and I had joined Jack Fernandez, a top criminal defense attorney, at one of Jack's favorite Cuban restaurants in Tampa. Jack, a proud Cuban American with a full head of hair, a broad mustache, and a great smile, had been his usual self that night: energetic and focused. Ours had been a social visit, but that night Jack had gotten to know Bill and the contours of his case. As Bill told his story, Jack had listened with a fiery intensity, his mind obviously racing. While at Labcorp, I had worked with Jack as counsel on three cases: none of them criminal, but each of them involving high financial stakes. During that time, I'd grown close enough to Jack to consider him like family. He had a brilliant mind and a great sense of humor, and he was a man of deep integrity. He also hated to lose.

As I thought back to that dinner with Jack, I knew what I needed to do. I looked up his cell number, and with Bill listening in, called him immediately.

"Jack, it's Marisa," I said, using the pet name Jack had given me while we had worked together years earlier.[12]

"Hey, Marisa," Jack said in a deep voice that belonged on radio. "How you doin'? How's Bill?"

---

12   Jack said I reminded him of Marisa Tomei, the actress from the film *My Cousin Vinny*. After dubbing me Marisa, he never called me Ellen again.

We excitedly updated him on our meeting with Barry Scheck and told him that he was the first person we thought of and the first person we called.

"I should always be the first person you call," Jack insisted. He then promised to look into the possibility of partnering with Barry's firm on Bill's potential lawsuit against the state.

I knew Jack well enough to know that could only mean one thing: Jack Fernandez, legendary for his tireless work ethic and near-maniacal ability to focus, was going to jump in with both feet.

CHAPTER 35
PEELING THE ONION

It was time for a change. I was in the midst of discussions with the board of DNA Diagnostics Center regarding the direction the company was taking. They wanted to go one way. I wanted to go another. After getting to know Bill and learning to see the world through his eyes, it was undeniable that my life was at a crossroads as well. I amicably separated from the company and left with a two-year noncompete clause in force, which I took as a sign that I should give Bill my undivided attention and support. Two years was plenty of time, I assumed somewhat optimistically, to research and write Bill's story.

Determined to get closer to the subject matter, Bill and I rented an apartment along the west coast of Florida. Unfortunately for Bill, the close proximity exacted a price in the form of nightmares and other symptoms related to his PTSD. He was always looking over his shoulder. If we passed a police car on the street, if we heard sirens at night, if there was an unexpected knock on the door—all such incidents triggered his fight or flight response. He worried the police might try to frame him for another crime, whether that meant planting a bag of drugs in his car or throwing him up against the side of his car and claiming he'd assaulted them.

Our only recourse was to keep digging, keep finding out all we could about his case and the various officials who had been involved. Shortly after his release, Bill had learned from Melissa Montel of the Innocence Project of Florida that his attorney, Frank Clark, had been the owner of a checkered past by the time he had served as Bill's attorney. Now, with plenty of time available for research, we began poring over news accounts and other documents. What we found was more than unsettling. Frank Clark, we discovered, was the victim of severe alcohol and gambling addictions. His vices were no secret within the legal and justice circles of Brevard

County, as his frequent, unsuccessful trips to Vegas often ended with him contacting a friend to wire money for a return ticket home. We learned that Frank had been reprimanded privately by the Florida Supreme Court in 1972 and 1973 for neglecting his clients. Two years later, while serving as an assistant public defender in Brevard County, he had been convicted of transporting a stolen diamond worth $62,500 across state lines—a felony! For that infraction, he had been suspended for three years—but had still somehow managed to keep his law license. The soap opera continued as we learned it was a well-known fact that Frank had had an illicit affair with one of his clients, a flamboyant prostitute whom he was defending against a charge of murdering her husband. Frank's reputation for wine, women, and gambling preceded him. Certainly Brevard officials had to have known Frank's history while assigning him to Bill's case. They had to have known that, with his career in near shambles, he would have no choice but to remain in the good graces of everyone, from Judge Wolfman to the state attorney's office. How hard could he possibly push against the very authorities keeping a watchful eye on his own conduct? We suddenly understood Frank's puzzling behavior during the trial. The attorney Bill had placed his faith in had shockingly been a convicted felon himself.

If Frank Clark had been hamstrung during Bill's trial, dog handler John Preston had operated free of serious scrutiny. It wasn't until 2006, when Bill began researching the possibility of applying for a post-conviction DNA test, that Bill learned about Preston's involvement in other cases. While investigating Preston's past, Bill learned that numerous individuals, including his former Avon Park softball teammate Wilton Dedge, had been wrongfully convicted based largely on bogus testimony from Preston. Now it was time to uncover Preston's shady past.

What we found was astonishing: Preston's story was anything but a secret. He had been thoroughly discredited by scent-tracking experts and multiple state supreme courts, and his work had been invalidated in everything from police training manuals to law review articles. Moreover, his work had been called into question not long after Bill's trial and imprisonment.

In 1982, the year after Bill's conviction, state attorney Norman Wolfinger, then a capital defense attorney, had represented Juan Ramos, one of the men later exonerated by DNA evidence. At the time of Ramos's trial, Wolfinger had told the press, "I wouldn't want my life to depend on what [Preston's] dog says." In other words, he had known then that Preston was suspect. But now that Wolfinger was heading up the state attorney's office, he had allowed his office to fight tooth and nail against post-conviction

DNA testing for Bill, Wilton Dedge, and others that Preston had helped convict.

We also learned that in 1984, Brevard County judge Gilbert Goshorn, since retired, had exposed Preston as a fraud by setting up a simple test for the dog handler and his dog. The results: Preston and Harass II had been unable to track a fresh scent the length of a football field. Goshorn gave Preston a second chance at the test, scheduled for the following day. Preston failed to even show up. Just one year later in 1985, Judge John Dean Moxley had reaffirmed Bill's conviction. One would have to suspend disbelief to think that Judge Moxley had been unaware that Preston had been exposed as a fraud. Yet the issue was swept under the rug, and no one told Bill.

Preston's exposure as a fraud hadn't been limited to Brevard County or even to the state of Florida. We soon learned that on October 3, 1985, the same year that Judge Moxley had reaffirmed Bill's conviction and one year after Judge Goshorn had embarrassed Preston, acclaimed television journalist Geraldo Rivera had traveled to Titusville, Florida, to expose Preston on the popular news show *20/20*. Speaking to a national audience, Rivera had called Preston "the dirty dog handler" after demonstrating that Preston's dog couldn't track at all unless Preston was fed information about the suspect beforehand. Rivera's scathing report had ultimately contributed to the exoneration of several individuals incriminated by Preston and Harass II in Brevard County, including Juan Ramos, released from death row a year later.

From there, we discovered that Preston's discrediting had snowballed. The Supreme Court of Arizona, for example, had declared Preston a fraud and a charlatan in 1986 and in the process had overturned every case that had involved Preston. Florida, curiously, hadn't followed suit. In fact, the state attorney's office in Florida had done everything it could to keep Bill, Wilton Dedge, Juan Ramos, and others like them in prison. Why?

In 2008, the year Bill was finally released, Judge Goshorn had publicly stated in a sworn affidavit, "The elected State Attorney at that time, Doug Cheshire, relied heavily on Preston in a number of cases and frequently offered him as an expert . . . It is my belief that the only way Preston could achieve the results he achieved in numerous other cases was having information about the case prior to the scent tracking so that Preston could lead the dog to the suspect or evidence in question. I believe Preston was regularly retained to confirm the state's preconceived notions about a case."

In each case we investigated, Preston's perjury had been bolstered by the testimony of a jailhouse snitch. Was it possible the state and county sheriff's department had worked in tandem, knowingly coordinating their efforts in order to make convictions stick? Had they groomed Preston as part of a two-pronged approach to put suspects away?

The press, along with Seth Miller and others at the Innocence Project of Florida, had begun to ask those very questions shortly after Bill's release. In response, state attorney Norman Wolfinger had been forced, little by little, to reveal more about what had taken place. First, Wolfinger told the media that his office had reviewed all of the Preston cases after Preston had been exposed as a fraud, and it had been determined that each case had contained enough merit on its own to make the conviction stand, with or without Preston's testimony. Later, in response to continued pressure from the public, Wolfinger's office had declared that it was the responsibility of each individual prisoner to seek relief, not the state attorney's office. "Defendants have had rights in Florida to challenge their convictions through a well-established post-conviction process," Wolfinger had said in June of 2009. "Those provisions have procedures which defendants must follow." Charlie Crist, governor at the time, had approved of the statement, declaring he would not appoint a special prosecutor to investigate the Preston cases.

Wolfinger and Governor Crist had been unable to quell the public outrage—or the media's interest in the ongoing revelations. "I left the state attorney's office because I could not abide by the fabrication of evidence," former Brevard County prosecutor Sam Bardwell told John Torres of *Florida Today*. "If Norm Wolfinger had one iota of integrity, he would say it's outrageous and investigate the cases. John Preston was a total fraud, and everyone knew it."

Now, nearly a year later, Wolfinger was still trying to defend Bill's conviction. Naturally, Bill and I were suspicious of Wolfinger's claims. To begin with, hadn't officials used the same excuse—that there was enough evidence from other sources—to deny Bill a new trial after Donna Parrish had recanted her testimony? Why, in the wake of Preston's discrediting, hadn't Bill been granted another trial? Why, for that matter, hadn't Bill been granted another trial when Roger Dale Chapman's testimony had been contradicted by Dencil Chapman in 1996? It seemed the more pieces of evidence were called into question, the deeper the state dug in its heels. Secondly, if the state attorney's office had truly looked into the Preston cases after Preston had been discredited, why hadn't Bill, his attorney, or his family heard anything about the internal investigation?

When reporters at *Florida Today* had asked for a list of Brevard County cases involving John Preston, Wolfinger's office had been unable to comply. Which prompted the question: had the state actually looked into the Preston cases? Or was Wolfinger blowing smoke?

Investigating the corruption at the heart of Bill's case was like peeling an onion: after each layer was removed, another appeared. Preston, we learned, had been the subject of a federal investigation by the US Postal Service in 1983, just two years after Bill's conviction. The report included this nugget: "Preston routinely asked investigators for information about a case before using the dog, and he led his dog to supply the wanted results. Newspaper accounts said Brevard agencies paid Preston at least $34,429 for work done in the first half of 1984."

Preston hadn't just helped send innocent men like Bill to prison; he had made a handsome profit from his work. Brevard County, too, had been culpable, having shelled out tens of thousands of taxpayer dollars to pay for his fraudulent services. The question was this: how much had officials known at the time about Preston's dubious methods? In January of 1984, Judge John Dean Moxley, chief assistant attorney under Douglas Cheshire during Bill's trial, had testified during a hearing for another man's post-conviction relief that he had known about the federal investigation.[13] Two years later, on May 1, 1986, Judge Moxley had been questioned about his knowledge of John Preston's abilities and had answered with a lengthy accounting of various cases he had worked on with Preston, including Wilton Dedge's. Moxley had also explained that he had rubbed elbows with other handlers, besides Preston, and had read extensively on scent tracking. By then, Harass II had been renamed the more politically correct Horace II. Moxley claimed he had never doubted the qualifications or capabilities of Preston or his dog. Surprisingly, Moxley had failed to mention Bill's case or the role Preston had played in Bill's conviction while listing what he said he believed to be a comprehensive list of *all* cases in which he used Preston's services.

As Bill and I continued with our research, we became convinced that a cover-up had been put into place the moment he had been convicted. When the US Postal Service and later the media had begun to investigate Preston, Judge Moxley and others had conveniently left Bill's case out of

---

13   The defendant was Nick Lennear. John Dean Moxley was the prosecuting attorney at Lennear's trial in March of 1983. Moxley, with the help of Wayne Holmes, state attorney, fought the post-conviction relief motion.

the discussion. Did Preston's shady involvement stop at Wilton Dedge, Juan Ramos, and Bill? Who else had been wrongly convicted on faulty evidence? Bill immediately thought of Gerald Stano, a man with a mental disability who had been known as the "serial confessor" and who Preston had helped convict for murder. Bill had met Stano in Florida State Prison before Stano had been put to death. At the time, Stano, who was portrayed by the state as one of the state's most prolific serial killers, had struck Bill as not quite all there—a happy-go-lucky guy who was always smiling, chuckling, and willing to agree to anything. At Stano's trial, Preston had made a remarkable claim: that his dog could track an eight-and-a-half-year-old scent. The con man explained his tracking results as if they were a scientific certainty. The sad truth is that Stano never stood a chance. In five of the eight unsolved murders he confessed to committing, he was represented by counsel that was playing a dual role. Attorney Howard Pearl was a deputized law enforcement officer during the period of time that he represented Stano and others charged with crimes. The court required that all persons sentenced to death when represented by Pearl be informed that Mr. Pearl's status as a law enforcement officer and a defense counsel violated the constitution. Nevertheless, Pearl was permitted to represent Stano, and the mentally disabled man likely never understood the conflict. Little did he know that while there was no legitimate physical evidence to tie Stano to any of the crimes, the state had multiple backup plans. When one trial ended in a mistrial, the state brought in reinforcements. At the retrial, the notorious Clarence Zacke appeared and willingly played the role of jailhouse snitch. The combination of Stano's confessions and the testimonies of Preston and Zacke locked in eight convictions including three death sentences.

Astonishingly, just before Stano's execution, he was asked by Brevard County officials to recant his confession in the Preston-assisted case after the real murderer had been identified. The county was in a bind: without Stano's recantation, the authorities couldn't prosecute the real killer. But Stano refused and was instead put to death for another crime he had also willingly confessed to committing.

Years after Gerald Stano's execution, Clarence Zacke, who had used up his favors from the state, would recant his testimony against Stano insisting Judge Dean Moxley and Brevard County prosecutor Chris White had put him up to it.

Many of the same Brevard County officials who had tried to put Bill away for life had routinely used John Preston to make other convictions stick. But the dog handler's role only accounted for half of the county's MO. The other half—the jailhouse snitch system—had also been honed to a T. In the case of Wilton Dedge, we learned that Clarence Zacke had been purposely put on the same transport vehicle as Dedge.

During a visit to our home in North Carolina, Wilton told us a horrifying narrative of the event. "When I was being transported back to the Brevard County Jail for a new trial, suddenly the van stopped in a small town in the middle of nowhere. Another transport van pulled up alongside of us, and all of the other prisoners who were going to the same place I was going were transferred to the other van. Zacke was put on my van. It was only the two of us on the van. It seemed strange, but I didn't know what was going on at the time," Wilton explained.

Zacke showed up at the trial and ended up falsely testifying against Dedge, saying that he confessed to him on the van and bragged about the brutality of the crime. Of course, there were no witnesses. Based on Zacke's testimony, Wilton Dedge was wrongfully convicted for a *second* time and given a life sentence. Zacke, it turned out, had a lot at stake and was looking for a deal. He was convicted of plotting to kill Dickie Hunt, a local car repossession man who was, incidentally, the brother of attorney Michael Hunt, the assistant prosecutor in Bill's case. Newspaper reports show that Zacke attempted to hire Dickie Hunt as a hit man. When the arrangement fell through, Dickie Hunt disappeared—forever. A notorious drug trafficker, Zacke had earned a 180-year sentence, which officials had routinely reduced in exchange for favors such as testifying against Dedge. Eventually Zacke had performed enough favors for the state to whittle down his sentence enough to qualify for parole. But when he had gone before the parole board, the same Brevard County officials who had used him as a jailhouse snitch to convict other people had, in an about-face, testified that he couldn't be trusted to tell the truth. They were afraid of their own snitch. Zacke was never granted parole. Years later, it was revealed that Brevard County was aware that Zacke was sexually abusing a family member during the years he was snitching for them but they didn't care. Zacke was their ace in the hole.

According to Dedge, this fact was never revealed to Dedge's attorneys when motion for discovery was filed. "At my trial, Zacke boldly claimed he was only testifying because he couldn't stand men that abuse women. If I had only known then about this!" Wilton exclaimed, still tormented by the reality of his wrongful conviction.

In Bill's case, we were appalled to discover that snitch Roger Dale Chapman's cozy relationship with the state had extended beyond Bill's trial as well. Chapman, in exchange for having the rape charges against him dropped, had falsely testified that Bill had confessed to Dvorak's murder. Records showed that a decade later, when Chapman was once again in trouble, state attorney Michael Hunt, in a rare move, had testified as a *character* witness on Chapman's behalf at a 1993 trial involving an aggravated assault and stalking case in Indian River County. Hunt's behavior was emblematic of a system whose players were willing to coddle known criminals while convicting innocent men and women. The state relied upon perjurers, who in turn learned they could gain leniency if they gave the state what they wanted to hear.

While we were researching corruption in Brevard County, Bill got a call from his sister, Debbie, who had heard from a woman whose brother had suffered the same fate as Bill at the hands of many of the same people. The man's name was Gary Bennett. Gary had been incarcerated for nearly thirty years after being convicted on flimsy evidence from Brevard County, including testimony from John Preston and a jailhouse snitch. Lo and behold, John Dean Moxley had been his prosecutor. Bill called the Innocence Project of Florida to see whether they could help and was told that Gary's case was already being handled by another group, Centurion Ministries, but that they would assist in any way they could.

The similarities between Bill's and Gary's cases went beyond the involvement of Preston and a jailhouse snitch. Like Bill, Gary had presented a credible alibi, which the prosecution had undermined. Like Bill, Gary had worked for years to qualify for post-conviction DNA testing and a new trial, only to be thwarted at every turn by Judge John Dean Moxley. And like Bill, when Gary had finally succeeded in gaining a chance to have post-conviction DNA testing, there were suspicious problems locating any DNA testable evidence.

Gary Bennett could do nothing but rail against a system seemingly hell-bent on keeping him in prison. Bill was all too familiar with the man's plight. It had been widely known for more than *two decades* that John Preston was a fraud, but no one had bothered to inform, much less help, those most affected by the dog handler's testimony. Buried deep in the system, Bill and others like him had been left to rot in prison, their stories untold, while the men and women who had put them there went on with their lives, unaccountable to anyone. Some of the victims, like Gary Bennett, are still awaiting justice.

CHAPTER 36

TOOLS

That same spring, while Bill and I were digging through the archives of *Florida Today* and other publications, Paula Zahn's documentary aired on the Investigation Discovery Channel. The usual players were interviewed, including Detective Thom Fair, who continued to double down on his belief that Bill was guilty.

Bill's lead prosecutor, Karen Thompson, meanwhile, told Zahn, "If Mr. Dillon was guilty, then he's done his time. But if he was not guilty, then a terrible injustice has been done to him, but not by me."

Bill stared furiously at the TV. The first responsibility of a prosecutor is to seek justice. How could Thompson so easily attempt to absolve herself of any role in the verdict that sent Bill to prison? Her statement suggested to us that, at the very least, she was determined to slither free of any responsibility. But it also hinted at the possibility that she knew something questionable had occurred and was determined to distance herself from the fallout.

At the end of the nationally televised episode, Zahn mentioned that Bill had become a songwriter while in prison and hoped to record his music someday.

A few days later, on a steamy morning in May, I left the apartment to buy some fresh eggs and bacon for brunch. Bill, ensconced in his makeshift studio, stayed behind to work on his music. I was just pulling into the store parking lot when my cell phone rang and Seth Miller's number appeared on the caller ID.

"Hi, Seth," I said. "What's up?"

"I just got a call from a guy named Jim Tullio who saw Bill on the Paula Zahn documentary," Seth replied. "He says he's a music producer and wants to get in touch with Bill. I don't know anything about him. Remember, a lot of strange people come out of the woodwork whenever something airs on TV. I thought you could check him out if you want to."

Not knowing what to expect, I dialed Jim's number as soon as I finished speaking with Seth.

Jim sounded excited to receive my call and began asking me all sorts of questions about how Bill was doing. The questions weren't intrusive or inappropriate. They were the kinds of questions a man with a compassionate heart would ask.

I immediately had a good feeling about him. I sat in my car for several minutes, and during that time we talked about Bill, music, and how Jim had first heard Bill's story. He had been sitting at the mixing board in his studio one afternoon when he got up to go get a bottle of water in the small studio kitchen. After turning on the TV that he always kept tuned to the Investigation Discovery Channel, he'd found himself engrossed in the Paula Zahn documentary. Before he knew it, his five-minute break had turned into an hour.

"I couldn't take my eyes off the TV," he said, "or get Bill's story out of my mind."

During the call, I was more concerned with what kind of person he was than what his musical credentials were, but Jim encouraged me to check into his professional background.

"If you're comfortable with it," he said, "I'd like to give Bill the opportunity to record some of his music in my Chicago studio. If anyone deserves a break in this world, it's him."

After hanging up the phone, I ran inside the store and grabbed the groceries and then raced home to tell Bill about the conversation.

As soon as I finished relating the news, we went online to check Jim's credentials. Jim Tullio, to our astonishment, was a Grammy-winning record producer who had worked with some of the greatest names in the music business, including Mavis Staples, Aretha Franklin, Levon Helm, Rick Danko, Steve Earle, and John Martyn, among others.

Bill didn't bother to hide his enthusiasm. "I just know that this is my chance," he said excitedly.

~ ❖ ~

Meanwhile, when we believed that we were connecting enough dots to prove wrongdoing in Bill's case, we knew we had to dig deeper. Bill formally requested information from Brevard County under the Freedom of Information Act (FOIA). Among the documents requested: Bill's case files as well as the personnel files of the prosecutors and detectives involved in his case. But *requesting* the documents, we soon learned, was much easier than *retrieving* them.

After Bill's request had been processed, we drove to Brevard County to pick up two sets of documents: one from the Brevard County clerk of the court and one from state attorney Norman Wolfinger's office. We arrived first at the clerk's office and were met by a friendly and helpful staff. After congratulating Bill on his release from prison, they quickly—and without hesitation—gathered the requested documents and presented them to us.

We had just turned to leave, our arms loaded down with files, when a young woman approached Bill. She was petite, with blond hair and bright eyes, and had tears streaming down her face. "I didn't know what I was going to say when I met you," she sobbed. "Oh, my gosh! I can't believe it's you!"

She tried to choke back the tears but finally gave up and buried herself in the arms of the young man standing beside her.

It took us a moment, but we soon learned the girl's story. Her name was Rebecca Bennett. She was the niece of Gary Bennett, the man whose story Bill had first learned from his sister, Debbie, and who was still serving a life sentence, having been convicted of murder in Brevard County. Like Bill, Gary had been put away with the help of dog handler John Preston as well as a jailhouse snitch. Rebecca had been trying in vain to get someone to reopen her uncle's case. The young man with her was her fiancé.

We left the clerk's office a half hour later with an invitation to Rebecca's wedding in hand—and two new comrades in our fight for justice in Brevard County. From there, we drove with trepidation to Norman Wolfinger's office. Yes, at the time of Bill's trial, Wolfinger had been a defense attorney, a man who had unsuccessfully defended Gary Bennett *and* Juan Ramos against John Preston's fabricated testimony, a man who had watched his innocent clients go to prison, one for life and one to death row. But power had changed Wolfinger. As the head of the state attorney's office, he did not support his former defendants' right to DNA testing. He had also refused to declare Preston a fraud, refused to publicly exonerate Bill, and refused to support Bennett's request for a new trial. Even after Wilton Dedge, Juan Ramos, and Bill had successfully had their convictions overturned by DNA evidence, Wolfinger had refused to reopen all the cases in which Preston had testified. What did Wolfinger have to hide? What did he know and how would his office treat us?

We were greeted by a woman seated behind a cut-out window. After Bill identified himself, her expression changed. She nervously took our FOIA request but refused to give her name or a receipt for the request we presented.

"We'd like to get proof it's been received," I said, certain that if we had no paper trail of the request, Wolfinger's office would likely ignore it.

"There's no procedure for giving receipts," she stated flatly.

"Will you sign a copy of the request?" I asked.

She balked at the request, and after I continued to insist, disappeared into the back room to speak to someone.

A few minutes later, she returned with the same answer: there was no protocol for issuing receipts for documents.

"Do you have a dated receipt stamp for mail or other paperwork?" I asked.

"No."

"Please ask someone how we can get a receipt for our request," I insisted.

Finally, after another trip to the back room, the receptionist agreed to print her first name on the request.

"Can't you sign it, instead of printing it?" I asked. "And can you put your last name on it, as well?"

"No, I'm not allowed to give out my last name."

"You're not allowed to give out your last name?" I asked in disbelief.

"No," she repeated.

I knew we were being given the runaround, and therefore insisted she date the document, which she finally, reluctantly, did.

"What's the procedure for retrieving the documents?" I asked.

"You'll have to make a call to find out," she said, without identifying who we had to call.

The cat and mouse game continued until we finally learned that a woman in human resources, who worked in the Viera office, was the person to call to arrange for a pickup.

While she retreated once again to the back office, Bill took photos of the huge emblem prominently posted on the wall, which read: Proudly In Search Of Justice. All we could do was shake our heads in disgust. Would we have been granted more cooperation had I put my name instead of Bill's on the request? It was hard to say. All we knew for sure was that the state attorney's office didn't seem happy to see William Dillon exercising his rights.

Three days later, Bill followed up with the human resources employee who eventually gave us a pickup date for the files, which she said numbered 1,200 pages and would have to be paid for in advance. Although we hadn't had to pay for any files from the county clerk of the court, since Bill was legally still considered an indigent, we readily agreed to pay the fee, not wanting to give Norman Wolfinger's office any reason to hold things up further. But when we traveled to the county courthouse to pick up the files on the specified date, the woman said the files weren't ready. Moreover, she explained, many of the files had been damaged in hurricanes and floods over the years and had been lost while being moved to other buildings. Now there were only eight hundred pages. She promised to refund us the excess charges. She added that the files were kept on microfilm and had to be scanned into the computer, which took extra time. On top of that, there was the issue of redacting all the personal information, such as Social Security numbers, from the files, which also took time.

We couldn't help but be wary. Just a few days earlier, she had counted 1,200 pages. Now there were four hundred fewer! Had more than just personal information been redacted? Something smelled bad.

We decided to stay in Florida to pick up the files, but when we called to arrange a pickup on the new date given us, once again said the files weren't ready. Now, we were told, they had to be reviewed by Wayne Holmes, the state attorney in the prosecutor's office who had fought against Bill's DNA testing and had successfully delayed it for more than a year. What was Mr. Holmes looking for? It seemed very suspicious that the prosecutor who tried to prevent Bill's freedom would be the one deciding what documents he could view. We could only assume this was another tactic to dodge their full legal responsibility.

By now we needed to return to North Carolina, so we asked whether Bill's father or brother could pick up the documents for us. The answer was yes, but when Bill's father arrived at the courthouse on the next date specified, he was met with the same delaying tactics. The files weren't ready. Mr. Dillon asked about the four hundred missing pages, and he was also told that hurricanes were the issue. Mr. Dillon went home empty-handed.

Another week passed. Finally Bill's brother Joe successfully picked up the files on May 23. The whole process reeked of manipulation, so Bill asked for a written explanation regarding the document count and said his father would be back to pick-up the letter on the specified date. Again, it took two trips to retrieve the the official response from the state attorney's office. The written excuse denied blaming hurricanes or moved files. Instead, a simpler but more puzzling explanation was offered: some of the documents had been printed on both sides. It didn't add up. If they had been printed on both sides, we surmised, we should have received additional pages not fewer. The swamp we were wading in was still as murky as ever.

Back at our Florida apartment, I sat down on the living room floor, surrounded by several boxes of files, and opened the prosecutors' files first. One thing immediately grabbed my attention. Karen Thompson, Michael Hunt, Norman Wolfinger, and John Dean Moxley had been in public service for years. Some had worked for Brevard County for nearly three decades, yet not one of them had a single blemish on his or her record. Not one negative comment, letter, reprimand, or review of any kind could be found in any of their files. Had they been scrubbed clean? Each file contained only glowing recommendations, commendations, and reviews.

We did learn that Karen Thompson had resigned from the state attorney's office just three short weeks after Bill's conviction. In her resignation letter, she had cited "circumstances" within the office as a reason for leaving. Also in the files was a letter from an Arizona sheriff to John Dean Moxley in which the sheriff thanked Moxley for teaching him how to use scent dogs to secure death sentence convictions. After reading the letter, we couldn't help wondering whether Moxley, while in charge of the state attorney's office in 1981, had stepped outside his role as prosecutor and acted as a detective by hiring John Preston in Bill's case and perhaps others. Had the state attorney's office just presented evidence given to them, or had they gathered and created evidence themselves?

We gained more insight into the prosecution's refusal to offer evidence to confirm witness Tracey Herman's flight date during Bill's trial—the lynchpin in nailing down the date of Bill's alibi. We found a subpoena from Douglas Cheshire and the state attorney's office. Signed by investigator George Dirschka and served to A. B. Dowdell, the custodian of records at Eastern Airlines, the subpoena was dated December 9, 1981, five days *after* Bill's conviction. It commanded the respondent to bring "copies of the list of passengers on Flight #103 and Flight #653 out of Atlanta, Georgia, arriving at Melbourne, Florida, at 9:37 p.m. and 11:23 p.m., respectively, on Sunday, August 16, 1981."

Bill and I searched the case files for a document regarding the outcome of the subpoena but came up empty. Did such a document exist? If so, where was it? Karen Thompson had, during her closing argument at the trial, ridiculously attempted to defang the issue by wondering aloud whether airlines erased their computer records after one week. But now we had proof that the prosecution had waited until *after* the trial to try to confirm Tracey Herman's claims that she had flown in on the evening of August 16. Had the airline ever responded to the subpoena? If so, where was that response? Had the evidence been destroyed when it hadn't conformed to Tracey's testimony and the state's assertions? Regardless, it was obvious that the state hadn't done its homework before the trial and that Thompson had chosen to obfuscate the point rather than admit her side didn't have all the facts it needed to prosecute Bill.

Our research unearthed a homicide investigation report filed by Detective Thom Fair, that showed how the police had, almost from the beginning, built a profile of Bill that didn't correspond with reality. Bill was described as an unemployed beach bum who was known to be anti-gay and who had bragged about "rolling fags to make easy bucks." According to Fair's report, filed September 1, 1981, a week after Bill was first brought in for questioning, Bill had stopped making such statements after Dvorak's murder and had begun dressing less casually. He had also been seen with bruising on his right shoulder and had recently shaved off his mustache. There was no evidence to support any of the claims—in fact, there was plenty of evidence to refute them—but the police memorialized the bogus narrative, nevertheless.

Similarly, the results of Bill's and Donna's polygraph tests showed how much the police's tunnel vision had prevented them from accepting anything other than what they had wanted to hear. We learned that contrary to what detectives had told him at the time, Bill had not failed any questions about the murder during his lie detector test. But Special Agent Albright, who had administered the test, had concluded that Bill "repeatedly showed deception when questioned about responsibility for receiving monies from Dvorak's death."

Albright, in his written report on Donna's polygraph, recounted Donna's reaction once the test had been concluded:

When Parrish was told the testing phase of the examination was finished, and before the components were removed from her, she asked,

"How many times did you catch me lying?" Parrish stated she knew she had not passed the examination because every time the questions were asked about rolling that man, she could feel her heart pumping. She stated that everything she had told me before testing was a lie. She said the real truth was that neither she nor Dillon was at Canova Beach on Sunday or Monday, 8/16/81 – 8/17/81. They both were together with Charles and Rosanna Rogers at their motel, the Ocean Star, in Cocoa from 1200 noon Sunday, 8/16/81, to 0800 hours Monday, 8/17/81. Parrish stated that she had only related to me what the investigators had told her about her whereabouts on 8/16/81 – 8/17/81, but the investigators were wrong.

Rather than entertain the possibility that the police had pressured Donna into accepting a preset narrative, Agent Albright had assumed the opposite:

> Responses to the relevant questions are consistent and definitely show deception. It can be inferred that Parrish was present when the man was rolled, and by not admitting her presence she responded as though she rolled the man herself.

It was possible Albright hadn't been competent in administering and interpreting the test. But it was also possible he had merely bought into his colleagues' narrative. In fact, the possibilities weren't mutually exclusive. Bill knew Albright's baffling conclusion did not jibe with the facts.

In any case, Detective Thom Fair's report from the following day showed that Donna was beginning to crack. In it, she admitted that her "emotional involvement with Dillon" had prevented her from telling the truth. The seeds of the prosecution's case—that Donna was a loyal girlfriend who had finally decided to tell the truth—were being sown.

The more we learned about the case, the more disgusted we became. Our emotions bottomed out when we found out the real reason why, during the trial, Frank Clark had never mentioned Donna's affair with Detective Slaughter: he had made a secret deal with the prosecution. If he stayed mum about the affair, the prosecution wouldn't seek the death penalty. It had been a devil's bargain, to be sure. To remain silent on the affair was to lend Donna and the state more credibility than they deserved. But to speak up could have meant sending Bill to the electric chair. Although the prosecution had claimed that Bill's case hadn't qualified for the death penalty while talking to the press, felony murder *had* qualified for the death penalty in the state of Florida in 1981. The excuse, however, deflected any further inquiry into the real reason why the state took the death penalty off the table. Withholding the torrid details of Slaughter and Donna's affair was more important; after all, it protected the code.

Bill had repeatedly asked Frank why he wouldn't mention the affair. So, too, had Bill's mother. And Frank's response had been the same each time: "His [Slaughter's] family has suffered enough." Now Bill finally understood what had been at stake. It was possible that Frank, by never playing that trump card, had made sure the jury spared Bill's life.

Any appreciation Bill had for the dilemma Frank had faced was offset by something else we found in the files. Frank Clark, in a letter addressed to state attorney Douglas Cheshire, had commended Thompson and Hunt on a job well done in getting a conviction in Bill's case! The letter read, "As you know, I have defended major cases on a statewide basis over a period of many years and I can say without reservation that this is the finest case I have ever seen from the prosecution," It continued, "It was a heavy blow to me from which I have still not recovered. However, that does in no way detract from a truly superior performance by the prosecution in a case which I believed to be extremely difficult to prosecute and even harder to win. Best wishes to you and your staff for the holiday season." Frank, at the end of the day, had been nothing more than an obsequious sycophant, a man whose own sketchy past had prevented him from effectively and ethically doing his job.

Frank, though, hadn't actively conspired to put Bill behind bars. That suspicion, it seemed, belonged to others, among them Detective Charles Slaughter, the intimidating cop who had conducted a one-man lineup at the courthouse on the night of August 25, 1981. Bill had been asked to pull his long hair to the side of his head while standing sideways in front of a mirrored window in order to emulate the profile of John Douglas Parker's bloody and shirtless hitchhiker. While perusing police files, we learned more about the fact that the half-blind eyewitness hadn't identified Bill that night. No one should have been surprised that John Douglas Parker hadn't originally ID'd Bill, given that the man Parker had described had possessed short hair and a mustache. In a television interview, we heard prosecutor Karen Thompson herself admit to a secret signal she had coordinated with the half-blind man. Parker, while on the stand, was to touch his ring if he was able to identify Bill as the man he picked up at the crime scene. If he gave the signal, Thompson would then ask Parker to identify the defendant. If he did not touch his ring, she would still allow him to tell his story to the jury without so much as a positive ID and would then default to Donna's testimony in order to place Bill at the crime scene. Ultimately, after working with detectives and the prosecution for three months, Parker, who had been unable to identify Bill just nine days after the murder, had testified at the trial that Bill was indeed the man he had picked up that night, although he "wasn't one thousand percent sure." What, we wondered, possessed Parker to improve his ability to identify Bill? Changing testimony seemed to be a pattern.

As Florida's balmy spring wore on, Bill and I continued to sort through the files. We heard back from Jane Ross, who in response to our formal question, informed us that the reason no complaints or grievances had been filed against anyone in the prosecutor's office was because they didn't maintain a complaint file. Such obfuscation only further fueled our fire. Bill was becoming increasingly motivated to file a civil lawsuit against the county, rather than wait for a compensation bill to be passed.

My routine, which I had established as soon as we'd gotten our hands on the files, was to stay up until midnight every night reading files, including trial transcripts, police reports, depositions, news articles, prison records, and so on. In addition to the prosecutors' files and the case files, there were thousands of pages of files from the Innocence Project to wade through. And when I wasn't researching, I was writing. I worked nonstop unless I needed to interrupt Bill in his studio to read him the latest damning detail I'd just found in the files. Eventually, though, the pace, not to mention the gravity of the material, began to take its toll on me in the form of nightmares and stomach aches. I spent a lot of time crying and clutching my stomach as I read through Bill's prison medical records and learned how much he had suffered year after year.

"Maybe this isn't good for you," Bill said one day. "Maybe you shouldn't write this book. Maybe I've brought too many bad things into your life."

The truth was the opposite. The deeper I delved into Bill's story, the more I wanted resolution. There would come a point when I would have to put the book down for months at a time in order to distance myself from the emotional ride I was on. But for now, I was determined to learn all I could and to share it with others.

In June, just after the summer solstice, Bill and I traveled to Evanston, Illinois, to meet Jim Tullio, or "Tools," as everyone called him. Jim's studio was housed in the oldest building in Evanston, a converted butcher shop and horse stable with refurbished meat freezers that now held state-of-the-art musical equipment. A huge mural of a New Orleans jazz band, painted by his brother, adorned one wall, while another showcased many of the award-winning albums Jim had produced. Proudly displayed over a grand piano was a black-and-white photo gallery of artists Jim had worked with over the years.

Jim, who lived in an apartment upstairs, looked and acted much younger than his years and exuded a down-to-earth, straight-from-Jersey vibe. His long, thick silver hair framed an expressive pair of eyes and a wide smile. Sincere, warm, the owner of a hearty laugh—Jim wore his heart on his sleeve. He had grown up playing the upright bass, following in the footsteps of his father, also a musician. Despite spending twelve hours a day glued to his mixing board, he still found time to teach music at Chicago's Columbia College as a part-time professor. As we would soon learn, he readily shared his knowledge with people he believed in, people like Bill.

Before we even unpacked, Bill and Tools went to work—and kept working late into the night. It was a pattern they would maintain for many weeks to come, during which time Tools's upstairs apartment would become our home away from home.

We made several trips to Evanston after that to visit Tools and his studio, but not all of them were strictly about recording. On August 14, less than two months after work had begun on Bill's first album, Bill played to a standing-room-only crowd at Space, the hottest nightclub and restaurant in Evanston. The gig had come courtesy of the venue's owner, Craig Golden, a charismatic local entrepreneur and friend of Tools.

A hush came over the crowd as Craig introduced Bill, who was the surprise opening act for headliner Tom Paxton. Along with several of Tools's friends, Craig had rallied around Bill and offered him his friendship and support. Now, with a lump in his throat, he was sharing Bill's story with everyone in the filled-to-capacity theater.

I could feel my heart pounding in my chest as Bill took the stage. Beside me was our friend Lisa Ray, who had flown all the way from California to support Bill and see the show.

With Tools accompanying him on guitar, Bill immediately connected with the crowd. His story, laid bare in verse after verse of "Black Robes and Lawyers," was as stark as it was powerful.

"This is my first show as a free man," Bill announced in between songs.

The audience cheered enthusiastically.

"It's also my first show in front of women."

The crowd, bursting with excitement a second earlier, fell silent. From that moment on, they hung on every word.

Bill, closing with a song called "Chasing a Dream," let loose on the final refrain: "I want to thank the Lord for DNA!"

The audience leapt to its feet, and Bill left the stage with a huge grin on his face.

"What an exciting night!" he said afterward, smiling in wonderment. "I knew I was meant to be up there."

CHAPTER 37
FISHING EXPEDITION

Jim Tullio wasn't the only one who watched the Paula Zahn documentary on the Investigation Discovery Channel. The episode, which was broadcast to audiences as far away as South Africa and Australia, played several times throughout the summer, and Bill received emails from supporters all over the world as a result.

In late August, Bill spoke with none other than Bill's alibi witness, Charles Rogers, who had caught a rerun of the Zahn interview at midnight a few days earlier while watching TV in his Alabama living room. With the help of his second wife, Jennifer, who had called the Innocence Project of Florida the next day, Charles had left a message for Bill to call him.

"They told me you were dead," Bill told Charles after greeting him.

Charles said he was shocked—and incensed—to learn that Bill had been convicted of the murder. "After testifying at the trial and flying home, I called Frank Clark to follow up," Charles explained. "I never could reach him, but eventually I spoke with his wife. I asked her if there was anything else I could do, and she said everything was fine and they didn't need me anymore. I assumed that meant you'd been acquitted. That was the last I ever heard from them. When I saw your face on the TV and heard them mention Canova Beach, I couldn't believe my ears!" Charles's voice grew angrier. "I've told the story a hundred times about how I testified in a murder trial, but I always ended it with you being acquitted."

Charles told Bill he would be celebrating his seventieth birthday in December and invited Bill and me to come to Georgia for the party.

Bill, who gladly accepted the invitation, was surprised to learn that Charles and Roseanna had enjoyed successful careers in the world of country music, with Roseanna earning a place in Maine's Country Music Hall of

Fame and Charles touring the country with her as her promoter. Charles was also a singer-songwriter. Some of his songs had broken into the top ten on the country music charts in the 1980s. After Charles and Roseanna had divorced, Charles had toured the country with Kitty Wells, queen of old-time country music, and had played with several members of the Grand Ole Opry. It seemed only fitting that Bill, just now coming into his own as a musician and songwriter, had country music in common with the man who had testified on his behalf at the trial.

A month later, in late September, Bill heard back from Charles.

"I just got a visit from two Brevard detectives. They didn't even call. They just showed up," Charles said in a disgusted tone.

Carlos Reyes and Ali Roberts, who were traversing the country and conducting interviews as part of the reinvestigation of the Dvorak murder case, had shown up unannounced at Charles's home in Seale, Alabama. Unbeknownst to them, sitting on the Rogerses' dining table when they walked in was a six-page letter addressed to the editor of *Florida Today*. Charles was on a mission to set the record straight regarding the events of 1981 and what he believed was a cover-up of the truth.

"I told them that I stand by my testimony from 1981," Charles said, "and that I'm furious with the sheriff's office for their shoddy and shady police work. They sure weren't happy to know I was adamant you'd been framed."

We later learned that Detectives Reyes and Roberts also called Roseanna Rogers, but after witnessing Charles's reaction to them, they never pursued an interview with her. Witnesses who wouldn't bolster their narrative, it seemed, were of little use.

Bill, already buoyed by Charles's support, got another shot in the arm a month later when, on October 29, Barry Scheck agreed to take on the civil suit he'd been contemplating. Having put investigators on the case, Barry concluded that the case had merit. Barry's New York City law firm, Neufeld Scheck & Brustin, had agreed to team up with Jack Fernandez from the acclaimed Florida firm Zuckerman Spaeder to represent Bill in a civil suit against the State of Florida.

Bill couldn't contain his excitement. He knew a civil suit could take years to resolve. He knew that he was going up against people who would do anything to cover up the truth, even if it meant ruining an innocent man. But he was determined to expose the cesspool of corruption in Brevard County, and he couldn't imagine assembling a better team to take on such a difficult task.

It was already getting dark on November 3, 2010, when we heard a knock at the door of our Chapel Hill home.

"Bill, there are a couple of guys at the front door!" I shouted from my desk.

We opened the door and were surprised to see two plainclothes detectives from the Brevard County Sheriff's Office. We'd known for a while now that Detectives Roberts and Reyes might pay us a visit, but we were still caught flat-footed by their appearance on the front porch.

"Mr. Dillon," the first man said as Bill opened the door, "we're from Brevard County. Can we speak with you?"

Bill was exhausted from having worked all day in his home studio. "Oh, sure," he said. "Come on in."

"You have nothing to worry about. We just want to see if you can help us. We have almost all of the information already, but you may be able to fill in a few details."

Detective Reyes, shorter in stature, with short dark hair and dark eyes, was clearly playing the good cop. He was dressed in a collared shirt, crewneck sweater, and baggy jacket—more than necessary, I thought, for a cool but relatively mild fall evening in North Carolina.

Detective Roberts, meanwhile, was somewhat taller, older, with a heftier frame. His hair was graying, almost white. He didn't say much.

"We're pretty close to being finished with our investigation," Reyes continued. "We're hoping you might be able to fill in some details for us, specifically regarding what happened back in 1981."

"I'd be happy to tell you what happened," Bill replied. "Follow me."

I was nervous about their intentions but offered each a bottle of water as Bill led them out to the screened porch.

Detective Reyes started in with his questions before they'd even taken a seat. "Can you tell us about the girl that was with you and your brother Joe in the car when you were questioned by detectives at Canova Beach?"

A puzzled look appeared on Bill's face. "No," he said, shaking his head, "there was no girl."

"Yes, there was," Detective Reyes insisted. "We have pictures."

"No," Bill said, this time more adamantly. "There was no girl."

Reyes acknowledged that he was referring to Sandra Weeks, the mysterious surfer girl who, after violating parole and while awaiting re-sentencing, had given shocking testimony just as Bill was anticipating his release from prison. According to the state, Weeks had alleged that she'd dropped Bill off at the Pelican on the night of Dvorak's murder. Moreover, she had claimed that she had owned several Surf-It T-shirts and that Bill might have gotten one of them from her while they were surfing.

When a furious Pirolo had exposed the state's shenanigans, Weeks had disappeared as quickly as she had appeared. Now Reyes was resurrecting the same claims, only this time he even placed her in the car with Bill and his brother Joe.

Reyes opened a folder he had with him and showed Bill a photo of a woman. "Can you identify her?"

"That's Donna Parrish," Bill said.

"And is this you?" Reyes said, showing Bill a photo of himself at the time of his arrest.

"Yes," Bill said.

Reyes, of course, couldn't produce a photo of Sandra Weeks in the car with the brothers since there wasn't one. What was he up to? Where was he going with his questions?

"I'll be right back," I said and went inside to call Seth Miller and the Innocence Project of Florida. Not surprisingly, given the detectives' arrival at the close of business hours, Seth had already left for the day. All I could do was leave him a message and hope he'd call back quickly.

When I returned to the porch, Detective Reyes asked whether he could audio tape the interview, now underway. Why had he waited until now, *after* he'd asked the questions about Sandra Weeks?

"It's a long drive to North Carolina," he explained. "This might be my only chance."

I glanced at the older Detective Roberts, who sat stone-faced and remained silent.

"I'll agree to that," Bill said, "if you'll let us videotape it too."

Reyes appeared surprised but approved of the arrangement, and I hurriedly fetched the video camera, thankful the batteries had recently been fully charged.

Reyes, still playing the good cop, led Bill through a series of questions, including one that struck me as odd: he wanted to know the exact timeline of Bill's residency in Brevard County. How was that relevant to the murder investigation? Bill had never denied living in Brevard County at the time of the murder. Was Reyes after something else?

By now Bill had been all over the country speaking to audiences, and no reasonable person who'd heard the details of his case doubted that he'd been framed. It was obvious he was relieved to finally be sharing his story with the police—the only audience that hadn't yet sided with him. Despite everything Bill had been through, he still had faith that justice could prevail, that the truth was on his side.

My phone rang. It was Seth.

I left the room and answered the phone with my hands shaking. "Seth, Brevard County detectives are here, and they're lying about the facts of the case."

"Ellen," Seth replied in a grave voice, "they are there for one reason and one reason only—to screw Bill. Can you shut down the interview?"

I walked back out to the porch. "Excuse me, guys. Bill has a phone call he needs to take. Can we have a five-minute break?"

Back inside, I handed the phone to Bill and watched as the color drained from his face.

After Bill finished with Seth, we returned to the porch.

"I'm sorry, that was legal material on the phone," Bill said, using a phrase he had learned in prison.

"Legal material?" Reyes asked.

"My attorney. He's advised me to discontinue this interview."

In fact, Seth was furious with the detectives, who knew full well that Bill was under counsel and had nevertheless shown up unannounced, hoping for an interview and eagerly preying on Bill's desire to finally be heard. It was likely they were planning to use Bill's words against him.

I, too, was furious, but with myself. Why hadn't I trusted my instincts when they'd first shown up at our door? Why had I so foolishly let them into my house? I suddenly understood why so many innocent people volunteer to talk to detectives without an attorney present—only to be arrested for their cooperation. After all, the only people who could fully absolve Bill of the murder of James Dvorak were working with the organization that had framed him in the first place. Bill was sure he could get them to see the truth, but they presumably had a vested interest in re-proving his guilt.

"Was that Barry Scheck on the phone?" Detective Reyes said excitedly. "Can we get his autograph?"

The detective had tipped his hand. It was obvious that the sheriff's office was concerned about Bill's pending civil suit. Attorney Barry Scheck, a well-known figure inside and outside of legal circles, was practically a household name. He had spoken freely to the press and announced that he was looking into the case. He'd also appeared recently on an episode of *Geraldo*, in which Geraldo Rivera had aired a follow-up segment to his famous 1985 exposé of "dirty dog handler" John Preston. In the episode, Barry had mentioned Bill's case, embarrassing Brevard County in the process. We believed Detectives Reyes and Roberts had come to our home to do more than investigate the murder of James Dvorak; they were here to build a defense against a possible civil suit.

"We'd like to continue this later," Detective Reyes said.

"Can I take your water bottles?" I asked as the detectives walked reluctantly to the door.

Reyes carefully held up his bottle, now empty, balancing it with two fingers affixed to the base. "I'd like to keep this," he said. "It was very good. I'd like to remember the brand so I can get some more."

Roberts, too, took his empty bottle with him. It was an odd response, but I didn't think much about it.

Glad to be rid of the detectives, Bill went back downstairs to his music studio, while I left for the bathroom to shower and color my hair.

Less than an hour later, just as I was finishing up, Bill appeared out of breath in the bathroom doorway. "Someone just rang the doorbell," he said worriedly.

It was almost eight o'clock. No one ever rang the doorbell after dark. Something was up.

We hurried to the door and found Detectives Reyes and Roberts waiting once again on the front porch.

"Would you be willing to give us a DNA sample before we leave town?" Reyes asked in a tone far less diplomatic than the one he'd used during their first visit.

"You already have my DNA," Bill said.

"Actually, we don't have it," Reyes said indicating that "we" referred to the sheriff's department. "We can't get it."

Something about that statement didn't ring true. "Why do you need it?" I asked.

Reyes reiterated that the sheriff's office didn't have possession of it but needed it for their investigation. It sounded like a trap. The results of Bill's DNA test were on file. Why would they need more?

"Where would you test it?" I asked.

Detective Roberts, silent until now, spoke up. "We use a variety of labs, including Orchid Cellmark and Bode Technologies."

Both were independent, fully accredited DNA testing companies that I was familiar with—and that Roberts likely knew I wouldn't object to using.

"How do you plan to transport the specimen in order to maintain the chain of custody?" I asked.

Reyes explained that they would collect a buccal swab specimen, put it in an envelope, and take it back to Brevard County. Reyes tried to reassure us as he patted the breast pocket on his jacket. "I'll put it right here in my pocket."

"That's not acceptable," I said.

It was obvious the detectives weren't concerned in the least about documenting and establishing a proper chain of custody for the specimen to assure us that it wouldn't be compromised or misused. I therefore suspected that the specimen, which would be collected from the inside of Bill's cheek, could be tampered with in any number of ways, including being used to contaminate evidence, intentionally or unintentionally. I started to ask more questions, but Reyes cut me off.

"Look," he said in a frustrated tone, "we know your line of work. But if you don't mind, we're talking to *him*." He pointed to Bill.

Bill put his foot down, clearly unhappy with the way the detective had just spoken to me. "We're working together," he said firmly.

Reyes, though, refused to give up and continued to try to sell Bill on a test.

"Not tonight, guys," I said repeatedly. "Not tonight."

Reyes lowered his chin and spoke toward his chest. "So you're saying you won't take the test?"

"No," Bill replied. "I'll take the test, but with my attorneys present. How about I show up on your doorstep one day with my attorneys?"

"Will you agree to take a lie detector test, just on what you told us tonight?" Reyes pleaded.

"I'm willing to take a lie detector test if my attorneys are present," Bill answered. "And I'll take a DNA test if it's handled the right way and with my attorneys present."

Reyes was persistent. "It's an awfully long drive to Florida. I just want to save you the trip."

"It's not as long as spending twenty-eight years in prison!" I shot back. "He'll make the drive. He's not going to do it tonight. Please leave. Please leave."

"If I really believed you were looking for the right guy, it would be different," Bill said, clearly irritated. "I'd hoped things had changed. It just shows I ain't learned nothing in thirty years."

"I was only two years old when you were convicted," Reyes protested. "You don't have any reason to be worried about me."

"I think this thing is bigger than you guys even know it is," Bill insisted.

I knew that somewhere in the back of his mind, Bill had to be thinking about Wilton Dedge, who had been framed *twice* by Brevard County before finally being exonerated through DNA testing. In Bill's case, multiple officials, from the county to the state level, could be implicated if the true facts actually came out. Even if Detective Reyes was on the level, others would make sure those facts never saw the light of day.

Finally the detectives gave up, and as soon as they'd left, we replayed the video we'd captured of their interview. Bill and I traded astonished glances as we watched what had happened when we'd left the porch to talk to Seth on the phone.

The two detectives, oblivious that the video was still rolling, did their best Keystone Cops impression.

"Let's check the girl out," Roberts whispered loud enough to be heard clearly on the video tape.

Reyes nodded and then motioned to the water bottle, which likely carried my fingerprints and DNA. In all probability, they were looking for some leverage to hold over my head.

Reyes then fumbled with his crewneck sweater and baggy jacket, tugging at and adjusting something beneath his clothes.

"Look at that!" Bill said. "He's wearing an illegal wire!" Bill and I stared at the tape in utter disgust.

CHAPTER 38

STALEMATE

The next morning, Bill and I sat down for conference calls with his Innocence Project attorneys in Florida and with Barry Scheck and his team of attorneys in New York. Letters were then sent back and forth between Bill's attorneys and Sheriff Parker. While Bill's attorneys put the sheriff on notice that Bill was still under counsel and that the sheriff's detectives had behaved deplorably and unprofessionally, Sheriff Parker insisted that Bill finish the interview and take a DNA test and lie detector test in order to be eliminated as a suspect. He also stated that Bill's original lie detector test, administered in 1981 by Special Agent Albright, had shown deception. The sheriff's use of the word "suspect" confirmed the worst fears of everyone on Bill's team. It was absolutely crucial, Bill's attorneys advised him, not to give the detectives anything they could use to frame him a second time. Even though Bill could never be tried again for the same crime of killing James Dvorak, they could destroy his name, shatter his chances at compensation and deviously cook up something to implicate him in another crime. All options seemed to be on the table.

Lobbyist Guy Spearman, acting as the mediator between the two groups, revealed to Bill's team that the sheriff had already spent more than $250,000, all of it non-budgeted, on the reinvestigation and that Bill needed to cooperate or face the negative consequences. "I believe in Sheriff Parker," Spearman said. However, the sheriff had sent a clear message that he would not support Bill's compensation if he didn't comply.

Thus negotiations began between the two camps. Bill's team couldn't understand why the state needed another DNA test. Weren't the results already in his case file?

Finally Sheriff Parker dropped a bomb: there was reason to believe that the DNA test Bill had taken in prison before his 2008 release had been compromised. According to the sheriff's office, an employee in the medical department at Hardee Correctional Institution, the prison where Bill's DNA sample had been taken, had allegedly told detectives during an interview that Bill's DNA sample had remained in the medical facility for a few days before mailing, and she postulated that it could have been tampered with as a result. On top of that, the sheriff claimed that Bill, as a prison trustee at the time, could have manipulated the specimen collection.

If all of this wasn't bad enough, the sheriff claimed that a prisoner, who wasn't identified, had alleged that Bill had offered him half of his future compensation to take the DNA test for him![14]

During Bill's trial, Karen Thompson and the prosecution had tried to suppress the state's own evidence, claiming it may have been compromised since they couldn't vouch for the chain of custody they had been in charge of preserving. This time it was the sheriff's office that was blaming the state's specimen handling and even alleging Bill had played a role in its manipulation. Bill, of course, had been a trustee in the band room and in the yard where he had picked up litter, not the medical department, and even as a trustee, he had never been able to wander the prison randomly. Any trip to the band room or the medical department had required authorization and a proper pass. Moreover, no prisoner had ever been left alone in the medical department and instead had always been in the presence of both a nurse and a prison officer. The prison snitch who claimed he took the test for Bill, meanwhile, was likely about as credible as the prosecution's other snitches. There was no telling what someone may have promised him in return for his bogus statement, assuming he even existed at all.

Several weeks passed before Bill's attorneys finally heard back from Sheriff Parker, at which time we learned additional reasons behind the sheriff's concerns that the DNA sample had been compromised: as dutifully reported by Orchid Cellmark laboratory in 2008, the outer envelope had arrived in perfect, unopened condition, but the inner envelope had not been sealed completely. Reading this, the sheriff had decided the sample couldn't be trusted. It didn't seem to matter that no regulations dictated the number of envelopes used in a DNA sample chain of custody mailing. No specific timeframe had to be met either for the chain of custody to remain intact. Orchid Cellmark had handled the documentation perfectly, and the state, after fighting tooth and nail to prevent the DNA testing in the first place, hadn't raised any red flags after it had been completed in 2008.

---

14   The prisoner's name has never been disclosed.

So what was really going on? Was Sheriff Parker just being extraordinarily meticulous? Or was he actively working to perpetuate a nearly thirty-year-old cover-up? Had the sheriff forgotten that just a short time earlier when Detectives Reyes and Roberts had ambushed us at our home, they thought it was perfectly fine to transport Bill's DNA swab in Reyes's front pocket with no concern for the integrity of the specimen at all. Whatever the case, it was clear Bill was still a suspect, at least according to the sheriff. Although a free man, Bill was being pressured to take another DNA test, finish the interview, and submit to another lie detector test, all of which could mean walking into another ambush. Guy Spearman tried to assure us that it wasn't a trap, that the sheriff was just doing his job, but how could we trust anyone after everything that had transpired?

Being the only DNA testing expert in the group and facing what was essentially a stalemate, I knew I had to step in and set some guidelines. I therefore stipulated that no one from the state was allowed to touch Bill's DNA specimen. Instead, I insisted that Bill complete a DNA test at an accredited third-party lab with absolutely no connection to the sheriff's office. Bill would go in person to a disinterested lab and hand over his swab to the lab personnel. Then, as soon as the lab had finished with the test, it would destroy the specimen. The sheriff would get his results, but his department would be unable to manipulate the testing in any way—or have access to the specimen itself.

Sheriff Parker, knowing full well that the test results were holding up any progress on Bill's compensation claim, demanded that we pick an accredited lab unaffiliated in any way with *me*, which was fine with our side, and then proceeded to reject all three of our subsequent suggestions. Instead, he offered up the names of three labs that were acceptable to him. A few minutes researching his choices showed that each lab was in some way affiliated with the Florida Department of Law Enforcement (FDLE) or had directors who had been employed by FDLE in the past. In fact, one of the labs the sheriff suggested was the same lab that was currently holding the evidence from the Dvorak murder case! How could we possibly trust such a lab given the performance of the state, which had claimed improper chain of custody, storage, and tracking of its own evidence during Bill's trial, and now the sheriff himself, who had cast doubt on Bill's 2008 DNA test despite Orchid Cellmark's by-the-book handling of the specimen? We had a real concern that someone intent on doing a favor for the state might allow the intentional contamination of the Dvorak case evidence with Bill's swab. We had to inform the sheriff that none of his proposed labs were an acceptable option.

There were dozens of accredited labs that were capable of conducting the test professionally and with no conflict of interest, but Sheriff Parker insisted only his three proposed labs were acceptable. Why? When it came to DNA testing, obtaining a DNA profile from a fresh buccal swab specimen is one of the easiest tests to perform in a lab, especially when compared with something far more challenging, like attempting to extract DNA from a thirty-year-old piece of evidence. Moreover, the test was needed merely to compare the results to the results from the DNA sample Bill had submitted in 2008. That would prove the test had been legitimate and no impostor had taken the test in his place. The sheriff, by insisting on using one of his own labs, suggested either ignorance or deception. It appeared he wanted to get access to the swab itself.

A similar stalemate had been reached regarding the unfinished interview. Sheriff Parker insisted Bill finish it at an FDLE facility, but I wouldn't agree to let Bill do an interview anywhere that the sheriff could entrap him in any way. Instead, I suggested conducting the interview at the Innocence Project of Florida's offices or at Sandy D'Alemberte's office, and we invited the sheriff to attend. Once again, Sheriff Parker refused. Why? When Detectives Reyes and Roberts had showed up unannounced at our front door, that location had been fine for an interview. But now the sheriff would only interview Bill at an FDLE facility.

"I'm not happy about it," Sandy told us one night during a conference call. "But you've got no other options, Bill."

Neither Bill nor I slept well that night. We were both convinced the police were planning to surreptitiously collect Bill's DNA from a desk, the men's room, a drinking glass, an armrest—anything he might touch. Bill's DNA markers could then mysteriously show up on the evidence from the Dvorak murder case or possibly on evidence from another cold case from 1981 that the police had yet to solve. Why else had Reyes so thoroughly quizzed Bill about the timeline of his residency in Brevard County? The state would then be able to rehabilitate its image, and everyone who had helped frame Bill the first time would be absolved.

Statistics show that the majority of people who are wrongfully convicted voluntarily walk through the front door of the police station to answer questions. From there, things quickly spin out of control. I was convinced the sheriff was laying a trap for Bill, and I wasn't alone. The next morning, Barry Scheck confirmed our worst fears.

"Bill, if you do the interview in an FDLE facility, you're insane," he said over the speakerphone. "You have your freedom. The letters the sheriff sent you are not friendly and they're making unreasonable requests."

Bill agonized over the decision. But after discussing the matter at length with Barry and his team, Sandy, Seth Miller, and Melissa Montel, he decided the price of compensation was too high. Maybe Guy was right about Sheriff Parker. Maybe the sheriff was a good man who was just doing his job. But the sheriff's refusal to agree to an arm's length DNA test at a reputable lab and an interview at a safe site for Bill raised too many red flags. Bill had already lost twenty-seven and a half years of his life; there was no way he would risk his freedom all over again.

The interview at an FDLE office was refused. It hurt Bill deeply to know that he might never see the compensation he was due. Worse, he'd lost an opportunity to once and for all prove his innocence. But he had no choice. He had to walk away.

In response, the sheriff's office accused Bill of being uncooperative. Like a black cloud that hung over everything, the reinvestigation remained open indefinitely.

CHAPTER 39
MOOT POINT

Despite the sheriff's ongoing reinvestigation, and despite my own obsession with learning all I could about the corruption surrounding Bill's case, Bill and I managed to go on with our lives as best we could. In fact, by the time we were celebrating Bill's two-year anniversary of his release from prison, we had traveled to twenty-six states, sightseeing at awe-inspiring natural wonders like the Grand Canyon and manmade wonders like the Hoover Dam. No longer imprisoned in a cell, Bill was free to drive the length of California, watch headliners in Las Vegas, jet-ski off the coast of Catalina Island, and even take a race car driving lesson in our good friend Lisa Ray's Roush-charged Mustang at Thunderhill Raceway Park in Northern California. We were living life in the fast lane, making up for lost time.

On December 17, on a sunny but chilly day, we arrived in Cartersville, Georgia, to help Bill's alibi witness, Charles Rogers, celebrate his seventieth birthday. A huge Christmas tree occupied the front lobby of the Country Inn & Suites, where we were staying along with other out-of-town friends and relatives. After checking in and leaving our bags in our room, we walked to Charles and Jennifer's suite and knocked on the door.

Charles opened the door while holding a Yorkshire terrier. "This is Boo-Boo," he said of the little dog, which he and Jennifer had rescued years earlier.

Bill and Charles enjoyed an emotional reunion, after which Charles introduced us to Jennifer; his sons Big Charlie and Little Charlie, both in their forties; and his mother-in-law.

White walls, old green carpeting, a wooden door—the small hotel suite could have been in any economy hotel in the country. An abundance of snacks and beverages were arrayed across the counter next to a small in-room refrigerator and wet bar.

Charles took a seat on a worn green sofa, and for the next three hours, Bill and Charles got reacquainted with each other while other guests came and went.

We all eventually made our way to Charles's big bash, which was staged at an American Legion hall, where Charles's brother ran the bar and concessions. The large old building, located on a side street off the main drag, boasted dark wood-paneled walls, a country-casual vibe, and an undeniably friendly clientele, from the regulars to those who had come solely for the birthday party. A huge square bar greeted us as we entered. A pool table, pinball machine, and other games lined the front walls. Beyond the bar, a cluster of mismatched tables, each covered with a paper tablecloth and small decorations, occupied the dance floor. Drums, amps, and a PA had been set up at the far end of the room and would be put to good use later by several of Charles's musician friends who had come to perform at the party.

Included among the star-studded artists was Leona Williams, former wife of country legend Merle Haggard. We had met Leona earlier, in the hotel lobby, and had sat around the Christmas tree with her and Roni Stoneman and talked about country music and wrongful murder convictions. Leona, the first female country artist to record an album in a prison, had written several songs for Merle, including a pair of number one hits. Roni was a phenomenal banjo player whose speedy picking and character acting had earned her a place on the cast of the hit television show *Hee Haw*. Roni's rendition of dueling banjos was as exciting as any ever heard, as she masterfully played both parts.

Charles invited Bill to perform at the party, and afterward, Charles and Leona were so impressed with Bill's performance and his original songs that they promised to do what they could to help his burgeoning music career. The evening was pure old-time country music gold.

There was a slight southern chill in the air later that month when Sandy D'Alemberte called and asked us to stand by for an important conference call with Guy Spearman. I ran downstairs to grab Bill, who was working in his studio. We then got comfortable on a couch in the living room and waited for the phone to ring. We answered it on the first ring.

"Bill," Guy said over the speakerphone, "I have good news and bad news for you. The good news is that the sheriff knows you're innocent. He also has new suspects." Guy went on to explain that it was at least two individuals, one of whom was living in Chicago. Then, the best news: "They have a DNA match on one of them!" he told us.

Bill whooped with joy, while I cried happy tears, overwhelmed by emotion.

Guy explained that he, along with Senator Haridopolos and Representative Crisafulli, the two officials sponsoring the compensation claims bills, had been called into the sheriff's office to be briefed for three hours on the findings of the Dvorak murder reinvestigation. Senator Haridopolos hadn't been able to attend the meeting in person—he was briefed later—but the sheriff had asked Guy to attend since he was representing Bill as his lobbyist during the claims bill process. Guy, along with the others present, had listened to hours of taped interviews and had been shown the results of the DNA testing that matched one of the new suspects.

"Like I said: the sheriff knows you weren't involved in the murder. The bad news is that he still wants to interview you," Guy explained. Allegedly, during the reinvestigation, the detectives turned up some unattractive things about Bill. Several witnesses claimed he used to brag about beating up and rolling gay men on the beach. There were also witnesses who claimed they saw him near the crime scene on the night of the murder."

Bill's smile disappeared, replaced by a bitter frown. "That's the same fabricated information they used to get me wrongfully convicted!" he hollered at the phone. "That's straight from the trial testimony of coerced witnesses! Are they still threatening these people with perjury if they change their story and tell the truth? How can they continue to lie and manipulate this situation? This is a pure, bald-faced lie! They haven't changed their ways at all. They're still trying to wrap me up in this thing any way they can."

Guy had no explanation for the ugly allegations against Bill, but he *was* able to clarify why Sheriff Parker still wanted to talk to Bill. The sheriff said he had reason to believe that Bill knew the suspects, who were juveniles, around sixteen years old, at the time of the crime.

Bill furrowed his brow. "I don't think I knew any sixteen-year-olds at that time. I was twenty-one and wouldn't have been hanging around with sixteen-year-olds for any reason that I can think of. If the sheriff will tell me their names, I'll gladly let him know if I recognize them."

"He won't disclose the names to you right now," Guy said.

"If he won't disclose the names," Bill replied, "I'd be awfully reluctant to go in for an interview."

Sandy sympathized but said that the sheriff had sent a stern message. He insisted that Bill do the interview—and both of us were to keep the information on the new suspects secret, especially from the news media. The message was clear to us: if Bill or I went to the press with the information, or shared it with anybody, Bill's compensation claim would be in jeopardy. The sheriff also seemed concerned that the suspects would run if the news hit the press prematurely.

We learned the suspects hadn't been arrested and they might never be. Guy explained that they were juveniles at the time of the murder, and the statute of limitations had run out, which might make it impossible to prosecute them. He informed us that Norman Wolfinger was trying to figure out a way to prosecute them.

My mind raced. Was there a statute of limitations in Florida when it came to murder? No, there was no statute of limitations on murder anywhere in America. Was state attorney Wolfinger trying to wrangle out of prosecuting them? In any case, the sheriff had made an abominable demand: despite knowing the real murderers had been found, despite finally having the ability to fully clear his name, Bill was to remain silent. But for how long?

Bill leaned back on the couch and frowned, his face knotted with worry and frustration. He'd waited forever for this moment, but because of the continued accusations against him and the enforced secrecy, he couldn't savor it. In fact, we felt like we were being blackmailed.

Bill had no choice but to honor the request, even if it meant continuing to live under the thumb of law enforcement and the state attorney's office. In stark contrast to the moment he'd been freed, when Judge Dugan had acted immediately after the DNA test and cleared him, Bill was now being forced to assist a sheriff who, though knowing Bill was innocent, was still capable of derailing his compensation claim if he or I dared talk. There were no well-wishers this time, no cameras or throng of reporters, and no articles would appear in the paper. Not yet. Bill had waited nearly thirty years for the truth to emerge. He would have to wait longer.

~❖~

In the waning days of 2010, Bill recorded the last of his tracks for his forthcoming album. Much work remained, including mixing and mastering those tracks. But the hardest part—capturing the energy and emotion of each song with just the right performance—was behind him. Jim Tullio had called in several well-known artists to accompany Bill on the songs, including Sam Butler from the Blind Boys of Alabama, who had done a magnificent job of singing background vocals on the title track, "Black Robes and Lawyers." A song that had been written on toilet paper by a frightened young prisoner was now ready to be mixed in a professional studio. Had someone told Bill in 1985, when he'd first written the song, originally titled "The Lords of Justice," that someday Sam Butler's hauntingly soulful backing vocals would one day grace a recording of it, Bill would have laughed in disbelief. Now here he was, working with the likes of Butler and other all-stars, including Jim Weider, the lead guitar player from the Levon Helm Band; Larry Campbell, a fiddler who had played with Bob Dylan and The Band at age sixteen and was currently in the Levon Helm Band; and Mark Tremonti, guitarist for Creed and Alter Bridge. A dozen of Chicago's best studio musicians, from Chris "Hambone" Cameron on keyboards to Billy Rupert on guitar, also contributed performances. The forthcoming album's liner notes would overflow with the names of numerous professional musicians with impressive résumés.

The *Chicago Tribune*, meanwhile, heard Bill was in town and came knocking at Jim Tullio's door. Mark Caro, one of their ace writers, was so impressed with Bill and his association with Tools that he produced a four-page spread entitled "William Dillon's Redemption Song." Caro described Bill's singing style in glowing terms in the article and went so far as to compare Bill to the legendary Johnny Cash: "Dillon's voice is deep, rich, with a slight burr, a touch of the South, and some of that "voice of God" quality for which another Southern singer is known."

Later that same week, the second week of January, we spoke on the phone with attorney David Menschel. David, though no longer with the Innocence Project of Florida, was still keenly interested in Bill's case and was a trusted adviser. Such dedication was typical of a man who had made it a big part of his life's work to uncover corruption and fight for justice across the country. Together we formulated a new plan to break the stalemate, still ongoing, with Sheriff Parker: Bill would go to an independent, accredited lab and have his DNA tested. He didn't need the sheriff's permission to do that.

"That way you'll have the results," David said, "and can prove in a court of law and to the sheriff that the original results were accurate."

With our plan in place, the Innocence Project of Florida scheduled the test to be performed at Fairfax Identity Laboratories in Virginia, a fully accredited lab within driving distance of North Carolina.

On January 24, 2011, Bill drove to the lab and met the forensics manager. After checking his driver's license and verifying Bill's identity, she collected four buccal swabs from his mouth, two from inside each cheek, and then transferred the swabs in a sealed envelope to the lab director who promised to have the results sent to the Innocence Project of Florida.

Four days later, on January 28, the phone rang at our home in Chapel Hill. It was Melissa Montel from the Innocence Project of Florida.

"It's just as we expected," she said. "They match."

None of us were surprised by the results, but we were nonetheless relieved to have the proof. Bill's team immediately forwarded them to Sheriff Parker.

The sheriff was in a tough position. He had to either accept the results as legitimate or accuse the scientists and director at a highly respected DNA testing institution of lying. Instead, he chose a third option: he never acknowledged the results. Either way, the DNA test issue was now a moot point.

CHAPTER 40

DEATH ON THE HOUSE FLOOR

Bill spent much of that winter nursing a fawn back to health after she had broken her leg and had been abandoned by her family. Bill had first discovered the injured animal while sitting on the deck and feeding the deer and the squirrels—a favorite pastime of his. Determined to help the fawn survive the winter, he offered her a steady supply of carrots and apples.

Sandy D'Alemberte, meanwhile, called to tell us that he believed the claims bill could be resurrected and that Bill should consider giving it a chance. Sandy and Guy were working diligently behind the scenes to encourage the sheriff to release the results of his reinvestigation.

On the first day of February, Judge Bram Canter, the special master for Bill's claims bill, issued a twelve-page report, which concluded with the following statement:

> I recommend that Dillon be compensated for the twenty-seven years he spent in prison, because there is no physical evidence linking Dillon to the victim or the crime scene, and Dillon probably would not have been found guilty with the credible evidence available to the prosecutors.

As encouraging as the judge's recommendation was, Canter also arbitrarily recommended that Bill only be compensated $30,000 for every year he had spent wrongfully incarcerated, instead of the $50,000 statutory amount, because Bill did not qualify for compensation under the clean hands provision *and* because numerous witnesses had placed Bill near the scene of the crime.

Bill made it clear to his attorneys that the amount, which totaled $810,000, or roughly half a million dollars less than what he was entitled to receive by statute, was unacceptable, especially in light of the fact that the sheriff knew he was innocent of the crime.

"I'd rather take my chances filing a civil suit," he said.

Confident that the compensation claim could still be tweaked, Bill's attorneys took his message to the legislators and the media in the hopes that the final total would be adjusted.

A month and a half later, on March 18, Governor Rick Scott issued an executive order stating that the Brevard County Sheriff's Office had completed its reinvestigation and had therefore asked the state attorney's office to review its findings. The governor went on to reveal that the state attorney, Norman Wolfinger, had voluntarily disqualified himself from heading up that review in order to avoid any appearance of a conflict of interest. Instead, another state attorney would oversee the effort.

Despite the announcement, the public was still in the dark. The average citizen knew only that the investigation was over. No one, other than Bill, me, and a handful of others charged with keeping the matter secret, knew about the four new suspects or the positive DNA hit on one of them. Likewise, the public didn't know *why* Wolfinger had recused himself. But we did. We knew Wolfinger and his office had shown a strong bias against Bill by forcefully fighting his right to DNA testing and later by fighting his compensation claim. Wolfinger, as the reinvestigation would surely show, had been petitioning against an innocent man for years while defending the likes of John Preston, a proven fraud. He therefore couldn't be trusted to objectively prosecute others for the crime.

The review was passed on to R. J. Larizza, a special prosecutor in Volusia County,[15] and Bill, still forced to remain silent, returned his attention to the completion of his album, which had been mixed and mastered and was ready for release. Before long, *Black Robes and Lawyers* would hit the airways and the world would finally hear Bill's story set to music.

With the recording of the album behind us, Bill and I traveled to Beverly Hills to celebrate Christmas with friends and ring in the New Year. The

---

15   Wolfinger retired a few months later.

legendary glamour of the iconic Beverly Hilton Hotel added to the holiday spirit. I spotted my friend Matthew behind the front desk and whispered our plans in his ear. In his usual enthusiastic fashion, Matthew escorted us to our exquisitely appointed three-room suite, a complimentary upgrade gifted to us by the hotel.

Later in the day, after searching for the perfect spray of blue flowers and finding the most decadent chocolate confection Gelson's had on hand, Matthew spirited us up the private back elevator, through the penthouse floor, to the rooftop terrace. "This is yours for the next hour," he said with a wink. "Don't ask me how I arranged it!" The Stardust Terrace's breathtaking panorama of the Santa Monica Mountains provided us with the ideal backdrop, as it had for decades of celebrities, dignitaries, and royalty as they graced the roof scape oasis with their most memorable events. We relished the irony of the setting, and with our dear friends Benji and Lee Shale by our sides, in a fairytale moment we tied the knot.

On March 29, 2011, Bill and I drove to Tallahassee to attend a state senate rules committee hearing that would determine whether or not the claims bill authored by Senator Haridopolos would be sent to the Senate floor for a vote. Roughly sixty people packed into the small hearing room, with the senators sitting in tiers in the front of the room and facing the assembled crowd of attendees and journalists.

Senator John Thrasher, a tall, robust figure with dark hair, a commanding presence, and old-fashioned movie star looks, called the hearing to order from the front and center tier. He then asked Judge Bram Canter to address the Senate members.

A slim man of medium height whose full beard made him look professorial, almost rabbinical, Judge Canter summarized his findings for the legislators. Although he thought Bill had been wrongfully incarcerated, based on information from the state, he believed that Bill hadn't been completely honest with investigators. Bill's alleged dishonesty, combined with the fact that some witnesses were standing by their 1981 statements locating Bill near the crime scene on the night of the murder, led Judge Canter to recommend that Bill be paid only $30,000 a year for his prison time.

Senator Thrasher took exception to the judge's assessment. He had studied the case himself, he told Judge Canter in a forceful voice, and he knew Bill had been wrongfully convicted. Moreover, he said, he didn't appreciate the judge's negative comments.

An emotional discussion ensued among the attending legislators regarding what they called the state's "deplorable behavior" toward Bill and the lack of any assistance offered to him while trying to assimilate back into society.

When Bill stepped up to the podium and spoke directly to the senators, he broke down in tears as he told them he was innocent of the crime being investigated. It was another painful moment for Bill, who, despite his release more than two years earlier, was once again having to defend himself against the charges of murder and against a state that was deeply invested in his wrongful conviction.

By the end of the hearing, the senators were ready to take Bill's side. The rules committee passed the bill unanimously. There was talk by Senator Thrasher of later amending the bill to increase the annual compensation from $30,000 to the statutory $50,000. However, if the current bill passed on the Senate floor and was later passed by the House, Bill would then be forced to choose between accepting compensation, at the possibly reduced total of $810,000, or taking his chances with a civil suit. As if that wasn't pressure enough, he had only until December of the following year to file a civil suit, after which time he would be ineligible for such litigation. That wasn't a lot of time to work with, considering the Florida legislature only convened for sixty days out of the year and had a record of delaying the voting on claims bills until the last few days of voting, if at all.

Guy Spearman and attorney Sandy D'Alemberte advised Bill that the sheriff as well as the legislators would not take kindly to being threatened with a civil suit while considering his claims bill. He would have to choose one or the other.

At the same time, Sandy and Guy began lobbying the sheriff to release the results of his reinvestigation. Although the Senate appeared amenable to passing a compensation claim, any bill would still have to make it through the House, whose representatives would be unlikely to pass anything without first knowing the results of the reinvestigation. It was time for the sheriff to stop dragging his feet and release his findings.

With spring came milder weather. The fawn, now strong enough to hobble around on her own, always came back to Bill whenever he called to her. Then one day Bill noticed tiny horns on the fawn's head. The fawn was a young buck, not a doe after all. Bill christened him "Bucky" and regularly watched for the growing buck, which was distinguishable not only by his limp but by a white tuft of hair that grew over his healed hind leg.

On May 3, of that year, joined by his newly formed band, Exoneree, Bill played at the famed Waldorf Astoria hotel in New York City. Aptly named Exoneree, the one-of-kind band consisted of five musicians who had honed their skills from behind bars. They had collectively spent over one hundred years wrongfully incarcerated for other people's crimes. Now they were playing at a black-tie Innocence Project fundraiser, at one of the great hotels of the world, in an effort to give back.

The very next day, Senator Haridopolos's compensation bill passed unanimously in the Senate, although it did so without the dollar amount being amended. Three days later, on May 7, the last day of the 2011 legislative session, it died, still in committee in the House. It never made it to the floor for a vote. We would have to wait at least one more year before the bill could be considered again by the legislature.

We weren't present at the session. In fact, we hadn't known which day it would come to the floor—or if it would at all. As State Representative Richard Workman had warned us the year before, the process of getting a claims bill passed was like watching sausage being made. "It will get worse before it gets better," he had said. In Bill's case, the Senate, encouraged by Senator Haridopolos, who had first-hand knowledge of the sheriff's reinvestigation results, had been willing to pass the claims bill by a vote of 39–0. But the House, even with Representative Crisafulli pushing his version of the bill, had refused to vote, explaining that it wanted to know more about the results of the reinvestigation before voting.

According to reports, several had stood up for Bill but the House members, angry with the Senate for not passing other unrelated legislation, had used the claims bill as leverage to get what they wanted passed and had refused to vote. From our point of view, the process was dysfunctional.

Mike Haridopolos agreed. The young senator broke down in tears as the bill died in the committee during the final hours of the 2011 session. "Politics got in the way today," he told the press, "and for that I am embarrassed."

Sandy and Guy, fearing just such an outcome, had for weeks been pushing Sheriff Parker to release the results of his reinvestigation, if not to the public, at least to everyone in the Senate and House. But by delaying the release of his findings, the sheriff had effectively let the clock run out on the legislative session, thereby ensuring that Bill would have to wait at least one more year for a chance at compensation. It was a Machiavellian tactic, not to mention a fitting outcome, considering everything the state had put Bill through over the last thirty years. In the interim, perhaps they'd work to find a way to sabotage his compensation altogether.

CHAPTER 41

BURNED

In early May, Bill shouted to me from his studio, "Ellen, I just got an email from a reporter who covered my trial in 1981!"

From the moment of his arrest, Bill felt many in the press had played the role of "stenographer" for the sheriff's office and the prosecution, credulously printing lie after lie fed to it by the state and "undisclosed" sources. I read the lengthy email and was encouraged to see that the reporter, after hearing of Bill's release and now the House's refusal to vote on a compensation bill, was reaching out to state attorney Norman Wolfinger asking him to support Bill in his compensation claim.

I turned to Bill and saw that he was deeply touched by the email. Since his release, of course, Bill had received more favorable treatment from the press, which had, for the most part, begun to show more skepticism toward claims from the sheriff's office and the state attorney's office. Although some news outlets had trotted out the claims of Sandra Weeks, the surfer girl who appeared in 2008 to claim she had dropped Bill off at the Pelican on the night of the murder, most reports, whether from *Florida Today*, the *Orlando Sentinel*, or the *Miami Herald*, had done an adequate job of showing the complexities of Bill's case and his fight against the state.

"The tide seems to be turning," Bill exclaimed. "People are beginning to understand what went on here."

Bill received a phone call the very next day from Senator Haridopolos.

"I want to apologize for not getting the claims bill passed," the senator said, "and I want to give you my assurance that I'll make it a priority next year."

Bill, feeling encouraged once again, thanked the senator for all his hard work and became even more determined to keep his story in the news and continue fighting for justice.

A week later, the national media came calling and the *Today Show* aired a four-minute segment, produced by the well-known journalist Mike Leonard, that included Bill performing his original songs. Media personalities Matt Lauer, Meredith Vieira, Ann Curry, and Al Roker offered nothing but praise for Bill's music, with Viera commenting on the deep resonance of Bill's baritone voice.

"Dare I say, he reminds me of Johnny Cash?" Curry said.

It was remarkable to think that just two years earlier Bill had been suffering abuse in a maximum security prison. Now he was being treated like a celebrity. Ironically, the clip was seen everywhere in the country but Florida, where the space shuttle's launch preempted it.

The sheriff's office finally went public with their eighteen-month-long investigation in mid-June, when they granted John Torres of *Florida Today* an exclusive interview and held a press conference. The result was a four-page feature article in the paper's Sunday edition entitled "30 years later, 4 new suspects in Dvorak slaying." The report was in many ways a replay of Sandy D'Alemberte and Guy Spearman's conference call several months earlier and contained good and bad news. The good news was that Bill had been cleared of the murder and four new suspects had been named. The bad news was that police still considered the case open and brazenly insinuated that Bill might have robbed someone on the night of the murder, possibly even the dead body of James Dvorak.

The four new suspects were Daryl ("J. D.") Novak, his brother Eric Novak, Phillip Huff, and James Alan Johnstone, three of whom still lived in Brevard County, with the fourth now residing in a Chicago suburb. Johnstone's DNA had been found on the infamous yellow Surf-It T-shirt, but it was Huff, opening up to investigators in February, who had supplied the police with details of the murder. According to Huff, the four men, all teenagers at the time except Johnstone, had been smoking marijuana with Dvorak in the woods by the beach. Dvorak and Johnstone had slipped away together at one point, and when the other three had gone looking for them, they had found the two in a sexually compromising position on the ground. According to reports, Johnstone, embarrassed, had leapt up, and in the chaos that had followed, the four boys had chased after Dvorak, eventually catching and beating him to death.

"You know," Huff said in a recorded interview with the police, "some of the screams and stuff haunt me to this day."

Dvorak, much older than his attackers but outnumbered four to one, had pleaded for his life, but to no avail.

Johnstone and the Novak brothers denied any involvement in the murder. Nevertheless, in addition to finding his DNA on the yellow Surf-It T-shirt, Police were able to further tie Johnstone to the crime, courtesy of three crucial details, all of which pertained to John Douglas Parker's nearly thirty-year-old testimony. First, the bloody hitchhiker Parker had picked up on the night of the murder had identified himself as "Jim." Johnstone's first name was James. Second, records showed that in 1981 Johnstone, twenty years old at the time, had owned a blue Dodge Dart, the car Parker had said had belonged to the bloody hitchhiker. And third, Johnstone still maintained a "manicured mustache," much like the man in the composite sketch the police had created based on Parker's description. His height and slim body shape were also a perfect match.

According to the article, the police had begun their reinvestigation focused almost solely on Bill as their lone suspect. Only after discovering a small piece of paper in the case file had agents changed course. The small note had included information from an anonymous caller, who had phoned in a tip in early September of 1981, just one day *after* Bill had been indicted by the grand jury. The tip? Johnstone and Huff had bragged about a fight they'd had with a homosexual man on the beach on the night of the murder. The caller believed the police had arrested the wrong man. The tip had allegedly been tossed into the file and ignored, never to be shared with Bill's attorney, Frank Clark. Withholding such exculpatory evidence is a clear Brady[16] violation. Who was responsible for burying this tip? Those details were not disclosed in the article, but we would later find out.

The article revealed that another tip had been given to the public defender's office while Bill was still in prison in 2008. This one implicated the Novak brothers, who had allegedly been heard bragging about beating a gay man on the beach and possibly even killing him. The person giving the tip had assumed Bill was guilty until reading news of Bill's DNA test and felt compelled to come forward.

---

16   *Brady v. Maryland*, 373 U.S. 83 (1963), requires prosecutors to disclose materially exculpatory evidence in the government's possession to the defense.

Daryl Novak's name had first emerged during the trial, of course, when Detective Barringer had casually admitted to Frank Clark that the police had never followed up on the potential lead. Both Bill and Donna had mentioned Novak as a possible suspect to the police, and during the trial Bill had testified that Novak had claimed to know who had committed the murder. Thirty years later, Bill racked his brain but couldn't remember anything about the Novak brothers, who were younger and had gone to school with his brother Joe.

Reporter John Torres had asked Bill about the Novak brothers in the run-up to publishing his story, but, although the name rang a bell, Bill had come up blank. "I don't know these people at all, or at least I don't remember that at all," Torres quoted Bill as saying. "I wish I could remember, but I can't."

In fact, Bill *had* mentioned Daryl Novak's name during his questioning in 1981, but he hadn't put stock in Novak's claim that he knew who the real killer was. Over the years, he had imagined instead that the real murderer had been a hardened serial killer, like Ottis Toole or Jeffrey Dahmer. The idea that a group of mostly school-age boys could have committed such a heinous crime had never occurred to him and even now left him troubled and in disbelief.

According to Torres's article, the police had turned their findings over to R. J. Larizza, a special prosecutor in Daytona Beach appointed by Governor Rick Scott. Whether the four would be prosecuted for the crime was now up to Larizza. Would he issue arrest warrants? For the moment, his office wasn't commenting.

Despite clearing Bill of murder, the police weren't ready to absolve him of guilt of some kind. Had he robbed someone else that night? Had he robbed Dvorak's dead body? According to Sheriff Parker and his investigators, numerous witnesses still claimed to have seen Bill near the scene of the crime. The same unsubstantiated rumors trotted out during the trial—that he was a bully and bragged about robbing gay men, that he had shown up shirtless and broke at the Pelican Bar on the night of the murder but had reappeared later that night with money and wearing a yellow shirt—all earned a prominent part in the police's final report. Worse, like a bad case of whiplash, Roger Dale Chapman had suspiciously reversed his recantation, referring police to his lawyers lest he be charged with lying to the legislative panel during Bill's compensation hearing in 2009 when he apologized to Bill and spilled the goods on the detectives who he swore orchestrated his trial testimony. In addition, Sheriff Parker was still concerned about how Bill's DNA had been collected and sealed in 2008, never mind the second test that had confirmed the first one was accurate. He still wanted Bill to submit his DNA to one of the three labs he had chosen, and he still wanted Bill to take another lie detector test.

The police continued to claim that Bill wasn't being forthcoming. "We just don't know what he did until he tells the truth," a sheriff's deputy insisted at the press conference.

It was an astonishing turn of events. The police had finished their investigation without actually finishing it, and rather than apologize to Bill for the role they had played in his wrongful arrest, conviction, and incarceration, they were continuing to drag his name through the mud while insinuating he had done *something* wrong and was withholding *something*. Meanwhile, when asked during the press conference to explain John Preston and his wonder dog's involvement in the case, a sheriff's detective had answered tersely, "human error." The Brevard County Sheriff's Office was still refusing to call Preston a fraud.

Bill, his attorneys, everyone at the Innocence Project of Florida—we were all furious. But there was nothing we could do. The police were in a position of strength. They couldn't prosecute Bill again for the same crime, which meant they didn't have to prove in a court of law anything they said about him, whether that meant calling him a liar or a gay basher. In short, they could allege anything and face zero consequences. By leaving the reinvestigation open-ended, by ignoring the second DNA test that had once again cleared Bill, and by demanding that Bill jump through still more hoops to clear his name, the sheriff had managed to divert attention from the corruption surrounding Bill's case. The police work had been atrocious from start to finish, but Bill was still the one on trial. No one who had helped put Bill behind bars would be held accountable in any way. If the reinvestigation had been about finding and convicting James Dvorak's true killers, Sheriff Parker's report wouldn't have stopped where it did. They would have called for the prosecution of the four new suspects. But it had been nothing more than a public relations exercise, a whitewashing of the truth.

Would it work? Could the police use old, tainted statements from compromised witnesses to continue to assassinate Bill's character? It was hard to say. To those of us who had followed the story and knew the details intimately, it seemed obvious the police had used the reinvestigation to rehabilitate their image and to further justify why they had come after Bill and made him their fall guy. They had a confession from Phil Huff, who had completely exonerated Bill. They had DNA evidence on the Surf-It

T-shirt matched to Jim Johnstone. But they were still insisting the onus was on Bill to clear his name.

In Torres's article, the sheriff had claimed that all of the witnesses from the 1981 trial were standing by their previous testimony. But who were these witnesses? The two barmaids, the Bocci brothers, John Douglas Parker, John Preston, and four of the detectives had passed away in the years following the trial. Another detective, Steven Kindrick, was too ill to give an interview. The only key witnesses remaining were Donna Parrish and Roger Dale Chapman. Each lacked credibility. Each had recanted their trial testimony at one time. Each had then been threatened with perjury and jail time and, after continued interaction with the police, we learned that once Bill was released, each had suspiciously reversed their recantation! In fact, Chapman had been in and out of jail once again, on unrelated charges, and therefore had plenty of reasons to tell the police whatever they wanted to hear.

Bill felt thoroughly burned. He'd held Sheriff Parker's secret for many months—only to watch as the police continued to cast suspicion his way, all while ignoring any evidence that suggested he was telling the truth. Charles Rogers, despite adamantly confirming his testimony that Bill was with him and his wife the night of the murder, was never mentioned in the article. Neither was there any discussion of the absent Eastern Airlines records that would prove Tracey Herman could not have met Bill and Donna the night of the murder. In fact, no real evidence was being used to muddy Bill's name, only innuendo, hearsay, and allegations. Once again, the police had been allowed to establish a narrative and promote it to the public.

Guy Spearman, ever conscious of the need to stay in the good graces of the authorities, recommended that Bill publicly thank Sheriff Parker for reopening the investigation, something the sheriff hadn't been required to do. But as thankful as Bill was that the real killers had finally been revealed, he also felt burned by the report. How many people would buy the police's description of him in his youth as a vagrant bully with nothing better to do than rob and beat gay men? When would the state discredit John Preston the way Arizona had and reopen the cases in which Preston had testified? Would there be a nonbiased review of the sheriff's report, or would it be allowed to stand on its own? Now that the new suspects had been identified, would they be prosecuted?

A month later, on July 6, Brevard state attorney Norman Wolfinger told *Florida Today* that he was "happy" for Bill. "This is precisely why I requested the governor to appoint an outside authority," he said. "I recognized that any future charging decisions would have to be made free of even the appearance of any perceived impropriety or bias, either for or against Mr. Dillon."

Sandy D'Alemberte, also quoted in the article, was less charitable toward the process. "I do not entirely understand why the Brevard State Attorney is not embarrassed by the sheriff's findings," he said. "If that office had not resisted DNA testing for so long, there could have been an earlier investigation. Even after DNA testing showed that Dillon was not connected with the shirt, the state attorney's office continued to defame Bill."

In 1981, while charging Bill with first-degree felony murder, the prosecution had initially sought the death penalty. Now, based on the confession from Phillip Huff, the description of the murder of James Edward Dvorak had been reduced to an assault and battery with a death. It was possible the four suspects would never be tried since all but one had been juveniles at the time and the statute of limitations on assault and battery with a death had conveniently run out. Bill, innocent of the crime, had been brutalized for twenty-seven-plus years in prison, but those responsible might never be held accountable.

CHAPTER 42
SECOND CHANCE

We were home in Chapel Hill when Jack Fernandez, Bill's new top-gun criminal defense attorney, called a few days after Independence Day in 2011. He was actively gathering information and evidence for the possible civil suit against the state.

"The investigator and I spent two full days interviewing witnesses," he told us over the phone. "I have to say I'm shocked by what I learned, but people are afraid to talk because Brevard County officials have already contacted some of them and told them not to talk."

Before we could get too disappointed, he informed us that three people *had* signed written deposition statements. The question was this: would they stand by their statements on the witness stand? So far, only one could assure us he would; the others had been too intimidated. We had to have solid evidence of misconduct before Bill could take the leap and abandon the claims bill process in favor of a full-blown civil suit. Even if several witnesses agreed to testify, the state would have the advantage, thanks to Florida's unusually strong sovereign immunity laws.

"We know who the ringleader is," Jack added. "One of the guys we talked to still lives in Brevard County and has a business there. He told us that if he talks, they'll ruin him. Like I said, people are afraid. We contacted Karen Thompson. She wouldn't even sit down and talk with me. I told her she had immunity and we believed she had valuable information, but she refused to talk. I gave her a chance."

Most of the people Jack and the private detective had interviewed had been detectives for Brevard County in the early eighties. One, Earle Petty, had been the chief of the homicide division for the Melbourne Police Department during the Dvorak murder investigation. He had been the detective John Douglas Parker, the half-blind eyewitness, had spoken to at the restaurant when Parker had notified the police about the bloody Surf-It T-shirt found in his truck. Although some of the details from Petty's deposition varied slightly from Parker's version of events thirty years earlier, they were damning. According to the transcripts Jack sent to us from Petty's interview, Preston had asked Petty for access to his case files and other information prior to conducting a scent lineup for a different case, but Petty had refused. "Preston even asked me to show him the exact items that had come in contact with the suspect." When Petty refused, Preston, upset, had told him that other officers in Brevard County allowed him access to such information and he couldn't understand why Petty was not cooperating with him. Preston's approach had been: "You help me, and I'll help you." Frustrated with Petty, Preston at one point had said, "Why are you being such an ass? You're here to help me." Petty said Preston's claims about his dog's capabilities had been "beyond the realm of belief." Nevertheless, he continued, "it was commonplace to see Preston inside a police station with his dog hanging around as he reviewed case files and listened to investigators talk about cases." Petty had brought his concerns to assistant state attorney Moxley, but Moxley, though cordial, had offered no response. Others had also voiced their concerns, according to Petty.

Another interviewee told Jack and the private investigator that Preston had been a fixture in the state attorney's office in the late seventies and early eighties and had often been "tethered to Michael Hunt's desk." The dog had been there so often, he said, that "you could smell him." He described a schism in the law enforcement community between those who had vouched for Preston and those who had doubted his abilities. Nevertheless, Preston had never lost a case. "He always hit a home run." Moreover, the state attorney's office had always had "inexhaustible resources when it came to Preston, even though he was quite expensive." Meanwhile, he added, longtime state attorney investigator George Dirschka[17] had allegedly led what he had called "jail sweeps," during which time he had called out certain inmates at the county jail and had made it known which cases he needed information on. The sweeps, more often than not, result-

---

17   George Dirschka was the investigator who signed the Eastern Airlines subpoena dated December 9, 1981, five days *after* Bill's conviction. The lynchpin in nailing down the date of Bill's alibi, the subpoena commanded the respondent to bring "copies of the list of passengers on Flight #103 and Flight #653 out of Atlanta, Georgia, arriving at Melbourne, Florida, at 9:37 p.m. and 11:23 p.m., respectively, on Sunday, August 16, 1981." The response to the subpoena was mysteriously missing from the files.

ed in a "jailhouse snitch" coming forward to assist, in return for favorable treatment.

Clearly, the one-two punch of using Preston and a jailhouse snitch to bring down a suspect was a pattern used over and over again. It was a winning strategy. Jack's interviews backed up the signed affidavit that Judge Gilbert Goshorn had produced while debunking Preston back in 1984. Goshorn had written at the time:

> It is my belief that the only way Preston could achieve the results he achieved in numerous cases was having obtained information about the case prior to the scent tracking so that Preston could lead the dog to the suspect or the evidence in question. In short, I believe that Preston was regularly retained to confirm the state's preconceived notions about cases, in an effort to provide independent scientific evidence.

With the statute of limitations on filing a civil suit approaching, Bill knew he would have to make a choice soon. The odds of him winning a civil suit were fifty-fifty, at best, despite the fact that his attorneys' investigations were uncovering more and more damaging evidence, and despite the fact that Jack's and Barry Scheck's teams grew more confident by the day.

Regardless, Jack's investigation confirmed what the Innocence Project of Florida aptly called a "culture of corruption" in Brevard County in the early 1980s. Nothing was off the table if it meant preserving a conviction. In Bill's case, that meant never prosecuting Donna's admitted perjury that had scored points benefiting the state; readily employing the services of Preston, who by then was already suspected of being a fraud; and of course, using Roger Dale Chapman as a snitch.

A little more than a month later, on August 16, the first single from *Black Robes and Lawyers* was released. The significance of the date, which marked the thirty-year anniversary of the beginning of Bill's long odyssey was not lost on Bill. On that very night, three decades previous, Bill and Donna had met Charles and Roseanna Rogers. A few hours later, while Bill and Donna and their hosts had slept at the Ocean Star Motel, James Dvorak, still in the prime of his life, had been ruthlessly murdered. Now, thirty years later, Bill was beginning anew. The long nightmare was coming to an end, while a long-held dream was coming true. It was a blessed sign, Bill thought, that life was worth living—and much of it still lay ahead of him.

Bill and his newly formed band played to standing-room-only crowds at his CD release parties in Florida and North Carolina, where he autographed CDs and posed for photos with fans. He was living his long overdue dream of sharing his songs with the world.

Bill's other great passion—baseball—found expression later that fall when Gary Yordon, a local TV producer in Tallahassee, invited him to play in the Roy Hobbs World Series, an adult male baseball tournament in Fort Myers. Bill wore the number twenty-seven on his blue Bombers uniform—a fitting number, given how many years he'd spent in prison. His teammates enthusiastically welcomed him even though his bad knees could barely carry him from base to base. The Bombers finished the tournament in third place, but Bill was able to once again feel the crack of the bat in his hands and hear the roar of the crowd in the stands. Bill was capturing time in a bottle—a time and a dream that had been snatched from his grasp three decades ago. Camera crews from ESPN, CNN, and CBS were on hand to document the extraordinary moment. "We're all little boys inside," Bill told the reporters, "and a ball player is always a ball player."

That fall, Bill's alibi witness, Charles Rogers and his new wife, Jennifer, visited us at our home in Chapel Hill. Since it was my first chance to cook for them, I prepared a Yankee pot roast, with carrots and mashed potatoes, to commemorate the meal Charles had served Bill and Donna on the night they had stayed at Cocoa Beach. After stuffing ourselves, we moved to the living room for dessert.

Charles, still devastated by the turn of events that had landed Bill in prison, couldn't help but remark on the injustice of it all. The fact that Bill had spent so many years in prison was still fresh in Charles's mind since he hadn't learned of Bill's fate until catching the Paula Zahn interview.

"I still can't understand why no one has been held responsible," he said, the rawness in his voice reflecting the emotions he was still processing.

"Charles," I asked, "would you mind giving me a short interview for the book I'm writing?"

"You bet," he answered, still angry at what he called a sham of an investigation. "I tried to tell them guys what happened thirty years ago, and no one wanted to hear it."

The four of us, seated on couches that flanked an oversized coffee table, got comfortable as Charles shared his version of events.

"Two sheriff's deputies came to the Ocean Star Motel to interview me and my wife shortly after the murder," he began. "They had the *nerve* to show up at two o'clock in the morning. I told them Bill and Donna were at the motel with me and my wife for the entire night of August sixteen through the morning of August seventeen and never left during that time. I also told them they could check the phone records because Donna had made several phone calls from both the pay phone and the phone in our apartment. In addition, I gave them the names of several people they could talk to who were stayin' at the hotel that night, including an Air Force colonel and a master sergeant. I also told them to speak with my boss, who was the vice president of the company I worked for. All of them knew Bill and Donna were at the motel. The police interviewed exactly none of them.

"I told them I was sure of the night in question because it was the same day as the Michigan 400 race on the radio. I also mentioned that the next day was my anniversary. They tried to convince me that I had the date wrong, but I told them I knew I was right." Charles took a deep breath, a bite of his pie, and then continued.

"Roseanna and I had to move to Georgia shortly after that, but when I saw in the paper that Bill had been indicted, I repeatedly tried to contact the sheriff's office to let them know they were makin' a terrible mistake. No one wanted to talk to me. Finally a female detective told me they didn't want to speak with me; they had all the information they needed. I knew that if they were trying to find the real killer, they would want to hear what I had to say but that obviously wasn't happening

"At that point, I tracked down Frank Clark and told him that I knew Bill was innocent. I knew the detectives were lyin' because the news article that came out in the paper the day before we testified said that they tried to pin the date down with *TV Guide*s and TV programs. I told them that I listened to the Michigan 400 on the *radio* that day. Back then, those races weren't televised; they were on the radio. Of course, they couldn't find it in the *TV Guide*—they knew they wouldn't—but they told a bold-faced lie to the press!"

Charles was not only passionate, the injustice seared into his heart and he felt personally betrayed.

Later that night, Charles mentioned that Leona Williams, the country star whom Bill had met at Charles's grand birthday bash the year before, wanted Bill to join her as a special guest performer when she was scheduled to host the *Midnite Jamboree*, the oldest radio show in the nation, broadcast from Tennessee. It seemed only fitting that Bill, the oldest performer to make his debut in country music, would perform on the oldest radio show in the country.

Thus on December 10, just before fall gave way to winter that year, Bill stepped onto the stage of the Ernest Tubbs Theater to make his Nashville debut. He'd come a long way from singing to murderers and rapists in a hot, dusty prison yard. Afterward, Leona generously invited Bill to join her at Ernest Tubbs Record Shop next door, where they autographed CDs.

Bill wasn't letting any grass grow under his feet. He was fifty-four years old but, as he put it, only "twenty-three years young in the free world." Having been given a second chance, he was determined to let the world hear his music.

CHAPTER 43

BETTER THAN JOHNNY CASH

The New Year passed uneventfully, but Bill's cause was gathering steam, especially in the state's legislative bodies, where Senator Haridopolos was still doggedly pursuing compensation for Bill. The senator, serving out his last year as president of the Senate, wasted no time lobbying on Bill's behalf. In a historic move, he introduced SB 2, which would award Bill $1,350,000, or the standard $50,000 per year for wrongful incarceration, on the very first day of an early legislative session on January 11, 2012. The president of the Senate rarely presented such bills, and it was rarer still for claims bills to be presented so early in the legislative session. Typically they were brought forth in the last days and hours, after more pressing state matters had been resolved. The Senate overwhelmingly passed the bill, which moved to the House of Representatives for approval.

It was time for Bill to make a decision. Should he accept a claims bill award from the state? Or should he take his chances with a civil suit where he could demand much larger damages? During a conference call in February with Fernandez and Debbie Cornwall, an attorney on Barry Scheck's legal team, Bill asked the two attorneys where things stood.

Debbie said Barry's team was ready and eager to move forward with the civil suit. But Jack, although clearly just as game to pursue the case, sounded a note of caution.

"I'm confident that we can show misconduct in the suit," Jack told Bill, "but it could take a very long time—maybe four or five years. It will be a grueling fight. You'll have to continually relive your wrongful conviction as we work on the case. Brevard County will continue slinging mud. It will likely get very mean, and it won't be a fair fight. Then, even if we win, they can appeal. The appeal process can take many additional years."

Jack reminded Bill that Florida has a crippling law that requires that all jury awards in excess of $200,000 and paid by the state need to get legislative approval. "So we'll have to go through a process very similar to the claims bill process that you are going through now, all over again after the trial. It could take an untold number of years."

We learned there was one very deserving individual who had won a jury award for physical damage and had been waiting a decade or more for payment—and the Florida legislature still hadn't approved that award.[18]

Jack's words were startling. We began to understand that, by claiming sovereign immunity and by making defendants jump through so many hoops, the State of Florida had superbly insulated itself from having to pay high awards for its own misconduct.

Jack paused to let everything he'd just said sink in. "Are you willing to wait anywhere from five to ten years or more to get paid, assuming you get paid at all?" he asked. "Look, Bill, I'm talking to you like you were my brother. You've moved forward with your life, and you're doing great things. You should think long and hard about settling for a smaller amount of money now and enjoying your life versus suing for a huge award and then waiting many painful and penniless years and maybe never getting paid."

"Aren't they supposed to help me now that they *know* what happened? Bill asked incredulously.

"Don't mistake me, we want to go to trial, but you need to know the cold hard facts."

Jack's position was predicated on Sandy and Guy's shared belief that they were getting closer to securing passage of a claims bill. They just needed a little more time. Barry Scheck's team, on the other hand, needed an answer as soon as possible, because if Bill decided to civilly sue, Debbie, Jack, and her colleagues would need to immediately start doing preliminary

---

18   A 1998 crash left Eric Brody, then eighteen years old, paralyzed and brain damaged after a Broward Sheriff's Office cruiser crashed into his car. A jury awarded him $30.6 million. But under Florida state sovereign immunity laws, damages are capped at $200,000. In order to get a larger monetary award from a Florida government agency, his claim required a special act by the legislature. In 2012 he was finally awarded $10.7 million by the state legislature. He would require 24/7 care for the rest of his life.

work in order to finish the filing before the statute of limitations ran out at the end of the year.

Complicating things was the fact that a lot of work had already been put into filing the claims bill, and the president of the Senate himself had put his own heart and reputation on the line for Bill. Bill was receiving advice from Sandy and Guy, who thought Bill's best option was to wait and see if the House passed SB 2—and at the statutory amount of $50,000 per year. If it did, they argued, Bill would be hard-pressed to turn it down since doing so would look terrible in the eyes of the legislators working on his behalf. Even if he later won a civil suit, how likely was it that those same legislators would approve his jury award after he had rebuffed them? It was an excruciating decision to make. His stolen years and suffering were worth far more than $50,000 a year, he knew that. But he also knew that many people who deserved awards got nothing.

Bill, after carefully weighing the pros and cons of each option, finally decided that if the Senate and House did indeed pass a claims bill at the statutory amount of $50,000 per year, he would accept the compensation and move on with his life. The alternative was to wade into the muck once more with the duplicitous state—with no guarantee of compensation.

A few weeks later, word came that the House was ready to consider the bill. We rushed to Florida on Friday, February 24, to attend the hearing and, once inside, found seats beside Sandy D'Alemberte in the visitors' gallery that overlooked the floor. Sandy wore a bow tie beneath a dark gray jacket, which, combined with his wire-rimmed glasses and silvery-white hair, made him look as distinguished as ever. Bill looked handsome in a dark suit and light blue tie.

Representative Steve Crisafulli introduced the bill, and a huge digital voting board high above the legislative chamber came to life. A contentious debate followed, with a handful of dissenting senators expressing their disdain for the claims bill process in general and pleading sovereign immunity.

"When the sovereign is wrong," Representative Richard Workman responded, getting to his feet, "the sovereign has to make it right. Let's be clear that thirty years ago people who resided in the great county of Brevard committed an atrocity. They lied. They cheated. They stole. They did whatever they could to get a quick conviction. And what that conviction did was give the residents of Brevard County some peace, because a convicted murderer was behind bars." Workman pointed up at the gallery where we were sitting and continued. "What else it did was put *that* guy in prison for twenty-seven years, where he went through untold horrors, time and time again, at the hands of rapists and killers and horrible people. One of the things we must do as a society is take a break from lowering taxes . . . and take a moment to give justice to a man who deserves it!"

Representative John Tobia took the microphone next. "Have you read *Florida Today* lately?" he asked. He then read aloud from an incendiary article that included information leaked by the state to a reporter who had parroted several unflattering allegations about Bill, repeating lies from the trial that accused him of "rolling fags on the beach." It mischaracterized his early discharge from the military and repeated the state's insistence that Bill had lied about his alibi. Tobia mentioned Bill's drug charge at the age of nineteen, before telling everyone assembled, "I believe the benefactor's character does not warrant special consideration."

Bill and I looked at each other in horror. Other than the drug charge, which did indeed happen, this was the same garbage the state had pedaled during the trial.

Incensed, I said, louder than I should have, "That's not true! That's how they wrongfully convicted him!"

"Calm down," Sandy whispered. "This is orchestrated. Someone got to him."

We were still seething when suddenly several dozen representatives, one by one, left their seats and walked determinedly, across the House floor to stand behind Representative Crisafulli in a powerful show of solidarity. Perhaps someone *had* gotten to Representative Tobia. But they hadn't gotten to everybody, not by a long shot. The mood in the chamber, moments earlier dark and foreboding, had just brightened considerably.

Representative Will Weatherford, the incoming Speaker of the House, spoke next. "I hope you don't believe everything you read in *Florida Today*," he said. "I am only thirty-two years old. The thought of me living my entire lifespan in prison for a crime I didn't commit is beyond my comprehension. It should be beyond *your* comprehension. There's no price tag you can put on that. There is no dollar amount that can give this man his twenty-seven years back. Mr. Dillon may have made mistakes in his life, as was pointed out. So have I. So has every person in here. We all live in glass houses. I've done a lot of things in my life that I'm not proud of. And you probably have, too. But I can be proud of voting for this bill today."

Visibly shaken, Representative Tobia slumped in his chair like a scolded schoolboy as the House passed the bill 107–5 and sent it back to the Senate. It needed a final Senate vote because the House committees had added two important revisions. The first was a single sentence noting that the Brevard County Sheriff's Office had excluded Bill as a suspect in the murder of James Dvorak. We were happy to see that, but the second, quietly slipped into the bill, further protected those involved in Bill's wrongful conviction. The original bill had stated that, if Bill accepted compensation, he couldn't bring a lawsuit against the state or the county for anything concerning his wrongful conviction. Now, with the reinvestigation still awaiting release, specific wording had been added to protect the current sheriff and his staff from legal action.

Bill's shoulders shook as he broke down in tears of relief beside me in the visitors' gallery. While I comforted him, Sandy smiled triumphantly and shed a tear himself. We knew the Senate would pass the bill swiftly.

It was apparent there had been some serious lobbying behind the scenes to protect the current sheriff's office. Sheriff Parker, still keeping the details from the reinvestigation under wraps, had given Representative Crisafulli the go-ahead to inform his fellow legislators that Bill had been cleared of murder and, in exchange, it appeared that someone had arranged for the sheriff to receive legal protection for himself and his staff. It was very revealing and convinced us that Sheriff Parker must have been afraid of something.

Less than a week later, on Thursday morning, March 1, we were on hand as the Senate voted on whether or not to pass the slightly tweaked version of the claims bill.

Senator Haridopolos, after proudly asserting that Florida lawmakers were traditionally tough on crime, suggested there were times when another approach was warranted. "When there are people in prison who've been wronged," he said, "who should have never been there, we need to stand up as a legislature and do what's right."

Bill looked on in amazement as the Senate stood to give him a standing ovation. The bill passed easily, 38–1. Senator Steve Oelrich, an ex-sheriff, was the only holdout.

After the bill had been passed, we were immediately escorted by Steve McNamara, the governor's chief of staff, to the governor's office. "This has never happened before," McNamara said. "The governor wants to hold a press conference and sign the bill right now."

But first, Governor Scott wanted to meet with Bill.

Bill and I, accompanied by Guy Spearman, Seth Miller, and Melissa Montel, entered the governor's large, handsomely appointed office.

The slim, bald-headed governor, dressed sharply in a blue-gray suit and a red tie, greeted us with a huge smile. He then shook Bill's hand.

Bill looked down at his hand in surprise.

"This is something I award soldiers coming home from war," the governor said of a specially minted silver and enamel medal he placed in Bill's palm. "I want you to have one."

I snapped a photo as the two men posed with the medal.

The rest of us took seats on two sofas, while the governor and Bill got comfortable in two armchairs facing us.

"It's an honor to meet you," Governor Scott told Bill. "I'm so sorry this happened to you. How are you doing?"

"Thank you, Governor Scott," Bill replied. "I'm doing much better. I'm really glad they didn't give me the death penalty, or I wouldn't be here talking to you right now."

"I know how it feels to be falsely accused," the governor said. "It happened to me many times during my campaign, but it was nothing compared to what happened to you. I admire your strength. How's your life going?"

"Life is wonderful," Bill answered. "I've seen you on TV, and it's a real pleasure to get to meet you in person. Thank you for believing in me." With that, Bill handed the governor a copy of his new album, *Black Robes and Lawyers*. "Do you like country music?"

"Yes, I do," Governor Scott replied.

"Well, it's a little bit of country, a bit of rock, and some folk mixed in. They call it 'Americana.' I hope you like it."

"I'll play it when I leave here today."

Steve McNamara popped in to inform us that the news conference was about to start.

As we stood to move to the next room, I took the opportunity to approach the governor. "Thanks so much for your support, Governor Scott," I said, "but most especially for the apology. That means the most."

I saw a twinkle in his eye. He understood completely.

Next door, the room bustled with camera crews and reporters. Several dignitaries had assembled at the front of the room, including Dean Cannon, the current Speaker of the House, and Jeff Atwater, the state's chief financial officer, who would be responsible for properly dispensing the compensation proceeds.

Governor Scott took a seat at the signing desk, behind which stood an American flag as well as the state flag. There he was joined by Bill, Senator Haridopolos, and Representative Crisafulli.

"On behalf of the state of Florida," the governor said, addressing Bill directly, "I apologize for what's happened to you."

What the governor was doing—apologizing to a wrongfully convicted man while the TV cameras were rolling—was unprecedented in Florida.

"What I really appreciate from sitting down with you," Governor Scott added, "is that you have such a positive attitude and you're doing something important with your life."

As he picked up one of several pens he would use to sign the bill, Scott said, "It's a real honor to be the governor who is signing this bill."

Each of the dignitaries spoke, including Speaker Cannon, whose branch of Congress had been so intractable for so long. He visibly softened as he turned from the microphone to Bill. "You showed incredible courage and class," he said, "probably better than I would have in the same circumstances."

Bill spoke next.

"Isn't God amazing?" he asked rhetorically. "Who else could put together a team that would bring somebody back from total death when you weren't supposed to be there? And it doesn't happen without Sandy D'Alemberte, and Guy Spearman, Steve Crisafulli, Mike Haridopolos—it doesn't happen. That's the greatest thing about this. There are people that actually believe in you enough to actually help you. There's so many names I could tell you about that were behind the scenes to make this team. The dollars and cents—they make sense for my life, but they don't give me back what was taken from me. But at the same time, it's such a joy to be here, because my life was gone. I can't do anything but look forward."

Bill continued poignantly, "I had this grandeur that everybody was going to see it and know it to be true. But it wasn't like that. When I was released, people thought I still committed the crime." Bill struggled to find the words as he fought back another round of tears. "The grandeur's faded away . . . and I never thought I'd ever . . ."

Overcome with emotions, Bill was unable to finish.

A moment later, though, the governor found a way to lighten the mood. "Don't you have a CD to plug?" he asked Bill. "Here's your chance. Tell the media. I hear you're better than Johnny Cash."

"Oh, yes," Bill said, smiling. "It's called *Black Robes and Lawyers*, and it's very good. You should listen to it. It's good. Um, I don't really know how to plug myself yet," he added with a laugh.

Governor Scott, after presenting Bill with the first pen he'd used to sign the compensation bill, shook his hand. Then the two men posed for several photos before we left for the long drive home.

The sun was peeking through the raindrops as we got into the car. Suddenly, the prism of a heavenly rainbow appeared above us. Bill said with a wink, "That's not a coincidence."

A few days later, after we returned home, we found a letter from Governor Scott in our mailbox. The governor apologized to Bill once again on behalf of the State of Florida, adding that it had been a pleasure to meet him. It was a lovely note and one worthy of a frame and prominent display in our home. Handwritten on the governor's own stationary, it included the following notice at the bottom: *NOT PRINTED AT GOVERNMENT EXPENSE.*

CHAPTER 44
SMOKE AND MIRRORS

Bill's long road to freedom had taught him much: patience, fortitude, faith. All three were tested once again in June of 2012, when Sheriff Parker finally released the written findings of his reinvestigation, this time offering up more than merely an exclusive interview to one reporter. Three months after the governor fully exonerated Bill and the legislature had agreed to compensate him for all that he had endured, the Brevard County Sheriff's Office, to the shock of many, seemed determined to sully Bill's name one last time.

The report, a one-sided document that served more as a careful defense of the sheriff's office and the state attorney's office than a legitimate investigation, offered a somewhat twisted replay of the trial. Roseanna Rogers was never interviewed. Charles Rogers's testimony was ignored. And Bill's reputation was torpedoed based on hearsay and second-hand reports from various witnesses who claimed to have known Bill back in 1981. *Wild Bill. Fucking crazy. A bully. A homophobe. A thief. A malcontent with no home and violent tendencies.* Bill was once again profiled as a lowlife who had deserved his fate, even if no proof had ever actually linked him to the crime.

In short, the report was a rearguard action, designed to retroactively make the state's case, even if there had been no case to make. To justify the police's attempts to link Bill to the yellow Surf-It T-shirt, some of the same old witnesses were quoted as saying they had seen Bill in a similar shirt on the night of the murder, never mind the fact that Bill's DNA had already proved he hadn't worn the shirt. How had the police persuaded those witnesses to double down on the baseless contention? It didn't take long to reveal that the state was employing the same tactics it had used to convict Bill the first time around.

Brian Kersey, sixteen years old and on parole for burglary at the time of the murder, was now incredulously being presented as the catalyst in the case against Bill. His baseless testimony was revived to show the police hadn't just stumbled upon Bill randomly during a general canvassing of the area; rather, Kersey's claim that Bill bore a passing resemblance to the sketch of the bloody hitchhiker ("except for the hair, the mustache and the cheeks") had caused the police to "be on the lookout" for Bill. However, in conflict to their contention, while digging into the case files, we had found prosecutor John Dean Moxley's own handwritten notes from September 4, 1981, the day *after* Bill had been indicted, which indicated that Kersey had backed off his original statement and had therefore been of little use to the prosecution. Nevertheless, he had been used at the trial, with Frank Clark and the jury none the wiser. Now the young boy's statement was playing an integral part in the sheriff's office's revisionist, C.Y.A. (a.k.a. cover your ass) history. John Preston and his wonder dog's involvement in the case, meanwhile, was minimized, as were those officials who had insisted on using his services. Any contradictions or malfeasance on the part of Brevard County officials were attributed to people like Charles Slaughter, who had already been discredited, or to others who had since passed away or were too sick to weigh in on the matter.

One of the biggest bombshells dropped in the reinvestigation report: Donna Parrish and Roger Dale Chapman were said to have each retracted their recantations and, more gallingly still, the Innocence Project of Florida was accused of manipulating the respective witnesses. No aspect of the report illustrated the police's built-in bias more than their treatment of these alleged recantations of their former recantations. Donna had testified in court that she had been pressured to go along with their version of events or risk being prosecuted herself. Chapman had told everyone assembled at Bill's claims hearing that he, too, had been strong-armed into lying on the stand. But the report, as if in denial that either recantation had ever transpired, claimed otherwise. The two recantations that took place in courtrooms for all to hear amounted to mere allegations. But two interviews recorded by the state's investigators—behind closed doors—amounted to unassailable facts.

Interestingly, the report showed that on July 26, 2010, when Reyes and another detective tracked down Chapman at a mechanic shop where he was working, he had declined to give an interview regarding his 2009 recantation and apology to Bill. However, two months later, after he had been arrested for the sale and possession of methamphetamine, Chapman had called the sheriff's office and asked to speak with Reyes. An interview was set up. During this subsequent interview, Chapman recanted his former recantation. But when it became apparent that his testimony wouldn't yield an audience with a drug task force agent, who might be able to help him with his current legal situation, he refused to give a sworn statement or submit to a polygraph test. After reversing his recantation, Chapman had used up all his favors from Brevard County Sheriff's Office. Like snitch Clarence Zacke, years earlier, he had outlived his usefulness, and Brevard County would let him rot in prison.

Much of the report had simply been regurgitated from the trial. But there were fantastic new claims meant to reinforce the state's assertion that Bill was extremely violent, such as one unsubstantiated allegation that Donna had regularly been seen with black eyes while dating Bill. Had this actually been the case, it would have been easy to prove since, although Donna and Bill had only dated off and on for two weeks, the police had begun questioning her as soon as Bill had become a suspect, long before any bruising could have healed. Indeed, had Donna shown any signs of abuse, the police and the prosecution would have jumped all over the issue during the trial, producing photos and so on. Other witnesses such as the Bocci brothers, Tracey Herman, or the barmaids would have mentioned it as well. But the vicious accusations didn't stop there. In an un-redacted version of the report, another "new witness" Bill had never heard of appeared out of nowhere and allegedly claimed he had run into Bill at a dojo next to the Pelican the night of the murder. Bill, he alleged, had been covered in blood and told him he had just beat up a "fag," hit him with a rock and enjoyed it. The sick nature of this accusation compelled us to look into it. Who was this new witness and why hadn't he come forward at the time of the trial or anytime in the last three decades with such damning information? His sudden appearance was suspect to say the least. Since Bill couldn't be tried a second time for the murder, conveniently, Detective Reyes had no obligation to follow up on the alleged claims—or even to determine whether they were credible. If this were a fair and impartial investigation, Reyes would have insisted on further exploration into this claim as would special prosecutor R. J. Larizza. Not surprisingly, neither official did. So if Reyes and Larizza were satisfied with the integrity of this new witness, we weren't. Our own private investigator didn't take long to learn that a man with the same name had criminal arrest records that were extensive. Multiple charges for various offenses from theft to battery to passing worthless checks. To our astonishment, numerous arrests in Brevard County not only made him a frequent acquaintance of the Brevard County Sheriff's Office but in addition, that same man was a frequent offender in Volusia County, the home of none other than special prosecutor R. J. Larizza. Once again, the foul stench of trading testimony for favors was nauseating. We had our answers.

We did learn from the reinvestigation report that it was Sergeant James Bolick[19] who had received the anonymous tip naming Phil Huff and Jim Johnstone as the murderers, the day *after* Bill was indicted. Sergeant Bolick was the officer who had allegedly been heavily involved in many of Preston's cases. Bolick told the detectives during the reinvestigation that he had no memory of receiving the tip, but a paper trail led directly from the sheriff's department receptionist who had taken the call to Bolick's desk. Bolick's ID number was on the tip, showing it had been received. The tip: someone had heard Huff and Johnstone bragging about beating up a gay man on the beach and had passed that information on anonymously to the sheriff's department, but by then, the police had already compiled a mountain of fabricated evidence against Bill and had secured an indictment. In short, they had their man. The tip was then buried in the file. Or was it? We couldn't help but wonder how many people had actually seen the tip. Why did it take detectives so long to find it if it was plainly there in the files? Or was it purposely ignored until it became useful to help rehabilitate the sheriff's department now thirty years later? And, most importantly, why hadn't the defense been presented with this exculpatory evidence before trial as is required?

Noticeably absent from the report was any mention of the state's misconduct in using Donna as their star witness. Her testimony had not only been tainted by her illicit affair with Charles Slaughter; she had admitted to serial perjury. And, although this was supposedly a reinvestigation into the murder of James Dvorak, Phillip Huff's explosive confession resulted in no charges being brought against him, Johnstone, or the Novak brothers. Huff's multiple statements to detectives that Bill had not been involved in the murder and had been wrongly convicted were given little weight in the report. But they bear repeating here. When asked whether justice had been served by Bill's conviction, Huff replied, "I would tell you right now, wrongly convicted." He later added, "Dillon was not involved."

Johnstone's DNA had been found on the yellow Surf-It T-shirt, and his face still bore a striking resemblance to that of the man in the composite sketch. But he faced no charges. He admitted that he'd once driven a blue Dodge Dart, the car Parker had attributed to the bloody hitchhiker, but claimed he hadn't owned it in 1981. Department of Motor Vehicle

---

19   Sergeant James Bolick stepped in to work on the Dvorak murder investigation, after Slaughter was demoted for having sex with the star witness, Donna Parrish.

records, according to the report, were no longer available, so his claim was allowed to stand. One witness alleged that Eric Novak had confessed to the murder to a friend, only to be shushed by his brother. Another witness claimed Dary ("J.D.") Novak had bragged about beating and possibly killing a gay man on the beach. The allegations were made by solid citizens, not criminals looking for reduced sentences, but neither Novak brother was charged with a crime.

There was no way to prosecute the four new suspects, the report concluded, because Huff's statements confessing to the crime and exonerating Bill were inconsistent and provided only circumstantial evidence. Moreover, his testimony was "not credible enough to provide the sole basis for such a circumstantial case." But what could be said for certain was that Bill had been uncooperative and less than forthcoming during the reinvestigation.

If the report seemed deceitful and sloppy, that might be because its list of supposed witnesses included parole violators, drug addicts and dealers, a burglar, a sex offender, two admitted perjurers, relatives of the aforementioned, and some who had hardly known Bill even in passing. The sheriff's office's reliance on people who were or had been in trouble with the law prompted an obvious question: had they pressured more people into bogus testimony, a la Roger Dale Chapman and Donna Parrish?

But therein lay the problem. None of the witnesses had been subject to cross-examination. No evidence had been offered to substantiate any of the numerous allegations. And it would stay that way, for the police weren't interested in investigating James Dvorak's murder in order to prosecute the true perpetrators. They were trying to rewrite history.

If there is truth to the saying that "living well is the best revenge," Bill was getting his in spades. While still struggling to put his past behind him, he was simultaneously living his visions of freedom to the fullest. A month and a half later, Bill's professional baseball dreams had come full circle. On July 17, Bill strode onto the infield at Tropicana Field in St. Petersburg, Florida. He wore a black T-shirt with the words Not Guilty emblazoned across the front. The Tampa Bay Rays were about to host the Cleveland Indians in a Major League Baseball regular season game. Robert Cromwell, a retired FBI agent and staunch believer in Bill, had contacted the Rays organization and sent them Bill's audition tape. Now the crowd roared as Bill was introduced and his story recounted.

Singing a cappella and by himself, Bill performed a starkly beautiful rendition of the national anthem, his baritone voice echoing throughout the brightly lit domed stadium.

In the seats were Bill's brothers, David and Joe, his nephew Brandon, the always supportive attorney Jack Fernandez, and dozens of members of the Innocence Project of Florida. Our hearts swelled with pride as Bill, after closing out the song, tossed out the ceremonial first pitch, a perfect strike.

"I'm a baseball fan," he told reporters afterward. "I love our country, and I have a great respect for what the national anthem stands for. Remember, you're talking to me about freedom."

The story hit approximately one hundred media outlets. The press was particularly interested in why a wrongfully convicted man would want to sing the anthem when his own government had turned on him.

Bill told them, "My country didn't do this to me. It was a handful of bad individuals who had too much power, no oversight and evil intentions. Our country has its problems but I'm a patriot."

In the days that followed, back-to-back appearances on *Fox & Friends* pushed *Black Robes and Lawyers* to the top ten on the iTunes charts and also afforded Bill an opportunity to personally thank Geraldo Rivera for exposing Preston as a fraud so many years earlier. Geraldo, in a surprise appearance, told Bill, "I'm so proud of you. I'm so proud that you didn't let bitterness consume you. I'm so proud of how you've grown up."

"The amazing thing," Geraldo told the audience, "is how long it took the system to exonerate him and how resistant the system is to allowing DNA testing. This man was convicted on the flimsiest of evidence. He was innocent from the get-go. He has a wonderful life ahead of him. I hope he sings his lungs out."

Despite everything he'd been through, Bill always knew he had a choice. He could be bitter or he could be better. He was still holding his head high. He was a man full of hope—and a proud American.

On Thursday, December 13, 2012, Bill and his pro bono attorney, Mark Schlakman, entered the hearing room at the state capitol building in Tallahassee. Shortly thereafter, Governor Scott and his cabinet filed in and took their seats at the front of the brightly lit room. Bill was in attendance for one last request from the State of Florida. Attorney Schlakman, a professor at Florida State University and former president of the Innocence Project of Florida, believed in Bill and stood solidly by his side. When his turn was called, Bill approached the microphone feeling cautiously confident.

"Hi Mr. Dillon, how is your life going these days?" the smiling governor asked.

"Oh, Governor, my life has taken off, like a flower that blooms big in the spring!" Bill's enthusiasm was palpable as he explained many positive things had been happening since being freed.

The state's chief financial officer, Jeff Atwater, held up Bill's newly released CD and asked, "How's the music going?"

Bill was surprised to see the cabinet member had purchased and brought a copy and was waving it in the air.

"Oh, it's going great!" Bill said as he addressed the cabinet members.

"The last time I met the governor, he told me I didn't know how to market myself. So, I want to tell you it's called *Black Robes and Lawyers*, and it's available on iTunes and Amazon."

The entire cabinet broke out in supportive laughter. Bill's energy was infectious and the tone in the room turned celebratory. Governor Scott stood and declared that he was granting Bill a full pardon, thereby wiping his record clean and nullifying the drug possession conviction from 1979 that had threatened to derail his compensation for over three years. The governor believed Bill's wrongful suffering at the hands of the state warranted having the drug charge eliminated from his record. As a result, all of Bill's civil rights were restored.

The irony was not lost on Bill that the one crime he was guilty of was easier to rectify than the crime for which he was innocent. It was a glaringly, brutally flawed system but at that moment, he was grateful.

The encouragement from the governor was buoying, but not everyone was working to rehabilitate Bill. R. J. Larizza, the special prosecutor Governor Scott had appointed to review the reinvestigation report, finally released his assessment on January 22, 2013. Rather than find fault with the state, which had been allowed to investigate itself and clear itself, Larizza, in true prosecutorial form, validated the reinvestigation *and* implicated Bill in the murder all over again, all while failing to move forward the investigation of the four new suspects. It was an outrage that reeked of cover-up and corruption.

Like the sheriff's office, Larizza all but ignored the alibi provided by Charles and Roseanna Rogers. Larizza downplayed Phil Huff's confession and testimony about the murder, concluding he couldn't be trusted, regardless, because he was a drug addict.

Several of Larizza's leaps of logic would have been laughed out of court, including this one: ". . . the wallet of the victim was taken during the murder," he wrote, "and Dillon is the only person reported to have unexplained funds after the murder." Dillon was also the only one reported to have an alibi, but the idea that Bill had been telling the truth and hadn't even been at the Pelican on the night of the murder wasn't up for discussion. Neither, it seemed, were the facts. Dvorak's driver's license, cash, and other personal items, normally stored in a wallet, had been found in the glove compartment of his car. His keys had been found in his shorts pocket. No evidence of James Dvorak carrying a wallet or being robbed had ever been produced.

Larizza's report, which began with the assertion that "further prosecution for the Dvorak homicide is not warranted at the present time," briefly explained why each suspect couldn't be prosecuted based on the available evidence. No one on Bill's team could understand the convoluted excuses as to why the combination of a confession by Phil Huff and a positive DNA hit on the Surf-It T-shirt identifying Jim Johnstone would not warrant a prosecution. A tighter case would be difficult to find.

From the first page to the last, the reinvestigation report never challenged the police's authority or its credibility. We were convinced that Larizza and the state officials were working hand in glove to cover up Bill's malicious conviction and the abominable behavior of the so-called keepers of justice in Brevard County. Bill, as he always had been, was considered guilty until proven innocent. The police used unsubstantiated claims that bolstered their unflattering profile of Bill and implied it was reasonable to accuse him of robbing *someone* on the night of the murder, with or without evidence. In the thirty-plus years since Bill's arrest, nothing had changed. The powers that be in Brevard County doled out justice on their terms— and protected their own. The sheriff's office, detectives would later tell the media, was just waiting for the right piece of evidence. In other words, the reinvestigation had been left unfinished and was, in fact, an ongoing investigation.

Regardless, we now believed we knew why Sheriff Parker had waited to release his findings until *after* Bill's compensation bill had passed—and why a last-minute clause showed up in the compensation statute preventing Bill from bringing a lawsuit against him or his staff. The reinvestigation was an act of defamation. In addition, it exposed law enforcement's suppression of exculpatory evidence—a violation of the Brady rule and a violation of Bill's civil rights. Safe from any legal repercussions, the report freely maligned Bill's character. It had presented hearsay as fact and ugly allegations as justification for nearly thirty years of wrongful incarceration. Bill had no legal recourse available to him to hold the current Brevard County Sheriff's Office accountable for any illegal or even criminal activity. The likelihood of the four new suspects ever being tried, much less convicted, for James Dvorak's murder is next to nil. How could the state and the county sheriff's office possibly turn around and use any of their "evidence" or investigative reports in a new trial against them? Having thoroughly discredited themselves, they would be torn apart by any halfway competent defense team. In short, by doubling down on their dirty tactics, by stealing nearly three decades from an innocent man, and by dragging Bill's name through the mud after the fact, the state has ensured that the real perpetrators will never pay a price for their crime. They have effectively destroyed their own case.

After the reinvestigation review hit the papers, Governor Scott mailed a second handwritten note to Bill reiterating his support and wishing him well. The governor didn't mention Larizza or his irresponsible report, but it was obvious he wasn't buying the snake oil his special prosecutor was selling.

CHAPTER 45
THE POWER OF INNOCENCE

Florida Coastal School of Law, located in Jacksonville, Florida, is an impressive, modern-looking school. The main building's largely glass facade carves an imposing-yet-elegant silhouette against the blue sky, all while mirroring the green surroundings. Even the nearby manmade lake sparkles.

Dressed in a dark blue tailored suit, a blue shirt, and a silk tie, Bill could almost pass as a professor. The cowboy boots, though, give him away. So, too, the silver "Freedom Eagle" pendant I gave him on his first anniversary of winning his freedom.

For several years, Bill had been coming every six months to speak to the new group of freshmen law students during orientation.

"The system works," he tells his audience, "if it's handled the right way. But some individuals misuse and corrupt it for their own purposes. We need the justice system. We need law enforcement. There are plenty of people who need to be prosecuted and put away for a long, long time. Believe me—I've met them. But there needs to be strict oversight of the system. No one should be so powerful that they're above reproach or beyond review. Justice doesn't happen by itself."

"If I can teach you anything today," he tells the students, "remember this: Justice is a word. If you want the soul of justice to be there, *you* have to put it there."

A young woman in the audience raises her hand. "Why don't you become an attorney?"

Bill smiles, his blue eyes twinkling. "I should become an attorney, but right now I'm one-for-one and I don't want to hurt my average. And I'm probably not smart enough to pass all those tests you have to take." He chuckles softly. "But seriously, I would be a great attorney. Not because I'm as smart as you, but because I have an open mind. A closed mind is a very dangerous thing. A big, fragile ego is even more dangerous. What you see on paper is not always the case. You must look through every door. If you become a prosecutor, don't be afraid to drop a case if you find out the man you thought was guilty is in fact innocent. On paper, I was guilty. They put all the evidence they needed on paper. They even had 'science.' But it wasn't true. It was what they now call 'junk science.' You have to eat and sleep your case if you're a defense attorney, because you're up against a very powerful thing. They have all the cards. And they can make people believe what they want them to believe, because they're the law. It's up to you to find the truth."

"Why aren't you angry and bitter?" a young woman shouted from the back of the room.

Bill's humble wisdom radiated throughout the auditorium. "They took twenty-seven and a half years of my life. I'm not going to give them one more day. Leaving bitterness behind is a choice."

"How did you survive all of this?" another future lawyer stands to ask.

A warm smile comes across Bill's face as he glances toward the heavens. "Innocence has such a power. It has a power all its own. It gave me the fortitude to endure. Now it gives me the courage to help create change."

Dog handler John Preston, the man perhaps most responsible for convincing the jury of Bill's guilt, passed away in June of 2008, just one month before the results of a DNA test proved Bill hadn't worn the infamous yellow Surf-It T-shirt. Preston, with the aid of his dog Harass II, had "expertly" tracked the shirt to Bill, and in the process, had helped the prosecution cement its case against Bill. But Preston had been wrong. His so-called science had been fraudulent. The shirt had belonged to someone else. He lived just a few months short of watching his third innocent victim in Brevard County walk free after DNA proved he was a charlatan.

Why have so many people worked so hard to suppress the truth? Plenty of questions linger to this day. We did learn, however, that on August 26, 1981, the exact same day Bill was originally arrested, Brevard County obtained its very first murder conviction courtesy of dog handler John Preston. Mark Wayne Jones reluctantly pled guilty in a double murder case in order to avoid the death penalty, but only *after* detectives insisted Harass

II had definitively connected his scent to the evidence. Preston's role in his easy conviction likely emboldened county and state officials as they went after Bill. Preston and his dog had already solved one murder case that day, why not a second?

Despite suffering unfathomable abuses by the system, Bill will be the first to tell you he's a lucky man. He has his freedom. He has the enduring love of his wife and family who are welded to each other by pain and ultimate victory. The legislators and the governor of the state of Florida have seen fit to officially exonerate him and compensate him for all the years he spent behind bars. He's making music, telling his story, answering to the same muse that kept him alive and sane so many years ago in Florida State Prison. In Avon Park. In Holmes, "the Rock," Polk, Okeechobee, and Hardee. Each stop along the way has marked his soul.

He moves forward each day by embracing the gifts he's been given, by remembering those children whose future was stolen by terminal cancer. He can never erase the past, but he can forgive the injustices done to him, both by the men and women who put him in prison and by the men who savaged him once he'd been locked out of sight. He can forgive those who would rather darken him with innuendo and outright lies than face up to their own sins.

But that doesn't mean he won't continue to advocate for justice, whether for himself or for those who are still languishing in prison. Some who played prominent roles in his incarceration, such as John Preston, lie beyond the grave. But that doesn't mean Florida can't follow the lead of Arizona and, along with officially declaring Preston a fraud, overturn every case ever tainted by Preston's involvement. Others who put Bill in prison are still hard at work suppressing the truth. They should be held legally accountable for all that they've done. Although the system has compensated Bill for the injustice done to him, the individuals who authored that injustice still owe a debt to Bill, as well as society.

Today, there has been a changing of the guard, and improvements made, in the Brevard County Sheriff's Department, as well as the state attorney's office. But only a thorough, impartial investigation will reveal the whole story of corruption and cover-up. Such an investigation will safeguard the future as much as it will unveil the past. It will protect anyone unlucky enough to find themselves the victim of unchecked power and corrupt tunnel vision.

In the meantime, Bill will continue to thank the many angels that have appeared in his life. The mysterious law clerk at Polk who encouraged him to file his own DNA motion; public defender Mike Pirolo who laid his job on the line for justice; everyone at the Innocence Project of Florida who tirelessly fought to expose corruption and injustice; Monica Levsen, the Brevard County clerk of the court who located the missing bloody Surf-It T-shirt; Judge David Dugan who followed his instincts and granted the DNA testing; attorney Sandy D'Alemberte who spent a lifetime fighting for the voiceless; Senator Mike Haridopolos and Representative Steve Crisafulli who were not afraid to stand up against the state; tireless advocate Guy Spearman who believed in doing the right thing; Governor Rick Scott whose wisdom saw beyond the surface; investigative journalist Geraldo Rivera and Judge Goshorn who exposed the fraudulent Preston; attorney Jack Fernandez whose legal expertise and heartfelt counseling were invaluable; attorney Barry Scheck who was ready to go to the mat with corrupt officials; investigative journalist John Torres who kept the story alive and worked exhaustively to report the facts; and lastly, two people Bill would never meet: James Watson and Francis Crick, the Nobel Prize-winning scientists who discovered DNA. Without any one of these heroes, injustice would have prevailed.

As free life moves on, Bill will continue to champion for justice and truth, as he pursues his quest to write the world's prettiest love song.

EPILOGUE

"It's incredible how many people it takes to free one innocent man," says William Dillon every time he reflects on his nearly three-decades-long fight for justice. In wrongful conviction cases, where the state and prosecutors are working overtime to preserve their convictions and reputations at all costs, it takes large teams of dedicated people, major expense, and years of innocent people's lives behind bars to right those wrongs. Why do many perpetrators of wrongful convictions find it worth it to double down on their own wrongdoings? Why the pile-on? Why the cover-up? There is only one conclusion we can fathom. The wrongful conviction was no mistake. It was orchestrated. In a just world, those guilty of malicious prosecution would find themselves behind bars, but the system doesn't seem interested in punishing the bad actors. What we do know, however, is that many of those who plotted to destroy Bill haven't faired very well themselves. The ensuing years have given new relevance to the word karma.

Like the Sword of Damocles hanging over their heads, one by one, many of those who were party to the case against Bill have suffered tragic consequences or early demise. Some found their careers in shambles; others had tragic car accidents, severe life-threatening diagnoses, and mental illness. One we know of became homeless, others had trouble with the law, and several have passed away at young ages. The Brevard County State Attorney's Office and the Brevard County Sheriff's Office have been exposed as substantially corrupt agencies, and the untold damage they have done has not been remedied for many who have suffered at their hands.

The four new suspects in the murder of James Dvorak have not been prosecuted and now only three remain. In November 2019, Daryl ("J.D.") Novak put a bullet through his head. It has been reported he left a note apologizing for things he had done.

In the end, no one ever really gets away with anything.

BLACK ROBES AND LAWYERS CD HITS THE TOP TEN ON I-TUNES

WISHING ALL OF OUR READERS, LOVE, PEACE, AND JUSTICE.

~~~ BILL AND ELLEN

www.ingramcontent.com/pod-product-compliance
Lightning Source LLC
Chambersburg PA
CBHW052052110526
44591CB00013B/2180